Colonial Australian Women Poets

Colonial Australian Women Poets

Political Voice and Feminist Traditions

Katie Hansord

ANTHEM PRESS

Anthem Press
An imprint of Wimbledon Publishing Company
www.anthempress.com

This edition first published in UK and USA 2022
by ANTHEM PRESS
75–76 Blackfriars Road, London SE1 8HA, UK
or PO Box 9779, London SW19 7ZG, UK
and
244 Madison Ave #116, New York, NY 10016, USA

First published in the UK and USA by Anthem Press in 2021

Copyright © Katie Hansord 2022

The author asserts the moral right to be identified as the author of this work.

All rights reserved. Without limiting the rights under copyright reserved above,
no part of this publication may be reproduced, stored or introduced into
a retrieval system, or transmitted, in any form or by any means
(electronic, mechanical, photocopying, recording or otherwise),
without the prior written permission of both the copyright
owner and the above publisher of this book.

British Library Cataloguing-in-Publication Data
A catalogue record for this book is available from the British Library.

ISBN-13: 978-1-83998-564-5 (Pbk)
ISBN-10: 1-83998-564-X (Pbk)

Cover Image: Macintosh, C. H. (1882), *Three-quarter-length Portrait of Woman Seated, Writing at Small Table*, Yeoman & Co., photographer. State Library Victoria.

This title is also available as an e-book.

CONTENTS

List of Figures   vii
Foreword   ix
Acknowledgements   xiii

Introduction: Rereading Colonial Poetry   1

1. Eliza Hamilton Dunlop: Anti-Slavery, Imperial Feminism and Romanticism: 1820–40   23

2. Mary Bailey: Hellenism, Bluestockings and the *Colonial Times*: 1840–50   51

3. Caroline Leakey: The Embowered Woman and Tasmania: 1850–60   81

4. Emily Manning: Spiritualism and Periodical Print Culture: 1860–80   111

5. Louisa Lawson: Fin de Siècle Transnational Feminist Poetics and the *Dawn*: 1880–1910   139

Conclusion: Beyond the *Dawn*   179

Appendix: Selected Poems   185
Notes   193
Bibliography   213
Index   227

FIGURES

1.1	Strutt, William, *The Burial of Burke*, 1911	47
2.1	Bailey, Mary, *View from Sandy Bay*, 1850	53
2.2	Vigée-Le Brun, Elisabeth, *Portrait of Madame de Staël as Corinne*, 1809	59
2.3	Hosmer, Harriet, *Zenobia in Chains*, c.1859	69
3.1	Bruce, Charles, *Miss Debney's Establishment for Young Ladies*, 1831	101
5.1	Nast, Thomas, *Get Thee Behind Me (Mrs.) Satan!*, 1872	147
5.2	Millais, John Everett, *A Huguenot on St. Bartholomew's Day*, 1852	151
5.3	De Morgan, Evelyn, *Love the Misleader*, 1889	157
5.4	Millais, John Everett, *The Somnambulist*, 1871	162

FOREWORD

Katie Hansord's *Colonial Australian Women Poets: Political Voice and Feminist Traditions* is the first major study of the work of five of the most significant of the many women who wrote poems in Australia during the nineteenth century. There are many reasons why their poetry has been neglected until now. First, much of it was published in newspapers and magazines rather than in volumes and so has remained difficult to access until recent mass digitization of newspapers from the period. This was especially so with the two earliest poets discussed here, Eliza Hamilton Dunlop and Mary Bailey. Both had published poetry in Britain before arriving in Australia, with Bailey producing several volumes. But after following her husband to Van Diemen's Land when he was transported for forgery, she was unable to afford the cost of further volume publication, although she remained a prolific contributor to local newspapers. A manuscript collection of her poetry, 'The Vase', which Dunlop prepared in the hope that it would be published, is now in Sydney's Mitchell Library. She too, it seems, did not have enough money to pay for it to be published as a volume in either Australia or Britain. And any writer without a volume of prose or verse surviving in a library failed to be included in later anthologies, bibliographies and histories of Australian literature.

The three other women poets discussed by Katie Hansord did manage to publish a volume in either Australia or Britain, as described in the chapters dealing with their work. Caroline Leakey's *Lyra Australis: Or Attempts to Sing in a Strange Land* was published jointly in London and Hobart in 1854 when she had returned to England after five years in Tasmania. Emily Manning's *The Balance of Pain and Other Poems* (1877) was also published in London; she had visited England earlier and contributed to London journals and so presumably had contacts there in the publishing industry. By the time Louisa Lawson published her collection, *The Lonely Crossing and Other Poems*, in Sydney in 1905 she had established her own press and so was the only one of the five women to fully control the production of her work. Even so, Leakey, Manning and Lawson are only briefly mentioned in bibliographies and histories of Australian literature and their poems have rarely been included in anthologies of Australian poetry, even those with a special focus on colonial or women's poetry. In *The Penguin Book of Australian Women Poets* (1981), edited by poets Susan Hampton and Kate Llewellyn, Ada Cambridge was the earliest poet included. They were not alone in selecting Cambridge as the first significant Australian woman poet. Two anthologies published over a century apart do the same: *The Golden Treasury of Australian Verse*, edited by Bertram Stevens in 1909, and *Australian Poetry since 1788*, edited by Geoffrey Lehmann and Robert Gray in 2011.

As Katie Hansord points out, there are two other main reasons for the neglect of colonial women's poetry. Until comparatively recently, literary studies have tended to be male dominated, with an inevitable bias towards works by male authors. While this has been increasingly challenged in the last 50 years by a growing interest in literature by women, feminist studies of nineteenth-century women's writing have tended to favour fiction rather than poetry. Hence much more attention has been paid to Caroline Leakey's novel, *The Broad Arrow* (1859), than to her poetry. Nineteenth-century poetry in general, whether by men or women, was also relatively neglected until recently, seen as a conservative and conventional hiatus between the innovations of the major Romantic poets and the experimental twentieth-century modernists. The emphasis in much nineteenth-century poetry by women on religion, motherhood, marriage and other subjects coded female rather than male meant that their work was even more neglected. The revaluation of nineteenth-century poetry, especially that written by women, in recent decades is discussed in the introduction to *Colonial Australian Women Poets: Political Voice and Feminist Traditions* and drawn on by Katie Hansord in her chapters on individual poets. As she demonstrates, each of her five women was well aware of poetry published outside Australia as well as of international events and important intellectual and social movements, such as protests against slavery and the sexual double standard, spiritualism and the fight for women's rights.

The neglect of women's writing has been even stronger in Australia than elsewhere in the English-speaking world because of the construction of Australian national identity as predominantly masculine. This developed initially because many more men than women were transported to Australia as convicts or came as part of the convict establishment and later as migrants. The discovery of gold during the 1850s in New South Wales and Victoria, and later in Queensland and Western Australia, also increased the male population. So those looking for what distinguished Australian from English or American literature focused on life in the bush rather than in the cities and on such masculine types as the bushranger, the gold digger, the squatter and the stockman. The best-known colonial poets – Henry Kendall, Adam Lindsay Gordon, 'Banjo' Paterson and Henry Lawson – were especially prized for their descriptions of bush scenes and characters. Mary Hannay Foott's 'Where the Pelican Builds' was, apart from Caroline Carleton's patriotic 'Song of Australia', the only poem by a woman to receive wide recognition in nineteenth-century Australia. This was the title poem of Foott's first collection, published in 1885, but only one other of her poems dealt with bush life. A similar nationalist bias remains obvious in more recent anthologies of Australian poetry where colonial women are usually represented by poems describing bush landscapes, characters or events.

Only two of the five women poets discussed here – Eliza Dunlop and Louisa Lawson – had any direct experience of bush life and neither wished to celebrate it according to the nationalist tradition. Dunlop was one of the first writers to focus on the impact of colonization on Indigenous Australians and to demonstrate an interest in their culture and languages. Lawson exposed the sufferings of women in the bush, caused as much by their brutal and unfaithful husbands as by isolation and loneliness. Mary Bailey challenged the masculine monopoly of translation from classical Greek and Latin poets as well as writing on local politics. Caroline Leakey focused on the sufferings of female convicts, especially those regarded as 'fallen', while Emily Manning investigated the changing roles of men and women, particularly in relation to the loss of traditional religious belief and a growing interest in spiritualism. All five were working within transnational poetic traditions but all made innovative contributions to Australian literature that are finally being acknowledged here.

Professor Emerita Elizabeth Webby AM FAHA
Department of English, University of Sydney

ACKNOWLEDGEMENTS

I acknowledge the traditional custodians of the land on which this book was written, the Wurundjeri people of the Kulin Nation, and acknowledge all traditional custodians' sovereignty across Australia. I dedicate this book in loving memory to my mother, whose strength, love and kindness continue to inspire me to grow and learn. My deepest thanks to both Ann Vickery and Elizabeth Webby for the outstanding intellectual generosity, guidance, enthusiasm and encouragement they have given. I would also like to extend my thanks to Nicole Moore, Katherine Bode, Lesa Scholl, Brigid Rooney, Lyn McCredden, Leonie Rutherford, Leigh Dale, Porscha Fermanis, Meg Tasker, Felicity Perry and my friends and colleagues for all their help in developing this book. My thanks to my family, whose support I am so grateful for. Thanks are due as well to all the librarians who have assisted me with the archival research. I would like to thank Deakin University as well as the Deakin University Library, the National Library of Australia, the State Library of Victoria (particularly Katie Flack), the Mitchell Library, the Sydney University Library, the British Library and also the University Library of Illinois at Urbana-Champaign.

A version of the first chapter was published as 'Eliza Hamilton Dunlop's "Aboriginal Mother": Romanticism, Anti-Slavery, and Imperial Feminism in the Nineteenth Century' in the *JASAL* Special Issue Archive Madness 11 (2011), a version of the chapter on Caroline Leakey in *ALS* (2015) and on Louisa Lawson in *Hecate* (2013). Material from this book was presented at the inaugural RSAA (Romanticism Studies Association of Australasia) 2011 conference 'Tyrannies of Distance'; the BARS (British Association for Romantic Studies) 2011 conference 'Romantic Identities: Selves in Society 1770–1835'; the AVSA (Australian Victorian Studies Association) 2012 conference 'Victorian Vocabularies'; and the ASAL (Association for the Study of Australian Literature) 2012 conference 'The Colonies'.

INTRODUCTION: REREADING COLONIAL POETRY

In this book I present a critical remapping of colonial Australian poetry to reflect the strong presence of settler women poets, particularly those writing in newspapers and periodicals. In examining this poetry in its original context of newspapers and journals, the political intervention as well as the reception of that poetry is made much more apparent. Five writers published in newspapers and periodicals have been selected as representative of particular periods in Australia (as well as globally), from the 1830s to the turn of the century: Eliza Hamilton Dunlop, Mary Bailey, Caroline Leakey, Emily Manning and Louisa Lawson. The aesthetic and political concerns of these five poets reveal a significant and cohesive imperial feminist movement in Australian settler colonial poetry. However, rather than seeing these poets as working within an insular colonial space, this book demonstrates an alternative networked tradition of imperial and transnational feminist poetics and politics beyond and around emergent masculine nationalism.

All five published in colonial and international contexts, particularly in Britain and North America. All were engaged in various ways in negotiating the domestic ideal in their expression of political voice. Ongoing relationships to political approaches are emphasized in these poets' engagements with earlier British and wider anglophone women's poetic traditions. In positioning settler women poets in Australia in relation to European and North American movements, this study challenges the dominant cartography of settler colonial Australian literature's relationship to Romanticism and its legacies. The connections of literary Romanticism with revolutionary thought, communitarianism and challenges to women's inequality are particularly significant to much of these women's poetry. I foreground their contributions, particularly in assuming and mobilizing a political voice, to a transnational feminist tradition. This significantly alters the current positioning of settler women poets in relation to Australian literary history. By resituating their work in its broader contexts, my book re-evaluates the political engagement of settler colonial women's poetry.

All five women published poetry extensively in journals and newspapers. The increasing recognition of the importance of periodicals and newspapers in colonial literary studies coincides with developments in print culture studies, and particularly the significance of print culture to political intervention, literary Romanticism and women's traditions. As Alexis Easley has noted of the British context, 'periodical journalism was instrumental in the rise of the woman author during the nineteenth century'.[1] In colonial Australia, especially for earlier settler poets like Dunlop and Bailey, newspapers were the main medium for the publication of poetry, as Elizabeth Webby's *Early Australian Poetry: An Annotated Bibliography* (1982) has shown. Such newspapers were spaces in which working-class and Indigenous Australian literature could find a place. The *Macquarie Pen Anthology of Aboriginal Literature* (2008) edited by Anita Heiss and Peter Minter includes letters by Aboriginal Australian authors written in English that were published in colonial newspapers. Heiss and Minter note that 'during the nineteenth century, Aboriginal people were dispossessed of their lands and many were interned on reserves and missions, institutions in which common human rights were rigorously limited by legislative machinery'.[2] They point out that

> Aboriginal authorship, as a practice and a literary category, first appears in genres that are common to political discourse: letters by individuals to local authorities and newspapers, petitions by communities in fear of further forms of dispossession or incarceration, and the chronicles of those dispossessed.[3]

Although my book is focussed on settler women's poetry, such writing as well as oral traditions are enormously important. Penny van Toorn's *Writing Never Arrives Naked: Early Aboriginal Cultures of Writing in Australia* (2006) examines Indigenous writing in the colonial period, including that of Aboriginal women, raising questions around understandings of pluralities in literacy and their relationships to empowerment. In reproducing Empire, newspapers and journals continued to be significant in terms of encompassing literary political dissent too. And these newspapers published original poetry by settler women, as well as popular British, European and American poetry, throughout the colonial period in Australia.[4]

This book aims to contextualize and re-evaluate these five women writers, since there has been little comprehensive study of them. It seeks to demonstrate the wider political contexts of nineteenth-century settler women's poetry by placing due emphasis on their international intertexts. The works of the women poets considered here were anglophone and Eurocentric and rather than situate white predominantly middle-class women's experiences as the norm this study seeks to examine their uses of political voice and imperial feminist discourses. As David Damrosch has suggested, all writing exists 'within a literary system beyond that of its own culture'.[5] These poets' address to identity and place problematically connected ideas of independent womanhood with the colonies, while at times simultaneously disrupting nationalist modes of thinking, especially emergent Australian masculine nationalism, and this is what I mean when I use the term transnational in the book. This is connected to Lynda Ng's point, following Susan Stanford Friedman and Damrosch, that transnational circulation is as much a mode of writing as it is a mode of reading.[6] These relationships to emergent masculine nationalism coincide with imperialist frameworks and are operating simultaneously. Themes explored in this study, demonstrating these poets' access to political discourses of gender, class and sometimes race, include abolitionism, Hellenism, eroticism and spiritualism. In considering the contributions of these women, particularly through print culture, this study seeks to recognize both the politicized nature of colonial Australian settler women's poetry and complicity with Empire in its engagement with imperial and transnational women's writing traditions and feminist discourses.

Have settler colonial women poets engaged with the European poetic tradition, political issues and imperial feminist concerns, via a polarized dualism between public and private? This divide is particularly important in relation to their questioning of local and cultural politics, as well as authorship. Clare Midgley's *Feminism and Empire* (2007) examines the foundational relationship of imperialism to the history of British feminist traditions, noting the connection both to ideas of 'progress' and to 'new imperial history'.[7] My study is concerned with the related historical poetic relationships of feminism to colonialism, literary Romanticism and emergent masculine nationalism. The idea of a so-called Australian national identity as applied to the literary is acknowledged as a later nineteenth-century construct, and this has also contributed to a lack of adequate study of colonial poetry as existing within a global context of imperialist Western expansion and colonization. An interrelated, often networked tradition of women's poetry is integral to the developments in settler women's poetry in colonial Australia. In foregrounding their connections to literary Romanticism, the relationships of these women's poetics to the British invasion and colonization of Australia are emphasized. Connections between the colonies and literary Romanticism can show numerous dialogues and imperialist responses to consider beyond those already elaborated on, such as British poet Letitia Elizabeth Landon's writing on India in poems like 'Hurdwar, a place of Hindoo Pilgrimage' (1832). The footnote to Landon's poem in *Hamilton's Gazeteer* expressed pro-colonial sentiment, for example, in suggesting that the fair following the pilgrimage 'thanks to the precautions taken by the British Government, has, of late years, gone off without bloodshed'.[8] Across the nineteenth century, the concerns apparent in Australian colonial women's writing reflect the strong influence and popularity of precursors and contemporaries including Felicia Hemans, Letitia Elizabeth Landon, Mary Robinson, Eliza Cook, Elizabeth Barrett Browning, Christina Rossetti and Ella Wheeler Wilcox. My study follows the British feminist revisionist work of Stuart Curran, Anne Mellor and Stephen Behrendt beginning in the late 1980s and specifically builds on Australian colonial studies by Elizabeth Webby, Ann Vickery, Patricia Clarke, Michael Ackland and Debra Adelaide.

Until recently, nineteenth-century women's poetry has tended to be excluded or marginalized in Australian literary studies, particularly in terms of its political significance. Such exclusions are even more pronounced for working-class women's poetry and Aboriginal poetries. Australian settler colonial women's poetry is often excluded or marginalized in broad studies of anglophone Romantic or Victorian poetry. Where such poetry has been included critics have tended to focus on ideas perceived to be specific to 'Australian literature'. The continuations of British and wider Romantic women's discourses in nineteenth-century colonial women's poetry rather suggests the ongoing significance of these earlier traditions. For example, the symbolic 'language of flowers' is important to Louisa Lawson's poetry as well as that of Caroline Leakey's and is part of a metaphoric poetic discourse on sexuality shared by colonial women poets and a wider anglophone poetic language, engaged across a range of geographical spaces. Leakey's use of a language of flowers can show how the emergence of a nationalist differentiation for settler Australian from British literature led to a misunderstanding of these women's poetry written in colonial Australia.

Australian colonial literature

Australian literary histories, as Webby notes, more recently have become concerned with 'the ways in which the terms "literature" and "history" have become increasingly contentious' as well as 'nation'.[9] In the introduction to *The Penguin Book of Australian Ballads* (1993) Philip Butterss and Webby note that

> by the middle of the twentieth century, a group of radical nationalists argued that the old bush songs and bush ballads embodied the anti-authoritarian, egalitarian and communal values which they felt were essentially Australian [...] Russel Ward [being] the most influential proponent of this view of Australian identity.[10]

Thus, bush nationalism had come to be considered the essential 'Australian literature' and the colonial writings which preceded it have, as Ackland suggests, 'customarily been treated as [...] sporadic and ineffectual attempts to found an Antipodean literature'.[11] The marginal position of many women poets to the canon of colonial Australian poetry allows a perpetuation of the assumption that settler women poets did not contribute and did not speak to political topics. In Leonie Rutherford, Megan Roughley and Nigel Spence's *Louisa Lawson: Collected Poems with Selected Critical Commentaries* (1996), Susan Pfisterer-Smith terms this exclusion the 'Louisa factor'.[12] This marginalization of the political significance of settler colonial women's poetry has continued, despite the fact that women poets consistently engaged with political themes, particularly in relation to their experiences of gender identity. Importantly, these themes were often accessed through an engagement with British imperialist and wider transnational women's poetic traditions.

Colonial poetry in Australia has generally tended to be interpreted through a lens of oppositionality or insularity. Richard White's *Inventing Australia* (1981) provides a re-evaluation which questions the various interests served by the construction of a national identity, valuable both when examining the kinds of ideas which have resulted in the exclusion of much settler women's poetry from the literary canon and the uses of ideas of national identity in their poetry. Michael Ackland's *That Shining Band: A Study of Colonial Verse Tradition* (1994) covers both settler men and women poets of the colonial period, but is in places superficial in its treatment of women poets. Emily Manning is only given a few pages, despite Rosalind Smith's assertion in the *Australian Dictionary of Biography* that 'together with her accomplished use of a variety of poetic forms [...] the intellectual weight of her poetry marks Emily Manning as a major nineteenth-century Australian poet'.[13] This is also true of the feminist revisionist studies from the 1980s, such as Debra Adelaide's *A Bright and Fiery Troop: Australian Women Writers of the Nineteenth Century* (1988), which coincided with a more general trend towards revaluing colonial writers. Ackland states that the earlier dismissal of colonial literature has been even more acute in relation to the poetry of women.[14]

Webby makes this point in 'Born to Blush Unseen: Some Nineteenth Century Women Poets', noting that novelists and journal writers have received greater critical attention than women poets.[15] Ann Vickery also contends that 'gender has tended to eclipse issues of genre [...] Focussing almost solely on the novel, poets remain absent or marginal figures'.[16] Women poets are included in other chapters of Debra Adelaide's *A Bright and Fiery Troop: Australian Women Writers of the Nineteenth Century*, where they also wrote novels. Yet while Caroline Leakey's novel *The Broad Arrow* is examined in Shirley Walker's chapter on her work, her volume of poetry, *Lyra Australis: Or, Attempts to Sing in a Strange Land*, rates only a mention. Jenna Mead has produced important research and critical re-evaluations of Leakey's life and works. However, again, Leakey's poetry has remained somewhat marginal in these discussions. This focus on areas of writing or public life other than their poetry is often true of the other poets in this study, alongside poets not included in this study, such as Ada Cambridge, and later poets such as Dulcie Deamer. The point made by Webby and Vickery that poetry tends to be bypassed in favour of novels in feminist constructions of an Australian settler women's writing tradition is worth considering in light of poetry's exalted position as a genre in literary history more broadly and its importance in nineteenth-century literature and political culture.

Much of the literature on Australian women's writing provides forms of 'group study' that examines critically and biographically or anthologizes women writers. The group study as a form offers a sample of writers, while also allowing detailed individual bodies of work to be compared with each other to demonstrate patterns and similarities suggesting their wider significance. Susan Lever's *The Oxford Book of Australian Women's Verse* was published in 1995 and offers a selection of women's poetry beginning from 1837 with Eliza Hamilton Dunlop's 'The Aboriginal Mother'. This collection includes early poets, whereas Susan Hampton and Kate Llewellyn's *The Penguin Book of Australian Women Poets* (1986) skips over many colonial poets, such as Eliza Hamilton Dunlop, Caroline Leakey, Emily Manning and Louisa Lawson, and includes only Ada Cambridge, Mary Gilmore and Mary Fullerton at the tail end of the nineteenth century.

While Vickery's *Stressing the Modern* is focussed on the period from 1900 onwards, it is a vital precursor to my research in being concerned with both women's poetry and politics in Australia. Vickery's 'A "Lonely Crossing": Approaching Nineteenth-Century Australian Women's Poetry' is also the only article in a special issue on Australian poetry in *Victorian Poetry* to examine colonial women poets such as Dunlop, Leakey and Lawson. Studies of Australian women's poetry, such as *Stressing the Modern*, have yet to extend earlier into the nineteenth century to examine connections, themes and concerns in the work of settler colonial women poets as a group. Although it makes no claim to cover all colonial women poets, this present work is intended to help fill the gap as a sustained critical and historical reappraisal of these five poets. Though the best-known poet in this study, Lawson's poetry has still been considered a secondary achievement to her feminist journal the *Dawn*, her historical significance as a campaigner for women's suffrage or her status as the mother of Henry Lawson. The first working-class woman poet of this study, Lawson engages with imperial and emergent nationalist feminist and working-class poetics. Sharyn Pearce writes that Lawson 'was a poet and a short story writer, though most would agree that her achievements in these areas were limited and uneven'.[17] Such assessments have not acknowledged that Lawson's poetry, like that of Dunlop, Bailey, Leakey and Manning, represents an influential contribution that was consistently politically engaged.

Susan Lever's 'The Social Tradition in Australian Women's Poetry' outlines a tradition of women's poetry in Australia concerned with social politics, which she contrasts with the more 'introspective' or 'confessional' tradition of British and American women poets. Often very conscious of place, the poetry of colonial women in Australia was also extensively connected with these British and American women's traditions. Isobel Armstrong's *Victorian Poetry: Poetry, Poetics and Politics* (1993) demonstrates the subversive strategies of Victorian British women's poetry. Paula Bennett's *Poets in the Public Sphere: The Emancipatory Project of American Women's Poetry, 1800–1900* (2003) examines women's poetry in American periodicals. Her study reveals that, contrary to previously held popular beliefs about Victorian women's poetry, women's writing in the nineteenth century was highly political and engaged in rethinking gender and sexuality. Through these women's poetic traditions, the extent of settler colonial women poets' political voices can be seen, operating within transnational and imperial nineteenth-century campaigns for women's rights. Lever notes a social emphasis in Dunlop's poetry, which she suggests is 'a firm political statement about the place of poetry as the preserver of humane values'.[18]

Critical appraisals, apart from those such as Lever's examination of Dunlop, have tended to overlook or underestimate the political nature of women's poetry in colonial Australia. The characterization of these women's poetry as having a so-called moral and civilizing function, particularly in relation to 'nation building' perpetuated at the time, has perhaps contributed to a false impression that these poets were disinclined to political radicalism or challenging gender roles. Yet within those predominant discourses these women's poetic expressions of anger and opposition to violence and inequality are considered structurally desirable and coded as 'civilizing'. Likewise, when these women's poetry is seen as specifically 'Australian', and isolated from European cultural concerns, much of its political content is blocked from view. Poetry in the colonial period was very much a public forum, often a persuasion in rhyme, so it was an important aspect of the development of political ideas and public debate. Hans Robert Jauss and the Constance School have argued that political significance derives particularly from the relationship between the text and its audiences. These poets were often writing for an English audience, sometimes both an English and colonial one, and sometimes wider transnational audiences. Clearly in dialogue with both the British and colonial poetic communities and wider anglophone readerships at the time, such direct relationships between author and audience are important for my analysis of these women's poetry. As works intended for specific audiences, their rhetoric and use of language to evoke particular emotional responses are significant.

How we respond as readers and critics to the concerns of these poems today is another important aspect of this relationship. Jauss argues that

> if the history of literature is viewed [...] within the horizon of a dialogue between work and audience that forms a continuity, the opposition between its aesthetic and its historical aspects is continually mediated. Thus the thread from the past appearance to the present experience of literature, which historicism had cut, is tied back together.[19]

My approach follows as well from Elizabeth Schüssler Fiorenza's coining of the term *Kyriarchy* as an analytical concept to replace that of Patriarchy, 'in order to highlight that the analytic object of feminist theory [...] is not simply woman or gender but the intersection of domination or Kyriarchy'. Fiorenza states that 'Kyriarchy is best theorised as a complex pyramidal system of intersecting multiplicative social and religious relations of superordination and subordination, of ruling and exploitation. Kyriarchal relations of domination are built on elite male property rights.'[20] For a feminist project, canonical and non-canonical literature alike must be re-examined as existing in a wider context in which its production fulfils agendas through that which it includes and that which it omits. Vickery questions assumptions about the role of women in the political sphere, pointing to evidence that while 'in the late 1880s, the *Bulletin* positioned feminism as antagonistic to national independence, arguing that women were naturally conservative, class-bound, and irrational [...] For women poets like Marie Pitt and Mary Gilmore, feminism paralleled socialism in their shared platform of equality'.[21] This entwining of feminisms with political activism is a frequent feature in earlier nineteenth-century settler women's poetry in Australia as well as internationally. Concerns within the development of various feminisms included the interrogation of women's roles, as well as the advocacy of pacifism and sometimes a breaking down of national boundaries. These are ideas closely associated with the writings of Saint Simonian socialists and Fourierists through to Marx, across the nineteenth century, and are evident in the work of these poets, particularly in that of Bailey.

The content of much of the women's poetry from this period, when closely analysed in relation to anglophone poetries, puts to rest claims that it was not politically engaged. The poetry examined in this study ranges broadly across themes of anti-slavery, anti-transportation, anti-industrialization, pacifism, utopian socialism, the religious crisis, republicanism and emergent nationalism. Most of these women's poetic concerns, however, do not acknowledge the rights of Indigenous peoples. Where they do consider First Nations Australians, appropriation and racism mark their approaches. This is because the political topics addressed are framed within a developing nineteenth-century imperial feminism present in the work of all these five poets. The so-called purity associated with the domestic ideal of nineteenth-century womanhood also excluded a public political voice for women, emphasizing wifely subjection, containment within the 'private sphere' and emotional sensitivity understood as existing in opposition to masculine intellectual expression and citizenship. All working-class women, as Patricia Ingram's *The Language of Gender and Class: Transformation in the Victorian Novel* (1996) argues, were coded as sexually impure, regardless of their individual situations. Similarly, as Jennifer DeVere Brody's *Impossible Purities: Blackness, Femininity and Victorian Culture* (1998) has shown, women of colour were also coded as impure, with the concept of purity an impossibility to begin with. Within these five women poets' approaches the white middle-class domestic ideal of nineteenth-century womanhood is negotiated and challenged in terms of political voice on issues like intellectual equality, moral and sexual equality, the right to financial independence, women's rights within marriage and the right to divorce.

It should be noted that Fidelia Hill and Ada Cambridge have not been included in this study due to a focus on poets working through the periodical press, for whom comparatively little critical research exists. Hill is regarded as the first settler woman to publish a book of verse: *Poems and Recollections of the Past* (1840). Ada Cambridge, also known as Ada Cross, contributed to journals such as the *Atlantic Monthly*, *Australian Ladies Annual* and the *Australasian*, serializing her novels under her initials, writing fiction and non-fiction as well as poetry. Her poetry was highly political and feminist, and included, prior to arrival in Australia in 1870, *Hymns on the Litany* (1865), *Hymns on the Holy Communion* (1866) and, after her arrival, *The Manor House and Other Poems* (1875) and *Unspoken Thoughts* (1887), all published in London. As Jill Roe notes, the poems in *Unspoken Thoughts* were regarded as being 'daring and even improper for a clergyman's wife' and were 'hastily suppressed'.[22]

The writers in this study have been chosen as poets who were represented in the periodical press. They also reflect a close relationship with women's poetic traditions and innovations outside Australia over the course of the nineteenth century. They all published in periodicals outside as well as within Australia. All the poets apart from Manning and Lawson were born elsewhere than Australia, and Lawson was the only one to have remained in Australia all her life. Dunlop also journeyed to India. Leakey came from England and later returned there, while Manning travelled to London and returned to Australia. Both published volumes of poetry in London, as Bailey had done prior to her arrival.

The poetry of settler women in colonial Australia is virtually unknown to many twenty-first century readers, and this raises many questions about canonicity and gender, fashions in literary styles and the constructed tastes of readers. The field of colonial poetry studies is much indebted to Webby's work and to her *Early Australian Poetry: An Annotated Bibliography* (1982), which lists every poem in surviving issues of newspapers and journals published before 1850. As Webby points out, this poetry was generally not published as volumes during this period owing to the expense.[23] Similarly, expensive volumes became unfashionable in the 1830s and 1840s in the British context, with women poets such as Hemans and Landon publishing in collections and annuals. Webby published Dunlop's *The Aboriginal Mother and Other Poems* (1981) using the original newspaper sources. However, the significance and extent of Dunlop's prolific contribution to Australian poetry is not conveyed through this small selection of poems as many of her poems remain uncollected in various early Australian periodicals. Dunlop's manuscript *The Vase, Comprising Songs for Music and Poems* is held at the Mitchell Library and more of her poems will be included in a forthcoming print collection.

Webby's critical introduction to Dunlop's *Aboriginal Mother and Other Poems* highlights her engagement with Aboriginal subjects, and her poetry is now increasingly included in Australian anthologies such as *The Penguin Anthology of Australian Poetry* (2008) and *The Turning Wave: Poems and Songs of Irish Australia* (2001). John O'Leary provides some New Historicist readings of 'The Aboriginal Mother' in 'Giving the Indigenous a voice: Further thoughts on the poetry of Eliza Hamilton Dunlop' (2004) and '"Unlocking the fountains of the heart": Settler verse and the politics of sympathy' (2010). Peter Minter reconsiders the poem in 'Settlement Defiled: Ventriloquy, Pollution and Nature in Eliza Hamilton Dunlop's "The Aboriginal Mother"' in *Text, Translation, and Transnationalism: World Literature in 21st Century Australia* (2017), making important points about how such ventriloquy relates to purgation following white violence and settlement. Dunlop's poetry, when viewed over the decades in which she published in various geographical locations, reveals a consistent engagement with European approaches to women's rights and Romanticism, including engagements with imperial campaigns against slavery and *Sati*, which, as Midgley notes, positioned white women as 'saviours of brown women'[24] rather than in solidarity with them. Dunlop's work has more recently begun to be more widely critically located.

Mary Bailey's poetry has remained largely unknown to an even greater extent, despite her prolific contributions to newspapers such as the *Colonial Times* of Tasmania. Although Bailey produced three volumes in Britain prior to her arrival (*The Months*, *Musae Sacrae* and *Palmyra*), she only published in newspapers after she followed her husband, a convict, to Van Diemen's Land.

This suggests again the dependence on the periodical press even of previously published poets in the early colonial period. Where volumes were produced, as with Leakey's *Lyra Australis: Or, Attempts to Sing in a Strange Land* and Manning's *The Balance of Pain, and Other Poems*, they have not been reprinted until recently. Both volumes were published in London, with Leakey's also published in Hobart. Lawson's collection, *The Lonely Crossing and Other Poems*, 'which she herself printed at the *Dawn* office just before it closed in 1905', as Megan Roughley notes, was not published again until 1996, when it was reproduced in *Louisa Lawson: Collected Poems with Selected Critical Commentaries*.[25] Morris Miller notes that a second edition was published in 1909[26] and Leonie Rutherford suggests that this edition was of sheets left over from the 1905 printing. Roughley also notes that a facsimile of the 1905 edition was published in 1986 by Maxwell Printing Co., Sydney. It is clear however that the periodical press was extremely important for these women's poetry even when they also published collections.

For many of the women poets there are still no published collections available. The University of Sydney has put together a collection of e-books freely available online, through the Sydney Electronic Text and Image Service (SETIS) project, now part of their Australian Digital Collections. Manning's *The Balance of Pain and Other Poems* (1877), Leakey's *Lyra Australis: Or, Attempts to Sing in a Strange Land* (1854) and Mary Hannay Foott's *Where the Pelican Builds* (1885), among others, are available through this resource, often the first time they have been republished since their initial publication. Additionally, these works are becoming more widely available through digitizations such as Google Books and the Internet Archive of the Library of Congress.

Archival research and the digital age

Contemporary projects recovering and formulating the importance of nineteenth-century Australian periodical literature include the important work of Katherine Bode's 'To Be Continued [...]' database,[27] Paul Eggert's indexing project for *AustLit*, and Ken Gelder and Rachel Weaver's *Colonial Journals and the Emergence of Australian Literary Culture* (2014).[28] Yet even as unprecedented digitization makes nineteenth-century periodicals, newspapers and rare texts widely available for the first time, there remain barriers to the visibility of settler colonial Australian women's poetry and a consideration of the wider relevance of that poetry. It is important to recognize that not all archival records and documents are digitally available. Examples include Caroline Leakey's letters, held at the British Library. Official bodies such as the Association for the Study of Australian Literature, the Australian Research Council, and digitization projects and databases such as AustLit, Australian

Poetry Library and SETIS have approached digitization and literature by mapping it out in terms of nation and published volumes. This impedes the visibility of much colonial poetry, given that much of it was published (and has occasionally been digitized) in countries other than Australia, including England, Ireland, America and India. Mary Bailey's poems, like numerous Australian and international journal and newspaper poems by women, remain absent from digitized poetry resources in Australia such as the Australian Poetry Library and would be valuable inclusions in such digitized resources.

Many of the poems published in periodicals have been included in large-scale digitization projects such as Google Books and Trove Newspapers through the National Library of Australia. Other nationalized newspaper digitization projects include New Zealand's Papers Past through Te Puna Mātauranga o Aotearoa, the National Library of New Zealand. However there need to be links from newspaper digitizations of poetry to other poetry digitization projects, as these poems will often not be revealed through online author searches, thus contributing to the lack of visibility. The AustLit database entry for Bailey for instance lists only ten poems, so does not begin to reflect the prolific extent of her publishing, though it does link these poems to Trove digitizations. International digitization projects such as NINES (Networked Infrastructure for Nineteenth Century Electronic Scholarship), the Poetess Archive and the British Romantic Women's Poetry Project at the University of California, Davis would also be enriched by settler colonial examples of women's writing. Projects on individual writers, such as the Rossetti Archive, show the significance of digital archival resources, but for settler women poets of colonial Australia resources are at present largely incomplete. This is the case for much nineteenth-century Australian periodical literature being uncovered through projects such as Katherine Bode's and Paul Eggert's.

This visibility of periodical literature is particularly important given the wider cultural contexts of colonial poetry. Critical scholarship has yet to catch up with the increasing availability of digitized texts and the implications for women's authorship in colonial Australia. The focus on published volumes of poetry and national categories in digital projects has meant that transnational flows in colonial poetry are elided rather than made more evident. For instance, while there is a mention that Mary Bailey produced volumes of poetry in England before her arrival in Tasmania in the biography section of her AustLit entry, they are not named, nor are they listed under her works. Bailey's volumes do, however, appear in J. R. de J. Jackson's *Romantic Poetry by Women: A Bibliography 1770–1835* (1993), which is a British text listing recovered volumes of Romantic women's poetry. This exemplifies the way relationships to Romanticism are obscured in the categorization of these women's poetry, due to the prioritizing of national categories.

Romanticism and its legacies

Critical work on women's poetry in Britain during the Romantic period and later nineteenth century has flourished since the 1990s, through the groundbreaking work of Anne Mellor, Stuart Curran, Jerome McGann, Judith Pascoe, Isobel Armstrong and many others. This has radically reshaped a long-held view that Romanticism in Britain was a movement limited to six canonical male poets: Wordsworth, Coleridge, Keats, Shelley, Byron and Blake. Stephen Behrendt's study, *British Women Poets and the Romantic Writing Community* (2009), was the first to include Irish Romantic women poets, so it is crucial to understanding the poetry of the Irish-born Eliza Hamilton Dunlop. Claire Knowles' *Sensibility and Female Poetic Tradition* (2009) is valuable in examining the Romantic women's poetic tradition, especially as a tradition with continuing significance. The important recent scholarship collected in *Romantic Sociability: Social Networks and Literary Culture in Britain* (2002) examines sociability and challenges the presumption of isolation typically associated with Romantic poets. This study is relevant especially in its approach to gendered aspects of Romantic sociability.

Romanticism, as a European phenomenon, is examined in Patrick Vincent's *The Romantic Poetess: European Culture, Politics and Gender 1820–1840* (2004), which includes British, French, Russian and German women poets. It is also apparent that poets such as Felicia Hemans and Letitia Elizabeth Landon were highly influential on colonial women poets, not only in Australia but also in America, Canada and India. British Romantic women's poetry was increasingly anthologized in the 1990s, making it available in collections including Paula R. Feldman's *British Women Poets of the Romantic Era* (1997), Duncan Wu's *Romantic Women Poets: An Anthology* (1997) and anthologies of nineteenth-century women's poetry such as Isobel Armstrong and Joseph Bristow's *Nineteenth Century Women Poets* (1998). These are important sources for examining settler women's poetry. More recently, increasingly global conceptions of Romanticism, and specific attention to the relationship of Romanticism to the southern hemisphere, have been considered in studies such as Porscha Fermanis and Carmen Cassalligi's *Romanticism: A Literary and Cultural History* (2016).

The consciously communal imperial feminist context of such networks is reiterated in women poets' choices of medium and genre. Anne Mellor points out for the British context that the

> poetic genres chosen by Romantic women poets […] function to create and sustain community. Frequently published in pocketbook albums and such annual gift books as *Forget Me Not* and *The Keepsake* […]

Women poets' choice of genre thus exists in contestation both with the eighteenth-century ordering of the arts and the masculinist poetics this hierarchy reflects.[29]

In *Lyric and Labour in the Romantic Tradition* (1998) Anne Janowitz similarly suggests that Romanticism might be usefully conceptualized as

> the literary form of a struggle taking place on many levels of society between the claims of *individualism* and the claims of *communitarianism*; that is, those claims that respond to identity as an always already existing voluntaristic self, and those that figure identity as emerging from a fabric of social narratives, with their attendant goals and expectations.[30]

Janowitz further positions 'the communitarian lyric as a romantic persistence in the nineteenth century life of lyric forms'.[31] These connections between popular print culture, the legacies of women's Romantic poetry and communal political approaches to literary production are crucial to colonial Australian settler women's poetry. These women often took what may be considered a cosmopolitan approach that extended beyond British or emergent Australian nationalisms, in which gender was recognized as a unifying category among white women more than nation or Empire. Their interests extended across ancient cultures, including Greek and Roman, as well as Indian, Italian, North American and French, and in some cases incorporated discourses around Indigeneity, slavery and so-called new- and old-world dichotomies.

Dunlop, Bailey, Leakey, Manning and Lawson, as representatives of women writing across the nineteenth century, all engage to varying degrees with arguments for gender equality. This is reflected in the inclusion of transatlantic anti-slavery discourses, the idea of the fallen woman and spiritualism in their work. The proximity of many of these concerns to specific legal reforms demonstrates the legislative political significance of this kind of protest poetry both abroad and in Australia. Issues addressed include the Myall Creek Massacre court trial, legislation around convicts and transportation, the cessation of convict transportation to Van Diemen's Land, the infant custody bill, the legal stature of woman as femme covert, divorce reform, women's education and women's constitutional right to vote. Settler women's poetry of this period in Australia is often presented as being concerned with nation building, and it should be remembered that nationalist agendas had a relationship with Romanticism. It is also important to consider the ways in which gender informed uses of patriotism and emergent masculine nationalism – in some cases its rejection. Romantic poetics did not necessarily reflect an isolationist approach to politics: on the contrary many of the political concerns are of a much more global scale, such as that of slavery. Anti-slavery discourses, although not predominant, were not uncommon in colonial Australia, despite the wider historical lack of recognition that the forced unpaid labour and servitude of Aboriginal peoples undoubtedly also warranted such language.[32] Yet such discourses often centred white women's and men's experiences or were appropriative. The example of slavery is also important in demonstrating the way in which the politics of race, class and gender are often constructed in terms of the discourses of the so-called old world and new world by these poets. The idea of the 'new' world perpetuates the myth of terra nullius, ignoring the reality of Indigenous Australian peoples as custodians of the oldest continuing cultures in the world.

The fall from law-abiding British respectability into 'exile' in Australia (a recurring theme particularly for earlier poets) manifests not only as personal experience in the poetry but also as political statements about law, class status, gender and the colonies. The importance of working-class British poets, such as Eliza Cook, and Chartist poetics to these literary approaches is also significant. Cook was a highly popular international presence, as was the later American poet Ella Wheeler Wilcox, although there are no studies of these women's significance for colonial Australian poetry. American models of poetry, such as in Emma Lazarus's depiction of the Statue of Liberty in 'The New Colossus', similarly operate through a more global envisioning of the politics of class and settler colonialism:

'Keep, ancient lands, your storied pomp!' cries she
With silent lips. 'Give me your tired, your poor,
Your huddled masses yearning to breathe free [...]'.[33]

Poetry celebrating the supposed breakdown of class structures in colonial Australia has a clear relationship to British imperialism that is elided by the insularity and oppositionality of masculine nationalist literary culture. For poets like Emily Manning, the ideal of colonial Australia as providing class mobility through opportunity to those who settled there, the so-called workingman's paradise, was not celebrated. Manning instead points to the poverty of Sydney's slums. By re-examining these women's poetry in colonial Australia within their connections to transnational anglophone cultural discourses, the political meanings of this writing are made more explicit.

Print culture

Without its inclusion in periodical literature, settler women's poetry in Australia during the colonial period would appear to have been fairly limited.

When periodical literature is taken into account, this picture is significantly altered and poets emerge as consistent contributors, often across a variety of newspapers and journals, who were well known, influential and connected with political figures and literary circles. In examining this poetry in the original context of the newspaper, the political significance of that poetry is often much more apparent than when poems appear in a published volume. For example, Dunlop's 'The Aboriginal Mother' appeared amid the newspaper debates on the trial of the men responsible for the Myall Creek Massacre and Lawson's 'The Squatter's Wife' appeared amid suffragist agitation for divorce reform.

In the colonial period in Australia, particularly in periodical print culture, Romanticism and settler women's poetry are strongly connected and very much present. Studies such as Mark Schoenfield's *British Periodicals and Romantic Identity: 'The Literary Lower Empire'* (2009) and Kim Wheatley's *Romantic Periodicals and Print Culture* (2003) have revalued the periodical for Romantic literature. As Behrendt observes,

> Literary history long nourished an image of the Romantic writer (usually a poet) as a solitary, flower-sniffing devotee of unspoiled nature. This myth entirely misses the reality that Romantic writers were characteristically directly involved in the leading social, political, economic and ideological contests of their era [...] Careful examination reveals that both the few canonical Romantic writers and many less familiar but equally active and committed writers knew the periodicals.[34]

Not only poetry but also serialized fiction, literary articles, reviews, criticism, rebuttals, correspondence and advertising of books and theatre were published in Australian journals, much as in the British literary periodicals. Australian journals and newspapers, including the *Dawn* and the *Colonial Times*, were also transmitted abroad. Further, the British Romantic poets figure heavily in the epigraphs of many of the Australian contributions, as well as being themselves published in Australian newspapers.

Despite the oft-cited arguments about distance, there are numerous examples where minimal delay occurred in the printing in Australian newspapers of new poetry from Britain. Wordsworth's 'Somnambulist' from *Yarrow Revisited* was published in the *Sydney Gazette* on Saturday 5 December 1835, the same year it was first published in Britain. The inclusion of British Romantic poetry in Australian newspapers appears to have begun with George Howe, editor of the *Sydney Gazette*, Australia's first colonial newspaper, which was established in 1803. Howe had previously worked on the *Times* in London and was a poet himself. The *Australian Dictionary of Biography* notes that 'his education was thorough [...] and he was well read in European literature'.[35] Poems by Byron, Shelley, Wordsworth and Coleridge appeared in colonial newspapers including the *Sydney Gazette*. Moreover, Romantic women poets including Eliza Cook, Hemans and Landon appeared in various papers, such as the *Argus*, the *Sydney Gazette* and the *Sydney Morning Herald*, often with notes about which periodicals or published books they were taken from. This trend is notable throughout the nineteenth century, with Lawson reproducing articles, stories and poetry from various journals and newspapers, including *Harper's Magazine* in the *Dawn*. Increasingly North American periodicals and writers were represented.

Those in influential political and literary circles often contributed to the colonial periodical press. In 1850 Henry Parkes, later a politician, who wrote poetry himself became the proprietor-editor of the Sydney newspaper the *Empire*, which Dunlop contributed to, demonstrating the tight-knit links between newspapers, poetry and politics in colonial Australia. The New South Wales–based poets Lawson, Dunlop and Manning all published poetry in the *Town and Country Journal* and Lawson and Manning both published in the *Sydney Mail* and *Sydney Morning Herald*. The poets in Tasmania, Leakey and Bailey, both published their colonial poetry in the *Courier* and Bailey also published poetry in the *Colonial Times* as well as in the *Hobarton Guardian*, of which her husband became the editor. Tasmanian periodical poetry by settlers was common in the period, with numerous writers, including Mary Leman Grimstone, contributing. All of the poets of this study also published in British and American periodicals.

Recognition of the uses and limitations of political voice in these women's poetry is bound up with the significance of print culture and international and imperial literary networks to colonial literature. Not only did newspapers and periodicals tend to be more widely read and speedily disseminated than printed books, they were also important spaces for poetry and reflect a far greater representation of settler women poets than published volumes of poetry in Australia, particularly prior to 1850. By the time Fidelia Hill's *Poems and Recollections of the Past* was published in 1840, a substantial body of poetry had already been contributed by settler women poets to the periodical press.

In *Print Politics: The Press and Radical Opposition in Early Nineteenth-Century England* (1996) Kevin Gilmartin, writing of Britain in the early nineteenth century, notes the radical underworld of high Romantic literature operating in the periodical press. Richard D. Altick's *The English Common Reader: A Social History of the Mass Reading Public, 1800*–1900 (1957) is also important to this study, as British periodical culture and its significance in Britain is so extensively connected with Australian colonial press and print culture, and is useful for theorizing readerships. Elizabeth Webby's 'Writers Printers Readers: The

Production of Australian Literature before 1855' provides important further information for an Australian colonial context.

The significance of periodical culture to women poets and to political voice is a key consideration of this book. A radicalism limited by imperialist and Eurocentric concepts in women's periodical poetry in Australia is also notable in American and British periodical poetry. Wide-ranging political affiliations are seen in the Tory *Blackwood's Edinburgh Magazine* and the Whig *Edinburgh Review*. Such affiliations are mirrored in colonial print politics and perhaps exemplified by Dunlop writing to Henry Parkes of the bias towards nationalist poetry in the *Empire*. Robert Dixon has noted Dunlop's assertion that the *Empire* did not publish her poem 'Carlingford Bay' because of preferential treatment of the white male Australian-born poet, Charles Harpur, and that the *Month* was more inclined to 'Old World' poetry.[36] These masculine nationalist values became increasingly prominent later in the nineteenth century and are exemplified by the particular projects of the *Bulletin* and the *Dawn*, in which the gendered nature of this divide is brought into sharp focus. In the light of this divide though, it is important to note that Dunlop did publish in papers such as the *Empire*, just as Louisa Lawson was published in the *Bulletin*. Dunlop and Bailey published their poetry in *Blackwood's*,[37] a very highly regarded magazine for poetry. The political divisions represented by particular papers extended to the emerging all-women's periodicals too, such as Louisa Lawson's the *Dawn*. For these women poets many of the periodicals in which they published were already a highly contested and often censorious poetic space.

Chapter 1 focuses on the poet Eliza Hamilton Dunlop and her significance, particularly as the writer of 'The Aboriginal Mother', a poem that voiced opposition to the horrific violence of the Myall Creek Massacre of Wirrayaraay Aboriginal people. Abolitionism as a key political theme linked to Dunlop's writing exemplifies some of the ways in which the discussion of a wider range of Dunlop's periodical poetry sheds new light on received conceptions of Australian women's poetry at this time as not only geographically isolated but also isolated from the major ideas, questions and concerns of the time and consequently not engaged politically. Dunlop's periodical poetry is important in the absence of a published volume and so the significance of periodical publishing is considered here, alongside questions of abolitionist literary culture and imperial feminist writing and their wide circulation at the time of Dunlop's writing. Importantly, Dunlop's political awareness not only presents a major challenge to representations of women's poetry as apolitical but also reflects her own preoccupations with questions of gender, race and class, and her attempts to bring questions of gender from the margins to a prominent space within the major political concerns of the day, in company with women poets writing on topics such as anti-slavery in Britain and Ireland. I argue that Dunlop's position also shows her awareness of the gendered nature of the divide between so-called native (a term which referred to white, Australian-born authors) emergent nationalist poetics and European literary approaches in Australia.

In Chapter 2, I consider the work of Mary Bailey, a classical scholar as well as a poet. Bailey followed her husband, convicted of forgery, to Tasmania, and the poetry she published in the *Colonial Times* and other newspapers after her arrival is examined here. I consider the political significance of Hellenism, concerned with ancient Greece, to Bailey's Tasmanian poetry as well as the continuity of the ideas and concerns of the poetry she earlier published in Britain. I first outline Bailey's negotiations with British Romanticism and Romantic Hellenism in her colonial poetry. Romantic Hellenism is evident in many of Bailey's poems on classical subjects and Grecian antiquity, as well as her translations from Latin and Greek, which she published in the *Colonial Times* in Hobart in the late 1840s. Bailey notably did not write at all on Aboriginal topics, and the significance of this, particularly in the wider context of the atrocities of Tasmanian genocide, is an important consideration. Bailey's use of utopian frames and anti-slavery discourse informs much of her writing against imprisonment, as did her standing as the wife of a convict, and these have important implications for questions of human rights and the development of a Tasmanian Romanticism. I argue that Hellenism is a template for Bailey's feminist poetics and her construction of a colonialist political engagement, based on classical ideals of democratic practices, equality, pacifism and education. Bailey's political engagements are complex and range from her involvement in local political matters, including those relating to prisoners' rights and the penal system, to far broader historical concepts. The lens of Hellenism is a major aspect of her work and is consistently suggestive of the political values espoused by a number of nineteenth-century utopians. Moreover, these values reveal both complicity with colonialism and a resistance very much concerned with gender. Bailey had an immense knowledge of European women writers and historical figures. I argue that Bailey's poems and translations from the classics articulate a strongly (Eurocentric) feminist approach in comparison with other existing translations, and that her publication of these poems in the *Colonial Times* reflects a politically engaged and feminist practice of making this classical knowledge and argumentation around rights freely available to her women readers.

In Chapter 3, the mid-nineteenth-century figures of the embowered woman and the fallen woman are discussed as pivotal to the poetry of Caroline Leakey. I resituate Leakey's volume within a transnational feminist tradition of women's poetry that raises these tropes and concerns. Through this shift in focus, Leakey's uses of the colonial space of Tasmania take on crucial differences from other examples, showing that her volume may be considered radical by the standards of writing on the figure of the fallen woman at the time. Tasmania and colonial Australia as a literary space may have been used to mask the intense compassion and sympathy with which Leakey approaches such narratives in her volume, given the increasing restrictions on women's sexuality at that time in Britain. Particularly in relation to the figure of the fallen woman, Leakey's use of Tasmania as an Antipodean space of 'exile' geographically critiques an imperial culture that approaches questions of women's sexuality in terms of law, morality and social position. Leakey, like Bailey, does not address the rights of Tasmanian Aboriginal peoples in her poetry, and the absence of an engagement with these issues is considered in relation to the development of Tasmanian Romanticism and the concept of exile. I offer a new perspective on Leakey's poetry as transnational and highly politically engaged with issues of women's sexual equality.

Chapter 4 considers the spaces of periodical print culture and spiritualism as significant aspects of the poetry of Emily Manning. It examines Manning's uses of Victorian-era spiritualism in relation to women's rights, marriage, women's poetry and Romanticism. Manning's use of ideas relating to occultism and theology reflects her position within a periodical print culture in which she was very much aware of international women writers including George Eliot and Harriet Martineau. Her political and feminist work includes important engagements with popular writers' positions on the role of the wife, such as Ruskin's, as well as questions relating to inequality and poverty. While Manning's colonial context reveals her involvement with influential and progressive intellectuals in Sydney, her literary context ultimately needs to be seen as imperial and transnational. As in the work of British Romantic women poets, typified by Hemans, Manning represents maternal love and womanhood as powerful elements throughout *The Balance of Pain, and Other Poems*, evoking 'The Cult of True Womanhood' and its associated feminized religion as a means through which women's rights and social reform were sought. This chapter will also consider Manning's poetry in terms of class and the absence of representation of the rights of Indigenous peoples.

Chapter 5 reconsiders the periodical poetry of Louisa Lawson, and particularly poems which she originally published in the *Dawn*. I re-evaluate Lawson's poems as literary interventions when recontextualized within major aesthetic and literary movements of the late nineteenth century and position her as highly engaged with transnational networks of women poets. Lawson's poetry, particularly in its broader contexts, emerges as gender and class-conscious writing that was intellectually occupied with wider late nineteenth-century women's traditions. I argue for the literary context of Lawson's poetry to be seen in the light of Romanticism and particularly Pre-Raphaelite aesthetics and the work of Christina Rossetti. When attention is turned to the literary contexts of the *Dawn*, Lawson's poetry was also closely engaged with related late nineteenth-century literary cultures, including the Aesthetes and 'New Woman' writers. I also consider Lawson's treatment of connections between ideas of whiteness and purity, particularly as they relate to colonial racism and the representation of Aboriginal women, as well as women's sexuality, in her poetry. This presents challenges to Lawson's reputation as a poet, as well as to histories that have marginalized the political significance and reach of her poetry, with most of the scholarship on Lawson tending to focus on her importance as a figure in the advancement of women's rights. In relation to Lawson's major role in the New South Wales women's suffrage movement, it is still vital to bring to the fore the transnational, aesthetic, social and political considerations of Lawson's poetry. I argue here that it played a crucial part in her political and imperial feminist activism.

This book is concerned with the historical relationships of these women's political writing and the entanglement of feminist discourses with imperialism, as well as colonialism, literary Romanticism and emergent nationalism. In prioritizing the contributions of settler women, particularly through print culture, and the themes and contexts demonstrating these poets' access to political discourses, this study seeks to recognize their poetry as influential, politically engaged and networked imperial literature rather than absent or apolitical and isolated. It also seeks to recognize how settler women's poetic voice engaged with developing feminist, imperialist and emergent nationalist discourses and approaches to questions of rights and justice in relation to literary Romanticism and its legacies, emphasizing rather than effacing imperial origins and connections. The inclusion of their poetry and these considerations reshapes understandings of settler colonial literary history beyond the lens of masculine nationalism into wider interconnected power dynamics, with a view to their deconstruction.

Chapter 1

ELIZA HAMILTON DUNLOP: ANTI-SLAVERY, IMPERIAL FEMINISM AND ROMANTICISM: 1820–40

Abolitionism, part of the wider political and literary context informing Eliza Hamilton Dunlop's best-known poem 'The Aboriginal Mother' (1838), presents a major challenge to characterizations of colonial women's poetry as apolitical. Abolitionist literary activism proliferated in the widely circulated European and North American print culture of the early nineteenth century. As Jennifer DeVere Brody suggests, the period between the abolition of the slave trade in England in 1807 and the end of the American Civil war in 1865 was central in the proliferation of narratives engaging with abolition, and 'an era of increasing philanthropy for the enslaved African fostered by abolitionist activism'.[1] Clare Midgley points out that it was during this period, from the 1790s to 1850s, that imperialist and feminist discourses ran parallel.[2] Dunlop's poetry, considered in the wider contexts of transnational Romanticism and anti-slavery literary culture, reveals her influence in transposing a gender-conscious Romanticism to colonial Australian poetry. Dunlop's periodical poetry, such as 'The Irish Mother' (1838) published in the *Australian* (1824–48) and 'Morning on Rostrevor Mountains' (1835) in the *Dublin Penny Journal* (1832–36), read within the contexts of transnational and imperial women's poetic traditions, challenges received conceptions of settler women's poetry in colonial Australia as not only geographically isolated but also isolated from the major ideas, questions and concerns of the time and consequently not engaged politically.

During her lifetime, Dunlop's poetry appeared in newspapers, journals and magazines in Ireland, as well as in England, India and Australia. She was known and highly regarded as a poet through her contributions to colonial Australian newspapers such as the *Sydney Morning Herald* (1842–54), the *Australian* (1824–48), the *Empire* (1850–75), the *Atlas* (1844–49) and the *Maitland Mercury and Hunter River General Advertiser* (1843–93). While the few biographical accounts tend to list only one or two newspapers, she was published widely over 50 years, and her verse appeared in at least two books. International journals noted in Margaret De Salis' biography include the *Belfast Magazine*, the *Globe*, the *Dublin Penny Journal*, *Blackwood's* and the *Bengal Hurkaru* in India.[3] The manuscript of Dunlop's collected poems, 'The Vase, Comprising Songs for Music and Poems', was never published in her lifetime, though there is a story that it 'had been despatched by mail coach from Wollombi to Sydney for printing and was lost on the way'.[4] The title, suggestive of Keats' *Ode on a Grecian Urn*, raises similar questions of immortality. Dunlop alludes to her poems as ephemeral blooms, a common trope within women's poetry of the period, perhaps suggesting the exclusion from canonicity faced by women writers. Recently her poetry has begun to receive increasing critical attention, most notably in Australia. Dunlop's positioning within both transnational and imperial women's writing traditions, including Romantic and abolitionist poetry, and her complex relationships with emergent Australian nationalist modes and Irish nationalism reveal her own preoccupation with gender and her attempts to bring questions of gender to more prominent spaces within literary engagements with major political concerns of the day.

Born in 1796 in Ireland, Eliza Hamilton Dunlop emigrated to Australia in 1838 and in the same year published 'The Aboriginal Mother'.

THE ABORIGINAL MOTHER

Oh! Hush thee – hush my baby,
I may not tend thee yet.
Our forest-home is distant far,
And midnight's star is set.
Now hush thee – or the pale-faced men
Will hear thy piercing wail,
And what then would thy mother's tears
Or feeble strength avail!

Oh, could'st thy little bosom,
That mother's torture feel,
Or could'st thy know thy father lies
Struck down by English steel;
Thy tender form would wither,
Like the *kniven* in the sand,
And the spirit of my perished tribe
Would vanish from our land.

For thy young life my precious,
I fly the field of blood,
Else had I, for my chieftain's sake,
Defied them where they stood;

But basely bound my woman's arm,
No weapon might it wield:
I could but cling round him I loved,
To make my heart a shield.

I saw my firstborn treasure
Lie headless at my feet,
The goro on this hapless breast,
In his life-stream is wet!
And thou! I snatched thee from thy sword,
It harmless passed by thee!
But clave the binding chords – and gave,
Haply, the power to flee.

To flee! My babe – but wither?
Without my friend – my guide?
The blood that was our strength is shed!
He is not by my side!
Thy sire! Oh! Never, never
Shall Toon Bakra hear our cry:
My bold and stately mountain-bird!
I thought not he could die.

Now who will teach thee, dearest,
To poise the shield and spear,
To wield the *koopin*, or to throw
The *boommering*, void of fear;
To breast the river in its might;
The mountain tracks to tread?
The echoes of my homeless heart
Reply – the dead, the dead!

And ever must the murmur
Like an ocean torrent flow:
The parted voice comes never back,
To cheer our lonely woe:
Even in the region of our tribe,
Beside our summer streams,
'Tis but a hollow symphony –
In the shadow-land of dreams.

Oh hush thee, dear – for weary
And faint I bear thee on –

> His name is on thy gentle lips,
> My child, my child, *he's gone!*
> Gone o'er the golden fields that lie
> Beyond the rolling clouds,
> *To bring thy people's murder cry*
> *Before the Christian's God.*
>
> Yes! o'er the stars that guide us,
> He brings my slaughter'd boy:
> To shew their God how treacherously
> The stranger men destroy;
> To tell how hands in friendship pledged
> Piled high the fatal pire;
> To tell, to tell of the gloomy ridge!
> and the *stockmen's human fire.*[5]

The poem uses the theme of motherhood to present a highly emotionally charged criticism of the horrific massacre of Wirrayaraay Aboriginal people at Myall Creek on 10 June 1838 and was originally published in the *Australian* on 13 December 1838, just five days before seven men were hanged for murdering an Aboriginal child at Myall Creek. This was, as Lyndall Ryan notes, 'the first time since 1799 that colonists had been arrested and charged with murdering Aborigines[sic]' while First Nations were not able to give evidence in court under the colonial laws.[6] As John O'Leary notes, the trial and retrial of these men resulted in much debate at the time about whether white men should be tried for the murder of Indigenous Australians.[7] O'Leary further points out that

> The claims that Indigenous people lacked the family ties that characterise human beings were not just part of the general discourse of the period; they were being made vociferously and energetically in several of the colonial newspapers in the weeks leading up to the appearance of 'The Aboriginal Mother' in print, notably by the *Sydney Herald* (later the *Sydney Morning Herald*), in what was undoubtedly a campaign to obtain the acquittal of the stockmen accused of the killings.[8]

Dunlop's poem emphasizes motherhood, grief and anguish, in an appeal for the recognition of shared humanity and the need for justice. Her poetic approach to the representation of the issues confronting Indigenous Australians is one aspect of a much broader use of transnational political and imperial feminist literary models within her work.

'The Aboriginal Mother': Anti-slavery and Romanticism

'The Aboriginal Mother', although set in Australia, engages with transatlantic abolitionist literary conventions, utilizing anti-slavery tropes. It employs both the reversal of the so-called civilized/savage dichotomy and the figure of 'the slave Mother bereft of her children' described by Mary Loeffelholz as 'the staple of abolitionist literature'.[9] Dunlop transfers these abolitionist tropes to a situation in which a massacre of Indigenous people had occurred. Her poem was criticized at the time in the *Sydney Herald* for being 'not calculated for the meridian of Sydney'.[10] Dunlop, in her reply, stated that 'it was not intended for any of the high southern latitudes, but [...] had its origin in the hope of awakening the sympathies of the English nation'.[11] It is significant that she specifies 'the English nation' as her intended audience, particularly as she was Irish, knowing that colonial newspapers were widely circulated and read by English as well as local readers. However, the criticism that the poem was not calculated for the location reveals how its connection to abolitionist literary tropes was used to dismiss it as inappropriate.

Dunlop's appeal to readers' sympathy in 'The Aboriginal Mother' lies in emphasizing the notion that women's natural maternal impulse transcended cultural difference:

> Oh! hush thee – hush, my baby,
> I may not tend thee yet.
> Our forest-home is distant far,
> And midnight's star is set.
> Now hush thee – or the pale-faced men
> Will hear thy piercing wail,
> And what would then thy mother's tears
> Or feeble strength avail! (4)

Abolitionist literature such as 'The Negro Mother's Appeal' (1833), an anonymous poem that appeared in *The Abolitionist*, is in this way very like Dunlop's 'The Aboriginal Mother' (1838). A dramatic monologue in the voice of the mother, 'The Negro Mother's Appeal' speaks directly to an audience of white women readers:

> White lady, happy, proud and free!
> Lend a while thine ear to me
> Let the Negro Mother's wail
> Turn thy pale cheek yet more pale.[12]

The appeal is specifically addressed to white women to 'plead the cause' with 'thy gentle voice' (160). This approach emphasized the shared experience of motherhood and love, in the lines 'By thy pure maternal joy / Bid him spare my helpless boy' (160), and the trope of the mother is a major similarity between Dunlop's 'The Aboriginal Mother' and abolitionist poetry like 'The Negro Mother's Appeal'.

Another similarity is the use of Christian language to support anti-slavery arguments, in the following lines:

> By thy pure maternal joy
> Bid him spare my helpless boy
> And thus a blessing on his own
> Seek from his Maker's righteous throne. (160)

Both the maternal and the Christian arguments are apparent in Dunlop's 'The Aboriginal Mother' and in examples such as Hannah More and Eaglesfield Smith's 'The Sorrows of Yamba' (1795) and the anonymous 'The Negro Mother's Appeal' (1833). 'The Sorrows of Yamba' was a popular example of such poetry, published in Hannah More's Cheap Repository Tracts series in London in 1795. As Alan Richardson notes, 'The Sorrows of Yamba', 'makes use of common antislavery tropes – for example, the reversal of the "civilized / savage" dichotomy, a reversal that casts the British slavers, not their African victims, as "savage" – that More also deploys in Slavery'.[13]

This approach is notable in Dunlop's poem, in which after the Aboriginal father and son have been 'struck down by English / Steel', the ventriloquized mother tells the surviving child:

> Yes! o'er the stars that guide us,
> He brings my slaughter'd boy:
> To shew their God how treacherously
> The stranger men destroy;
> To tell how hands in friendship pledged
> Piled high the fatal pire
> To tell, to tell of the gloomy ridge!
> And the *stockmen's human fire*. (4)

Dunlop's inclusion of 'their God' recalls the Christian references of 'The Sorrows of Yamba' (1795):

> Cease, ye British Sons of murder!
> Cease from forging Afric's Chain;

Mock your Saviour's name no further,
Cease your savage lust of gain.[14]

Such poetry was related to women's rights activism as well, and these maternal and religious themes would be significant to the development of imperial feminism. Jane Rendall discerns that early feminists 'had to challenge the view that citizenship was possible only for male heads of households [...] that challenge came, eventually, from two sources: from the republican notion of the increasing and moralizing domestic power of motherhood, and from the feminised language of evangelicalism'.[15] Clare Midgley points out that these feminist discourses on women's rights and anti-slavery began a long and problematic relationship between feminism and imperialist attitudes. Colonialism, Christian evangelism and Enlightenment values are interrelated in nineteenth-century political developments more generally, as well as in some feminist discourses.[16] As Midgley argues, by modelling its discourse on those of imperialist progress, the women's rights cause came to be tied up with assumptions of Western superiority. Midgley notes that there are important contemporary implications 'resulting from western imperialism, and the associated problems of racism and Eurocentrism in white western feminist thought and practice'.[17] This connection to imperialist values is what Tanya Dalziell suggests when she calls the figure of the 'sympathetic white woman' in colonial literature 'unsettling'.[18] The imperialist genealogy of some feminist approaches continues to be unsettling as it remains unresolved. As Peter Minter has noted, 'Dunlop's iteration of a disembodied, ventriloquised Aboriginal subject produces the classical dramatic figure of the *pharmakos*, whose function is to enact a Levitical demarcation and purgation of the defilement of the massacre and, in an act of disembodied repossession, to sublimate the violence of the colonial dispossession of land'.[19]

Romantic women poets and anti-slavery

Dunlop's 'The Aboriginal Mother' reflects her grounding in the Romantic tradition of British women's poetry, including in the work of Hannah More, Ann Yearsley, Anna Letitia Barbauld, Amelia Opie and Mary Robinson, and Irish women poets like Mary Birkett, who were all engaging with anti-slavery discourse. As Roxanne Eberle points out, the contexts in which women's anti-slavery poetry appeared were varied:

> Unlike Hannah More and Ann Yearsley, who had published poems in the 1780s under the auspices of the Anti-Slavery Society, the abolitionist verse of Opie and Robinson appeared in volumes of poetry

largely innocent of overt political critique. Opie's 'Negro Boy's Tale' for example was first published among rather conventional Romantic and Sentimental fare.[20]

'The Aboriginal Mother' was a part of Dunlop's 'Songs of an Exile' series published in *The Australian* from 1838. Apart from it, the poems in the series more broadly may be categorized as Romantic and Sentimental, dealing with her personal emotional responses to aspects of motherhood, grief and her memories of Ireland.

Sentimental poetry was typical of such enormously successful and well-known British women poets as Felicia Hemans and Letitia Elizabeth Landon (L. E. L.). Although she is not as widely known to readers today, Felicia Dorothea Browne (later Hemans) 'was the best-selling poet of the nineteenth century'.[21] The first line of 'The Aboriginal Mother', 'Oh! hush thee – hush my baby', recalls Hemans' 'The Bride of the Greek Isle', published in *Records of Woman* in 1828:

> Oh! hush the song, and let her tears
> Flow to the dream of her early years
> Holy and pure are the drops that fall.[22]

Hemans was published widely in colonial Australian newspapers, such as the *Sydney Gazette and New South Wales Advertiser*, during the 1830s and 1840s. The emphasis on both motherhood and Christianity as sources of feminist challenge was also being actively addressed through women's poetic traditions. Hemans' 'Indian Woman's Death Song', published in *Records of Woman* (1828) 10 years prior to Dunlop's 'The Aboriginal Mother', ventriloquized the Indigenous American woman. This poem portrays what the prologue describes as a 'woman, driven to despair by her husband's desertion of her for another wife' and the scene in which 'Her voice was heard from the shore singing a mournful death-song, until overpowered by the waters in which she perished':

> Proudly, and dauntlessly, and all alone,
> Save that a babe lay sleeping at her breast,
> A woman stood. Upon her Indian brow
> Sat a strange gladness, and her dark hair waved
> As if triumphantly. She press'd her child,
> In its bright slumber, to her beating heart,
> And lifted her sweet voice that rose awhile
> Above the sound of waters, high and clear,
> Wafting a wild proud strain, her Song of Death.[23]

The poem attempts to present women's emotional pain and sympathy with other women's experiences as transcending culture, as the mother speaks to the child, 'And thou, my babe! Though born like me for woman's weary lot, / Smile! – to that wasting of the heart, my own! I leave thee not' (179). These lines are ventriloquized and concerned with promoting a sympathetic understanding of emotional experience. A sympathetic readership is addressed as an alternative to societal judgement of white women's financial dependency, vulnerability and shame within and especially outside of marriage, rather than in terms of the specific political or cultural contexts of the Indigenous American woman's experience.

However, Hemans' influence is apparent in Dunlop's model of approaching the political through the domestic and motherhood. O'Leary notes that Dunlop's 'poem belongs to what the critic Isobel Armstrong has called "the expressive tradition" of nineteenth-century women's poetry, exemplified by writers such as Felicia Hemans and Letitia Langdon [sic]'.[24] The work of both precursors and contemporaries like Felicia Hemans was also frequently based on accounts of specific events, just as Dunlop's 'The Aboriginal Mother' was a response to the Myall Creek Massacre. Hemans wrote the 'Indian Woman's Death Song' based on a tale related in Major Long's account of a scientific expedition, *Narrative of an Expedition to the Source of St. Peter's River* (1824).[25] Tim Fulford describes Hemans' 'The American Forest Girl' (1828) as a poem rich with a 'sentimental and proper Romanticism in which pity overcomes cultural difference and women save men from their masculine violence by appealing to their feminine better natures'.[26] This is the kind of reading that Dunlop's 'The Aboriginal Mother' (1838) has been given by critics such as Elizabeth Webby and O'Leary.

Earlier examples such as Anna Laetitia Barbauld's 'Epistle to William Wilberforce, Esq.on the Rejection of the Bill for Abolishing the Slave Trade' (1791), published in London, suggest the tradition of Romantic women poets interceding in political issues followed by Dunlop. Barbauld's poem, written in response to the rejection of Wilberforce's bill, opens as

> Cease, Wilberforce, to urge thy generous aim!
> Thy Country knows the sin, and stands the shame!
> The Preacher, Poet, Senator in vain
> Has rattled in her sight the Negro's chain;
> With his deep groans assailed her startled ear,
> And rent the veil that hid his constant tear;
> Forced her averted eyes his stripes to scan,
> Beneath the bloody scourge laid bare the man,
> Claimed Pity's tear, urged Conscience' strong controul,

And flashed conviction on her shrinking soul.
The Muse, too soon awaked, with ready tongue
At Mercy's shrine applausive pæns rung;
And Freedom's eager sons, in vain foretold
A new Astrean reign, an age of gold:
She knows and she persists — Still Afric bleeds,
Unchecked, the human traffic still proceeds;
She stamps her infamy to future time,
And on her hardened forehead seals the crime.[27]

Barbauld's 'Epistle' appeared shortly after parliamentary debates regarding the abolition of the slave trade were published in 1791 and William McCarthy speculates that 'she must have started writing it soon after reading the published debate'.[28] Her poem is particularly strident in its demands for political change. While Dunlop was writing much later than Barbauld, contrary to the 'narrative of progress' there were then more constraints on what was acceptable for women to write about. As Stephen Behrendt notes,

> Although nineteenth century women writers were increasingly constrained by the expectation that they should 'civilize' a 'fractious citizenry' by providing both models and exhortations of harmony, tranquillity, and feminine submissiveness, according to Marlon Ross, this was much less the case during the early part of the Romantic era.[29]

While Barbauld's poem is perhaps more overtly radical, Dunlop's 'The Aboriginal Mother' was also an immediate political intervention into a public debate around laws and human rights, and so also resistant to the more conservative context of the 1830s.

Dunlop expressed disappointment at the negative reception of 'The Aboriginal Mother', suggesting that such attitudes may have been more extreme in the colonial context. Following criticism of her poem, Dunlop wrote to the editors of the *Sydney Herald* expressing her dismay that Australia had not yet arrived at the view that racist attitudes and violence towards Aboriginal peoples were unacceptable:

> But the author of the Aboriginal Mother did hope, that, even in Australia, the time was past when the public press would lend its countenance to debase the native character, or support an attempt to shade with ridicule, ties stronger than death, which bind the heart of woman, be she Christian or savage.[30]

She did use the term 'savage' in this published response, even as she attempted to emphasize shared humanity. Her letter to the editor also emphasizes a sense of humility about her poetic talent that functions in a similar way to many prefaces to women's poems, including Mary Birkett's *A Poem on the African Slave Trade Addressed to Her Own Sex*, published in Dublin in 1792:

> In presenting this juvenile attempt to the eyes of the public, I am sensible how much I lay myself open to the censure of those, whose superior discernment shall point out all its errors in their full magnitude. – I can only hope that the merits of the cause will in part plead my excuse; for the rest, I submit to their candor.[31]

Birkett's opening lines following this preface, however, are not concerned with diffidence: 'OPPRESSION! Thou, whose hard and cruel chain / Entails on all thy victims woe and pain' (1). Another Australian example can be found in the preface to Caroline Leakey's *Lyra Australis, or Attempts to Sing in a Strange Land* (1854) in which she suggests her poems are 'of a wild and wilful nature' to 'show to greater advantage the better spirit of resignation and trustfulness' and were written 'during a long illness'.[32] Dunlop's letter to the editors of the *Sydney Herald*, like Birkett's and Leakey's prefaces, is evidence of the need for women writers at this time to work within particular kinds of conventions, both poetic and social, of what women could write about and say. It seems that in appealing to the essentialist notion of women's sympathy in expressing thoughts on political issues, sentimentality had to be paramount and modesty exaggerated, in order to position poems within acceptable boundaries of early Victorian femininity and the domestic ideal.

Women's Romantic tradition and the colonial context

Given her marginalized representation in Australian literary history until recently, it is telling that Dunlop was so active on the literary and political scenes and moved in influential political and literary circles in Ireland, England and Australia. Isaac Nathan, who had set Byron's *Hebrew Melodies* to music, would later set 'The Aboriginal Mother' to music. Dunlop specifically mentions Isaac Nathan's setting of Byron's *Hebrew Melodies* in the note to 'The Aboriginal Mother' in her manuscript poetry collection 'The Vase, Comprising Songs for Music and Poems'. Writing to Dunlop in a letter De Salis reproduces in her biography, Nathan says, 'I shall not set a line […] to any words of the Sydney writers while I may calculate on […] your powerful pen' (105). The piece, which O'Leary notes was performed at a concert in

Sydney, sung by Nathan's daughter Rosetta, was credited in the *Sydney Gazette* with bringing the audience to tears, although, 'competent as Nathan's setting was, the true force of the piece lay in its text'.[33] Dunlop's poetry, including 'The Aboriginal Father' and 'Pialla Wollombi', also appeared in Nathan's *Southern Euphrosyne* (c.1849), published in both Sydney and London. Dunlop had earlier also published her poetry in collaboration with her cousin William Hamilton Maxwell, and one of Dunlop's poems, 'The Virginia Voyager to his Mistress', was included in Maxwell's novel, *The Dark Lady of Doona* (1834). In addition to literary relatives and friends, Dunlop had connections and was in correspondence with such politically significant figures as Bulwer Lytton (the writer and, later, politician) and W. T. Copeland (a Whig politician and later Lord Mayor of London). In Australia, Dunlop wrote elegies on political figures including Lady Gipps, the wife of Governor Gipps. She was also in correspondence with Henry Parkes. A newspaper proprietor and poet, Parkes later became a politician. A. W. Martin points out that Parkes was advised by Charles Harpur (1813–68), a canonical colonial Australian poet, on intellectual matters, and 'came to be associated with most of the colony's radical patriots'.[34] Dunlop should certainly be regarded as a politically engaged figure and, importantly, one whose political voice is distinctly gender conscious.

De Salis, in *Two Early Colonials*, says that Dunlop 'was a friend of Bulwyer Llyton [sic]; as evidenced by two books in our library autographed by him' (11). De Salis also notes that 'a complete dinner service and […] teaset were given to her by the Lord Mayor of London on her departure for Australia' (11). The friendship between Dunlop and W. T. Copeland provides clues to Dunlop's own political leanings, as Copeland was a Whig candidate elected in Coleraine in 1831 before becoming Lord Mayor of London in 1835.[35] De Salis points out that 'There are many letters from Alderman Copeland, who represented the borough of Coleraine for several terms. In 1833 he writes to Eliza, who is just as active in politics as her husband' (30). Another of Copeland's letters to Dunlop included in De Salis' biography, dated August 1837, states:

> Now that adversity has assailed you I will try to show that I am a friend. If Dunlop has made up his mind to go to Sydney, I will give him letters of introduction but with the government I cannot serve him […] If a change of government takes place, which I verily believe it will, what between Dawson and myself it will be hard if we cannot get Dunlop a berth. (32)

This friendship suggests the Whig political leanings of Eliza Hamilton Dunlop, as do the anti-slavery themes suggested by her poetry. She was not only aware of current concerns in British women's poetry but was also connected with extended Romantic social circles before emigrating.

'The Aboriginal Mother' has tended to be considered in the historical context of colonial and Victorian values rather than its wider relationship to Romanticism. Tim Fulford and John Kitson note that 'it is surprising that, with some recent exceptions, Romanticism's relationship with colonialism has been little studied'.[36] Of the specific overlaps between Romanticism and the colonial period in Australia, Paul Kane asserts that

> almost the whole of what we associate with the flowering of romanticism took place while the settlement in Australia struggled to become a self-sufficient colony [...] the primary concerns of the people were local – insulated, as they were, from any sense of participation in the political and cultural convulsions of Europe.[37]

Kane posits Charles Harpur as a lone Romantic poet in a country whose literature would not follow that tradition. Harpur's 'An Aboriginal Mother's Lament' (1853), like Dunlop's 'The Aboriginal Mother' (1838), recounts the story of an escaped mother and child from the Myall Creek Massacre, ventriloquizing the voice of the mother. Kane argues that Romantic poetry is concerned primarily with two things: first, a reverence for nature and, second, a revolutionary impulse. Consequently, he argues, these two aspects are not found in settler poetry in Australia, where 'nature, it turned out, no longer corresponded to *Nature*, [...] not only were the seasons backwards, the plants and animals strange, but the land itself was thought by many to be irredeemably ugly' (11).

This is apparent from Harpur's 'An Aboriginal Mother's Lament', which reads very much like Dunlop's poem. Harpur's poem was originally published under the title, 'A Wail from the Bush', in the *Weekly Register*, 26 July 1845, and was republished in 1853 in *The Bushrangers: A Play in Five Acts and Other Poems*. The poem had the following note at the time of its publication in 1883: '[About the year 1842 a party of Stockmen, several of whom were afterwards hanged for the crime, made a wholesale slaughter of a small tribe of defenceless blacks; one woman only, with her infant, escaped from the murderers].'[38] Harpur's 'An Aboriginal Mother's Lament' evokes a picturesque landscape:

> No more shall his loud tomahawk
> Be plied to win our cheer,
> Or the shining fish pools darken
> Beneath his shadowing spear;

> The fading tracks of his fleet foot
> Shall guide not as before,
> And the mountain-spirits mimic
> His hunting call no more!
>
> O moan not! I would give this braid –
> Thy father's gift to me –
> For but a single palmful
> Of water now for thee. (102)

Harpur's descriptions of nature, while not sublime, are still revered, as in 'the shining fish pools', but Dunlop's poem offers no description of the natural environment at all. Yet Kane acknowledges the trope of the link between human nature and nature, and Dunlop's 'The Aboriginal Mother' does make use of this model.

If we are to conceive of nature not literally as the Australian landscape but as transcendent human nature embodied by the mother, human emotion associated with the protection and love of children is developed specifically in order to display a common maternal nature. As Kane points out, while 'theories of the sublime may present nature as Other, that sublime Other is generally recuperated within an economy of human reason [...] the representation of nature therefore forms a system of reference [...] that governs thought in ways that can be seen as ideological'.[39] Such ideological representations of nature are clearly present in Dunlop's 'The Aboriginal Mother':

> To flee! my babe – but whither?
> Without my friend – my guide?
> The blood that was our strength is shed!
> He is not by my side!
> Thy sire! oh! Never, never
> Shall *Toon Bakra* hear our cry,
> My bold, my stately mountain-bird!
> I thought not he could die.
>
> Now, who will teach thee, dearest,
> To poise the shield, and spear,
> To wield the *koopin*, or to throw
> The *boomerring*, void of fear;
> To breast the river in its might;
> The mountain tracks to tread?
> The echoes of my homeless heart
> Reply – the dead! the dead!

This conception of nature leads to Dunlop's ideological position. By representing the nature of motherhood, O'Leary argues that Dunlop engages in 'a deliberate, strategic contribution to the newspaper debate' that was going on at the time regarding the trial of men for the massacre at Myall Creek. O'Leary argues that Dunlop's poem was in fact designed to 'help bring about an amelioration in the treatment of Indigenous people'.[40]

So 'the revolutionary impulse' that Kane feels to be lacking in colonial Australian poetry is evidenced in the poem, through an ideological alignment with French revolutionary values such as liberty, equality and fraternity. However, these ideals are fundamentally undermined by their complicity with Western imperialism and imperial feminist thought in this context. Anne Mellor discerns that within a

> feminine Romantic tradition, the sublime combines with the beautiful to produce, not the experience of *sehnsucht*, of solitary, visionary transcendence sought (however futilely) by several male Romantic poets, but an experience of communion between two different people, that very 'sympathy' or *domesticated* sublimity [...] a sense of participation in a human community.[41]

Sympathy as an acceptable literary space for women is expanded to encompass grief, anger and despair and subsequently to draw attention to and question its political context in 'The Aboriginal Mother'. As Mellor further points out,

> In addition to offering an alternative definition of the sublime as an experience that produces an intensified emotional and moral participation in a human community, this tradition of Romantic women writers specifically condemned Burke's and Wordsworth's representations of the sublime as a moment of masculine empowerment over female nature. (105)

This is an important aspect of Romantic women's poetry, and the concern with a wider human community in Romantic and Victorian women's poetry has a complex relationship to the imperial feminist strategies poets utilized.

Isobel Armstrong suggests the use of dramatic monologue could allow such women poets a 'protection against self-exposure and the exposure of feminine subjectivity'.[42] Such strategies, however, centred white women and included cultural appropriation and ventriloquizing through identifying with the enslaved woman as a common metaphor for women's oppression in the West. Clare Midgley describes a 'triple discourse' in which first, British women's oppression was likened to slavery, second, their marriages were likened to sexual slavery such as that of a harem and third, their position as women was likened to that of women in polygamous societies. Midgley adds that 'engagement with the radical intellectual and political currents of the period' was intertwined with 'attempting to bring questions of women's subordination from their margins to centrestage'.[43] Dunlop's 'The Aboriginal Mother', particularly in its reverence for motherhood, should be read not only as an example of political intervention into the debates around laws and the human rights of Indigenous Australians but also as a part of an international imperial feminist discourse and Romantic women's poetic tradition.

Irish identity and nationalism

As an Irish woman writer, Dunlop was aware of both British and Irish literary and political figures. As Claire Connolly notes, the Act of Union 'created a professional literary culture characterized by movement between and across the two islands'.[44] Dunlop was likely also conscious of Ireland's relationship to the slave trade. Nini Rodgers notes that Daniel O'Connell

> frequently claimed a long anti-slavery tradition for Ireland, quoting the Council of Armagh 1171 which prohibited Irish trading in slaves [...] He also announced that the one benefit brought by the Union was the anti-slavery attitudes of Irish MPs from all parties; their presence enabled the English to abolish the trade in 1807, slavery itself in 1833 and apprenticeship in 1838.[45]

It was during the 1830s that Margaret De Salis suggests Dunlop was active in Irish politics. It should also be noted that county Armagh, notable for its slavery prohibition, was her birthplace, so it is probable that Dunlop associated anti-slavery with her home and Irish nationalism.

Claire Connolly points out that 'Ireland emerged from this period with a renovated reputation as a naturally distinct and national culture; this in turn fostered and supported new theories of nationality and nourished the cultural nationalism of the 1830s and 40s' (408). Dunlop's poetry reflects a concern with both gender and nationalism. Originally, 'The Aboriginal Mother' was the fourth poem in the series 'Songs of an Exile' published in the *Australian* from October 1838. The poem which followed 'The Aboriginal Mother' was 'The Irish Mother' (1838), a song seemingly addressed to Dunlop's eldest daughter Mary Georgina, from her previous marriage to James Law. Neil Gunson notes that Dunlop 'arrived at Port Jackson in February 1838 in the *Superb* with the four children of this marriage'.[46] This suggests that Mary Georgina Law did not travel with the family. However, there are records of

Mary Georgina Law as an artist in Australia, in the Dictionary of Australian Artists Online. So it seems that she joined them, perhaps later. In 'The Irish Mother' (1838) Dunlop writes partly in a phonetic and anglicized Gaelic, and a footnote explains:

> The last line is the Irish cry of a broken heart, of which there can be no adequate translation. The name Varia is MARY. The other Irish words are expressions of fondness for which the English tongue offers no sounds half so tender.[47]

While not suggesting experience comparable with the massacre of Wirrayaraay people, Dunlop clearly intended this poem to be read alongside 'The Aboriginal Mother' (1838) and the other poems in the 'Songs of an Exile' series. These other poems, voiced in the first person, articulate her own experiences with maternal grief and love and her deep sense of loss and longing for her home following her arrival in Australia.

'The Irish Mother' (1838) was later republished anonymously under the title 'The Emigrant Mother' in Sir Charles Gavan Duffy's popular *The Ballad Poetry of Ireland* (1845) in Dublin. A note in *Irish Minstrelsy Being a Selection of Irish Songs, Lyrics and Ballads* (1887) explains that 'Sir C. Gavan Duffy found this touching little ballad in an Australian Newspaper, and was charmed with its fresh feeling and grace, but was not able to discover the writer's name'.[48] The second poem in 'Songs of an Exile', published in the *Australian* in 1838, is similarly concerned with motherhood and is an elegy for her daughter Jane who had died in Ireland in 1831. It had no separate title and Dunlop noted in the newspaper publication that it was 'adapted to the music of *I stood among the glittering throng*', a popular ballad. Dunlop's version reads:

> SHE WAS – yet have I oft denied,
> Veiling the secret in my heart,
> SHE WAS my dearest – my pride;
> For whom those bitter tear drops start.
> Now happy voices fill mine ear,
> And dancing footsteps timing around –
> Yet hers amid them all I hear!
> A sound of music from the ground.
> Still, MY lorn spirit, seeks the clay,
> Where her young limbs in darkness rest –
> While her's, in light of endless day,
> Reposes on a Saviour's breast.[49]

As Anne Janowitz suggests, 'the ballad was crucial to the founding of romantic lyricism: simultaneously dated and fashionable, oral and written, choric and monologic, the ballad expressed the pan-cultural possibility of a democratic poetry'.[50] As Florence Boos has also pointed out, 'it has often been assumed [...] that subtle allusions and metrical refinements thought to characterize respected genres of Victorian poetry bore little kinship with the forms of song, verse and recitation indited by the seventy-five to ninety percent of Victorians who were not middle- or upper-class'.[51] Although she was not working class, Dunlop's second poem in the 'Songs of an Exile' series is an example of a personal response to original lyrics. This was, as Boos notes, a strategy of many working-class women poets. Dunlop's adaptation subverts the lighter emotional tone of the original song. The original was a love song, of happy courtship from the perspective of a man to a young woman:

> I stood among the glittering throng
> I heard a voice, its tones were sweet,
> I turned to see from whence they came
> And gaz'd on all I long'd to meet;
> She was a fair and gentle girl,
> Her bright smile greeted me by chance,
> I whisper'd low! I took her hand!
> I led, I led her forth to dance[52]

The popularity and memorability of the ballad form and song are important aspects of Dunlop's poetry in its periodical publishing context. Her adaptation of the lyrics builds from a sense of shared cultural memory and prior joy in the love song, at the same time as it undoes this emotional connection and transforms the perspective into that of a heartbroken mother's isolation in grief and love for a child she has lost. The title 'I stood among the glittering throng' takes on a very altered sense of emotional isolation within a crowd, replacing a romantic attraction with a heartbroken maternal grief that is experienced alone. The emotional significance of this is heightened by the temporal and contextual displacement, quickly establishing a sense of memory and loss, and of the speaker's distance both from a joyful past and from those whose 'happy voices' and 'dancing footsteps' now surround her and yet remain unaware of her pain. The poem's retelling of the song is a clear articulation of a gendered and maternal difference of emotional experience. This is reiterated by the simultaneous connection to and emotional removal from the original song lyrics. The poem centralizes motherhood and grief, and the emotional experiences of both, emphasizing the speaker's ongoing pain as a bereaved mother while those around her are joyful and her daughter's spirit 'in light of endless day / Reposes on a Saviour's breast' (3). This sense of isolation and difference in the experiences of both motherhood and grief is, however, vocalized as a point of sympathetic and emotional connection with a broader community. Behrendt notes of Irish Romantic women writers that

> As women writers grappled with the conflicting demands of retaining their Irish cultural identity at the same time that they participated in a cosmopolitan Anglophone discourse field, one characteristic theme began to be apparent: 'the tension between feeling included and excluded by society', a tension that is expressed at times as inseparable from 'the female condition' and at other times as part of 'being Irish' – and often both of these. (*Writing Community*, 248)

So she may also be signalling her alterity as an Irish woman writer.

Dunlop's concern with negotiating the politics of her own identity is conceptualized within both an Irish and a broader anglophone tradition. As Armstrong notes more generally of women poets in this period, literary themes revealed a heightened interest in cultural differences. She points out that

> As a child Letitia Landon invented a fantasy country located in Africa [...] very much as the Brontë's were to do when they constructed Gondal and Angria [...] This need to move beyond cultural boundaries manifests itself in the work of the earlier poets as a form of historical and cultural syncretism which both juxtaposes different cultures and reshapes relationships between them [...] Felicia Hemans brings together British, French, Indian, German, American and Greek narratives from different historical periods in her *Records of Woman* (1828).[53]

Dunlop likewise over the course of her poetic output references place repeatedly, through iconography specific to Ireland, India, Africa and Australia. Dunlop herself travelled widely, having been to London, Scotland and India before Australia. She was no stranger to colonialism: De Salis notes her father Solomon Hamilton was a Judge of the Supreme Court in India, and Dunlop travelled to India in 1820, when he died (19).

In a poem published in the *Dublin Penny Journal* in 1835, 'Morning on Rostrevor Mountains', Dunlop describes 'other waters' in Romantic tones, where

> To gladden scenes more fair than earth –
> The sea – the sea and heav'n!
> Yes! And where the Gunga's mighty streams

> Their sacred waters spread
> I've seen beneath thy worshipped beams
> Ten thousands bow the head.[54]

This poem juxtaposes the landscapes of Ireland, India and South Africa. Dunlop reiterates the line 'In solitude I stand' in the three locations: Rostrevor Mountains in Ireland, 'beside Cloch-mhor', India and South Africa, giving a sense of the speaker as a culturally isolated traveller, 'A stranger on my natal shore / And this, my father-land' (42). This line reflects Irish nationalist feelings of what Stephen Behrendt calls 'being neither British nor Irish', stemming from British colonization of the Irish and their increasing hardship following the Act of Union (246). As much as it is possible to place Dunlop in a British literary tradition, neither this poem nor her others can be properly understood outside the context of Irish Romantic women's poetry.

In 'Morning on Rostrevor Mountains' (1835) Dunlop's imagery evokes the practice of *sati* (sometimes anglicized to 'suttee'). Midgley points out that 'The most important of the Imperially focused campaigns were for the abolition of colonial slavery and for the eradication of *sati*, or widow burning, in India' (8). Dunlop describes the location of the temple of Jagannath, or Juggernaut, in Puri, Orissa, a Hindu temple where *sati* took place, as 'Where the dark domes of Juggernaut's / Profane pagoda's stand' (42). Although she never directly mentions *sati* or widows in the poem, Dunlop's descriptions of the 'the tainted air' of 'Calcutta's graveyard gloom' evoke the negative representations of *sati* in the literature of Western women's rights circles. Lata Mani points out that 'The prohibition of *sati* – widow burning – in 1829 has been canonized by colonialist and nationalist texts as a founding moment in the history of women's emancipation in modern India.'[55] She contextualizes this within the so-called civilizing mission of colonialism and adds that rather than centring the perspectives of the women that *sati* involved, Western evangelical discourse was centred in these debates and in the colonial intervention into the practice, in ways similar to those of anti-slavery literary culture.

Dunlop's poem appeared amid many British women's poems that addressed *sati* or Indian culture more generally, such as Letitia Landon's 'Hurdwar, a place of Hindoo Pilgrimage' (1832) and Maria Jane Jewsbury's 'Song of the Hindoo Women, While Accompanying a Widow to the Funeral Pile of Her Husband'.[56] As Clare Midgley points out, 'white women, too, were able to position themselves as saviours of brown women and, thus, actively contribute to the moral justification of Empire and simultaneously to justify their active engagement in missionary work overseas and in petitioning parliament', adding that this 'laid the grounds for the emergence of imperial feminism'.[57] Dale Spender notes that Dunlop's trip to India in 1820 resulted in her discovery of her 'two Indian half-sisters whom her brothers refused to acknowledge. Helen Heney (1985) suggests it could have been this experience which set Eliza Dunlop thinking about "racism" and the suffering and injustice that it generated'.[58] The speaker in 'Morning on Rostrevor Mountains' addresses the sun's 'sick'ning rays' which echo

> The Brahmin's funeral pile
> In that far hemisphere,
> Sunrise, alas! I've met thy smile,
> Mocking the burning bier! (42)

These lines suggest despair at the sunrise, symbolic of continued life, rather than at the burning bier, yet the sun is also represented in the poem as a departed unfaithful husband:

> Yon orb – the beautiful, the bold,
> Hath left his ocean bride,
> And from her couch of wavy gold
> Comes forth in regal pride
> Fair sun, I've seen that crown of rays
> As gallantly put on,
> And mark'd thy robes of crimson haze
> O'er other waters thrown. (42)

Much like British women's poetry on the subject, the poem is concerned with marriage and with the expression of experiences that fall outside of the middle-class British domestic ideal held up for women.

This emphasis on marriage and double standards of devotion in women within the domestic ideal is reiterated in the line 'In solitude I stand', suggesting the speaker's differentiation from these ideals. 'Morning on Rostrevor Mountains' (1835) was later altered to contain an additional Australian stanza and republished in 1845 in the *Atlas* (an Australian newspaper), 10 years after its initial publication in Ireland:

> Where the wild Emu leads her brood
> Across the trackless plains
> And lord of nature's solitude –
> The stately cedar, reigns;
> Even there, through exile's cheerless hours,
> Lighted by Austral skies,
> I've lingered amid orange flowers,
> To catch thy scented sighs.[59]

This new verse fits in fairly seamlessly because the poem is already shifting through geographical boundaries and juxtaposing different locations. Dunlop was already representing specific places under British colonial rule, including her own 'fatherland' of Ireland. In this case, by declaring herself as Irish in the line 'I stand beside Cloch-mhor' (257), Dunlop articulates her Irish nationalist position.

Elegiac poetics, E. B. Kennedy and gender: Women's Romanticism and emergent masculine nationalism in colonial Australia

As active as canonical colonial Australian poets like Harpur and Henry Halloran in the quest for poetic fame, Dunlop was also engaging in emergent nationalist poetics. She did this with a resistance to its masculine bias rather than its inherent oppositionality to equality and Indigenous rights. The editors of the *Sydney Morning Herald* described her nationalist poem 'Star of the South' as 'bad poetry', and following this criticism she wrote to the editors that

> To have given poetry unslurred to your readers by prejudicial remark, would have been no more than justice to a pen, not a paid one, but proud of contributing its quota to the original literature of the colony.[60]

Webby has pointed out that the *Sydney Morning Herald*, which 'had strongly opposed the execution of the men involved in Myall Creek was for many years very hostile to her and her work'.[61] This response to her poem should be viewed in the context of this particular newspaper. Dunlop's letter about 'Star of the South, an Australian melody' reveals tensions over the intersections of Romanticism, nationalism and gender.

This hostility also seems to have in part reflected a growing white masculine nationalist agenda. Webby notes that

> As well as being the inaugurator of a poetic tradition which continues through Mary Gilmore and Judith Wright [...] Eliza Dunlop can also be seen as the inaugurator of a tradition of patriotic poems, extending from Caroline Carleton's 'Song of Australia' (1858) to Dorothea Mackellar's 'My Country'.[62]

This emergent nationalist poetics was often understood as a political mode constructed as the domain of the white male poet. Robert Dixon in an article on the hostilities between two colonial publications, the *Month* and the *Empire*, notes that they reflected a division between so-called old world and 'native' (white Australian-born) literary approaches and describes how

> An extant letter from Eliza Dunlop to Henry Parkes (now in the Mitchell Library collection of Parkes MSS) suggests the way in which she was affected by the conflict between the two factions. In her letter, she complained that her poem, 'Carlingford Bay' had been rejected by the *Empire*, while the same newspaper was willing to publish the verse of the native-born poet Charles Harpur; still deeply involved in English poetic traditions, Eliza Dunlop cautioned Parkes that he may be neglecting the needs of 'old-world readers'.[63]

So as early as the 1850s Dunlop was aware of how a feminization of the so-called old world connected to the 'racially and ethnically exclusive construction of "Australianness" and of the "native" (that is, white Australian born)', which Susan Sheridan notes as an important development of the 1890s.[64] Importantly, this feminized connection to transnational Romantic as well as imperialist writing traditions, rather than exclusive engagement with an emergent nationalist mode, situates Dunlop's writing much more clearly in its relationships to British imperialism, where these connections have been obscured or minimized within white masculine nationalist traditions.

Harpur was an early proponent of this masculine tradition, proclaiming himself the first native-born Australian poet and publicly criticizing his rivals as 'not even Australian born!' in what Dixon states was 'purely personal abuse'.[65] Dunlop's choice of the title 'Native Poetry' for the appropriative verses she transliterated may have been intended as an attack on this discourse. Anna Johnson writes of her wordlists that 'Dunlop's notes record that some terms are linked to the "Northwest Cumeleroy Tribe"' and 'Liverpool and Wollombi Tribes' adding that 'the "district" terms Dunlop records are nascent and imprecise, but they mostly bear a phonetic relationship to the language groups that are now listed under the designated AIATSIS category "Gamilaraay /Gamilaroi /Kamilaroi language [...]"'.[66] Dunlop's position also shows her awareness of the gendered nature of the divide between an emergent masculine nationalism and 'old world' literary schools in Australia. This would become the dominant nationalist masculine literary tradition, which, as Sheridan has noted of fiction, 'excluded women and all those un-Australian cultural phenomena attributed to the feminine'. Sheridan states that 'in much literary-nationalist critical discourse, popular forms of Romantic fiction – no matter whether they looked back to Walter Scott or Jane Austen or to Gothic and sensationalist fiction – were marginalised. And "feminised" at the same time'.[67] Within poetry, masculine nationalism could be seen as a mode also working within the Romantic tradition. Nonetheless, it is also arguable that women's poetry associated with European concerns and Romantic traditions was not prioritized within the emergent nationalist literary culture. Dunlop's ongoing poetic engagement in Australia with Romantic women's poetry demonstrates a resistance to the emergent masculine nationalist construction of identity through a differentiation from European traditions within imperial feminist approaches.

Dunlop's 1849 poem 'To the memory of E.B. Kennedy', an explorer, was published 11 years after 'The Aboriginal Mother'. Memorializing a white man killed by Aboriginal people, this poem is engaged with a different kind of politics to 'The Aboriginal Mother' and undermines the attitude towards Indigenous people expressed in the earlier poem. While Dunlop was highly critical of the massacre of Wirrayaraay people by white men at Myall Creek, 'To the memory of E.B. Kennedy' is not concerned to make moral judgement for the death of Kennedy. However, it suggests her positioning, as a settler woman poet, in the processes and politics of grief for a public figure. Dunlop refers to Aboriginal people as 'savage' in the later poem, in the same way as she had earlier used the word in her letter to the editors defending 'The Aboriginal Mother'.[68] The poem, published in the *Maitland Mercury and Hunter River General Advertiser*, is overtly focused on Kennedy and his so-called glorious quest. Like the newspaper discussion of Kennedy's death, and other emergent nationalist elegies, this explorer mythology is paralleled in the visual arts in paintings such as 'The Burial of Burke' (1911) by William Strutt, which commemorates the explorer Robert O'Hara Burke (Figure 1.1). Although painted much later, it is emblematic of the celebration of a masculine nationalism.

Henry Halloran published a poem on the death of Kennedy, 'The Late Mr Kennedy' (1849), in the *Sydney Morning Herald*.[69] Halloran and Dunlop both also published elegies following the death of Isaac Nathan's daughter, Rosetta. O'Leary notes that it was she who performed the vocals for Nathan's setting of Dunlop's 'The Aboriginal Mother', which had 'moved its audience of colonists to tears'.[70] The publication of poems such as Harpur's 'Aboriginal Mother's Lament' (1853) and Halloran's 'Rosette' (1843) demonstrates the community of colonial poets in which, as a woman poet, Dunlop was actively involved. This was perhaps a reason for Dunlop's use of a line from Hemans's 'The Siege of Valencia' as the epigraph for 'To the Memory of E.B. Kennedy', as a means of aligning the poem to a women's literary tradition, flagging the precedent of women poets addressing such topics. The epigraph, 'O'er that forsaken sepulchre banner and plume might wave', is misattributed to L. E. L. However, its inclusion shows that after 11 years living in colonial

Figure 1.1 Strutt, William, *The Burial of Burke*, 1911.

Australia, Dunlop still wished to highlight the connections of her own writing to the British Romantic women's poetic tradition.

The inscription on the title page of Dunlop's *The Vase* reads 'Within this simple Vase enshrined / Are the undying flowers of mind', reflecting Dunlop's resistance to women's poetry being considered ephemeral.[71] Such connections between women, flowers and transience are elaborated by Brandy Ryan, who asserts that 'in Landon's elegy for Hemans, the evanescence of flowers becomes a symbolic identification for women. To have a "vain" love for something that, while beautiful, cannot last, suggests an unconsciously acute premonition of the fate of nineteenth-century women's poetry'.[72] As Ryan notes, Hemans, Landon and Elizabeth Barrett 'developed an elegiac dialogue that set in place a poetic economy of shared and negotiated values that flourished throughout the nineteenth century'.[73] Ryan discusses the elegies of Hemans on the death of Mary Tighe, Landon on Hemans's death in 1835 and Barrett's response to Landon's elegy on Hemans as using the traditionally male elegiac form as a space for the recording of the woman poet. Hemans died in 1835, three years before Dunlop's arrival in the colony, and Landon in October 1838, eight months after. It is possible that Dunlop's 'To the Memory of E.B. Kennedy' had a double meaning in the light of the women's elegiac tradition, which focused on issues around 'the temporary heights of female success'.[74] Dunlop exclaims:

> Bewail him not! – Oh, Bewail him not! –
> Though sunk to his rest in his spring-tide of fame
> For, oh, there are hundreds, who, mourning his lot,
> Yet sigh for the triumph that circles his name.[75]

Dunlop also appears to be in dialogue with Halloran's poem 'The late Mr. Kennedy' which contains the line 'And thou shalt still be named with many sighs' (Halloran, *Kennedy*, 2).

The first stanza of Dunlop's elegy on Kennedy is placed between the epigraph attributed to L. E. L. and Dunlop's signature at the end of the poem, juxtaposing the talent of women poets as public figures with the 'fame' that society assigns a male explorer like Kennedy. The line Dunlop quotes in the epigraph from Hemans's 'The Siege of Valencia' (1836) refers specifically to a woman and the denial to her of glory in death:

> Scorn not her tomb – deny not her
> The honours of the brave!
> O'er that forsaken sepulchre,
> Banner and plume might wave.[76]

The women's elegiac tradition signals the restrictions on attaining immortality through verse for the woman poet. One of the great difficulties in recovering earlier work published in periodicals by Dunlop in Ireland is the fact that they are signed with initials, or even with a single initial 'E', if anything at all.

Dunlop's ongoing abolitionist and Romantic women's poetics also reveals how significant these connections were to negotiations with the increasingly restrictive domestic ideal that settler women poets were engaging with by publishing in the periodical press. These wider literary contexts give further insight into how gendered expectations could be interpreted to allow for the expression of political voice. The themes of motherhood and Christianity, as consistently employed approaches in anti-slavery literary culture and women's rights discourse, demonstrate the entanglement of Western feminist and imperialist discourses, as does poetry that addressed *sati*. Poetic concerns with revolutionary values around ideas of equality, like imperial feminist linking of women's emancipation with colonization, are problematically approached in ways that presume Western superiority and engage with various nationalisms.

Empathy with experiences considered particular to women and the encouragement of sympathetic engagement from readers included the use of tropes around motherhood and religion as a means of establishing a political intervention into public debates. Appearing amid the 'debate' around the trial of the white men responsible for the massacre, 'The Aboriginal Mother' as a poem centred in ideals of feminine sympathy and nurturance was critiqued in the *Sydney Morning Herald* as failing to reflect the 'real' character of Aboriginal people, in line with predominantly racist views. Through these feminized ideals, the right to equality and justice for both Aboriginal people and white women connected by maternal sympathy is suggested by Dunlop's poem. Yet as commentators on Dunlop's 'The Aboriginal Mother' such as John O' Leary have already noted, 'her verse is open to charges of colonialism and cultural appropriation'.[77] O'Leary, like Webby, nonetheless argues that the value of Dunlop's poetry lies in her concern for the welfare of Indigenous peoples, especially in the context of the racist views being expressed in the newspapers at the time. 'The Aboriginal Mother' can be viewed as an instance of political intervention seeking justice for the Wirrayaraay people. Dunlop's other 'Songs of an Exile' poems, in the context of Romantic women's poetry, may be viewed as explorations of her personal alterity as an Irish woman poet in relation to gendered expectations and British imperialism. There seems a desire in Dunlop's poetry, like that of precursors such as Hemans, for representations of a universal, transcendent moral power in women, as well as women's suffering, through motherhood. Such an approach situates Dunlop's writing of 'The Aboriginal Mother' within broader anglophone women's writing traditions. Complicit with imperialism and colonialism, there are some elements within this of resistance to women's subordination bound up with Dunlop's poetry, reflecting the interconnected relationships of imperialism, colonialism, various nationalisms, some feminist approaches and gender.

While Dunlop expressed resistance to the violence and racist discourse around the massacre of Aboriginal people at Myall Creek, she was yet complicit in colonialism, including cultural appropriation. Her poetry, while conscious of and resistant to limitations on women, also functions within the expectation of bringing a feminizing and so-called civilizing influence to the colonies. These aspects signal constraints posed by the category of gender, as well as the ways emotion and sympathy could function as acceptable spaces for women's political expression. Their poetic expressions of anger at violence have similarly been coded within expectations of white women's so-called civilizing role, and these contexts require attention in criticism of women's writing. An inclusive approach to colonial women's poetry involves incorporating the findings of nationalized approaches into broader knowledge of the complex historical relationships between feminism, Empire and political contexts, in which complicity is acknowledged. Dunlop's poems are frequently politically motivated and highly gender-conscious interventions into political and popular discourses, including those around slavery and abolition, the massacre of Aboriginal people and discourses associated with the construction of an emergent white masculine nationalist poetics. Dunlop's experience with the

Empire also suggests that the emergent masculine nationalist mode in colonial Australia was differentiated from feminized connections to wider anglophone literary cultures from relatively early on. Her poetry involves negotiations with women's Romantic poetic traditions and the domestic ideal for women that strive to undermine the limitations it imposed through public articulations of women's political voices.

Chapter 2

MARY BAILEY: HELLENISM, BLUESTOCKINGS AND THE *COLONIAL TIMES*: 1840–50

Mary Bailey's feminist concerns about women's intellectual equality access political themes through classical models. Bailey was born Mary Elizabeth Walker in Gestingthorpe, Essex, in 1792, and married Reverend William Bailey in 1832 when she was 40 and he 25. A prolific poet, Bailey produced three volumes in England (*The Months, Palmyra* (1833) and *Musae Sacrae* (1835)) as well as the prose work *Reflections Upon the Litany of the Church of England* (1833).[1] She also contributed to the London reviews and *Blackwood's Edinburgh Magazine* (1817–1980). In 1844, she and her son followed her husband to what was then called Van Diemen's Land and later renamed Tasmania by settlers, known as lutruwita in palawa kani, after he was transported for life following a conviction for forgery of a promissory note in favour of his sister.[2] Her volumes are listed in J. R. de J. Jackson's *Romantic Poetry by Women: A Bibliography 1770–1835*, although there are no comprehensive studies in either Britain or Australia of Bailey's poetry.

Having been educated in England by her grandfather the Reverend William Jones, an eminent scholar, Bailey also produced translations from Greek, Latin, Italian and French poetry.[3] These appeared in the Tasmanian newspaper, the *Colonial Times* (1828–57), and included her series of translations of the Greek 'Odes of Anacreon' (1849), as well as translations of Italian poets Taso and Metastasio. Although Bailey's work is particularly associated with the *Colonial Times*, her poetry also appeared in the *Hobart Town Courier* (1827–39), later known as the *Courier* (1839–1859), the *Geelong Advertiser and Squatters' Advocate* (1845–47) and the *Hobarton Guardian* (1847–54), of which her husband became editor in 1847. Her later poetry appears in the *Sydney Freeman's Journal* (1850–1932). Bailey's writing exemplifies both Romantic Hellenism, which is concerned with ancient Greece, and the legacy of bluestocking women. These traditions are part of a nineteenth-century feminist approach that prioritized Western understandings of egalitarian principles, pacifism and education with the assumption that these ideas were universally applicable. Acknowledgement of the presence or claims of Indigenous people, however, is absent from Bailey's poetry, as it is from later poets including Caroline Leakey and Emily Manning. This absence of acknowledgement, particularly given the wider context of the atrocities of Tasmanian genocidal war, has a clear relationship to imperialism and colonialism. In a letter to the *Colonial Times* comparing Tasmania and England, Bailey described Tasmania as 'Elysium itself', despite its 'legalised slavery in a penal colony' while condemning the 'rampant iniquity' in England as the '*free* but infernal bondage [...] by the hardest of all taskmasters and slavedrivers – the Devil!'[4]

Gender, and the negotiation with the nineteenth-century domestic ideal, is an important consideration in both Bailey's Romantic Hellenism and her publications in newspapers and periodicals. Shanyn Fiske points out that Hellenist writing by women was considered heretical and suggests that

> The erotic appeal of forbidden knowledge [...] clung heavily to the classics, which was seen as an exclusively male prerogative. While for boys classical knowledge was a mandatory part of the curriculum, the attainment of the same knowledge for girls was heretical [...] involving zealous, self-motivated, and independent pursuits of learning that transgressed into male territory.[5]

Through these publications Bailey became known as a woman to her readers and challenged women's exclusion from intellectual and political discourses and classical knowledge.

Bailey's Romantic Hellenism looks to the deep past, and particularly to Greece, as an idealized point of comparison for subjects including rights around gender and imprisonment. In correspondence published in the *Colonial Times* entitled 'Contamination! And Pollution! Or, England and Tasmania compared', Bailey makes her colonial applications of Romanticism explicit; she compares Tasmania to Elysium, in a feminized personification of the natural environment viewed in terms of the value of liberty, associated with the French Revolution,

> We might naturally suppose that any comparison of such a concentration of the luxuries of freedom with our manacles of bondage would only tend to deepen the doleful sorrow of the children of legalised slavery in a penal colony [...] But let the Irrepressible eloquence of facts speak [...] A penal vassalage beneath the embracing sway of such a gentle and gracious mistress, is Elysium itself in comparison of the free

Figure 2.1 Bailey, Mary, *View from Sandy Bay*, 1850.

but infernal bondage riveted in its galled possessors by the hardest of all taskmasters and slavedrivers – the Devil!⁶

Bailey's watercolour painting 'View from Sandy Bay' (Figure 2.1) similarly demonstrates her desire to represent an idealized Van Diemen's Land – despite its convictism.

Her approaches to the natural environment as well as gender and imprisonment are articulated through idealization of Greco-Roman antiquity, from which modern democracy was modelled. Yet as Elizabeth Schüssler Fiorenza points out of this model, 'In Greco-Roman antiquity the socio-political system of Kyriarchy was institutionalised either as empire or as a democratic political form of ruling that excluded all freeborn and slave wo/men from full citizenship and decision-making powers.'[7] Bailey's uses of Romantic Hellenism extend to an implicit ideological support of colonization as an idealized space in which she hoped white women's inequality and political exclusions from democracy might be challenged. Bailey frequently aligns ancient Greek culture with the colony of Tasmania, in terms of questioning the rights of white women and, as the wife of a convict, questions around law, penal servitude and transportation as connected positions. An avowed supporter of women's equality, Bailey was no doubt aware of imperial feminist discourses linking white women's oppression with slavery.

Bailey's concerns with convict rights and women's rights do not encompass the relationships that some settlers articulated between anti-slavery discourses and the situation of First Nations peoples, nor the horrific atrocities of the Tasmanian genocide and the Black War (c.1828–32). Shayne Breen notes that 'international writers and scholars, including Raphael Lemkin, have long seen the Tasmanian extermination as a clear case of genocide'.[8] While the Black War was genocidal, and was both martial and informal, Palawa Tasmanian Aboriginal people survived and assert their sovereignty and continuous culture. As Lyndall Ryan's study attests, Tasmanian Aboriginal people resisted British colonization and 'did not die out in 1876 or any other period of Tasmania's history'.[9] Ryan notes of the period of pastoral settler invasion in Tasmania in the early decades of the nineteenth century, that 'in 1818 the editor of the *Hobart Town Gazette* had argued for the newly emerging humanitarian view, arising from the abolition of the slave trade in 1806, that the Tasmanian Aborigines[sic], like slaves, were part of the "flesh of all nations" assigned by God and deserving of settler sympathy and support'.[10]

In the 1820s the *Colonial Times*, however, is noted to have 'advocated the immediate forcible removal of the Aboriginal nations in the Settled Districts to an island in Bass Strait' (80). James Boyce notes that the removal of 'hostile' Indigenous people became a government policy in 1831, a policy which 'never bore any relation to practice' with removals occurring without consent, regardless of 'hostility' and continuing after the war.[11] Boyce points to the illegality of the practice and the extremely high rates of death among those removed. Bailey herself, following her arrival in 1844, seems to have made no mention of Indigenous peoples in her poetry. At the time of Bailey's arrival, while convicts were still being transported to Tasmania, Palawa and Tasmanian Aboriginal people had been removed, Boyce states 'by force or trickery', from Western Tasmania during 1832–33 to Bruny, Flinders and Hunter Islands.[12] This included those removed to Wybalenna on Flinders Island, which was abandoned in 1847.

The absence of any acknowledgement of Indigenous people in Bailey's work reflects colonial and imperial erasures of genocidal practices and human rights abuses. While different in important ways from mainland histories, it is clear that where anti-slavery tropes were engaged with in relation to Wirrayaraay Aboriginal people in Eliza Hamilton Dunlop's poetry, Bailey's writing is concerned with convict transportation and utilizations of anti-slavery discourse in relation to that practice. Many of Bailey's translations, hymns, original poems and scholarly essays were written and published in the context of her husband's convict status and (subsequently her own) financial and legal situation. Her husband was convicted in 1843 and was later reported in Tasmania as an insolvency case in 1858.[13] She published a series of long argumentative essays on 'Imprisonment for debt' (1848) in the *Colonial Times*, in which she aimed 'to show from the legislative records of antiquity, how ancient lawgivers regarded the blighting curse inflicted so uselessly upon the impoverished debtor, by his deprivation of liberty and incarceration in the gloom of prisons'.[14] Drawing on comparisons with Roman law, she argued that 'a debtor's goods and not his body should be answerable for his debts' (4). These essays reflect her lived experience as both a classical scholar and as the wife of William Bailey. Deirdre Coleman notes that 'White apologists for the slave trade like lieutenant John Matthews [...] argued that there was in essence no difference between enslavement and transportation.'[15]

While Bailey opposed both slavery and transportation, the idea that there were connections between these practices was similarly understood by those who supported their abolition or reform. Angela Davis points out that 'most people are quite surprised to hear that the prison abolition movement also has a long history – one that dates back to the historical appearance of the prison as the main form of punishment'.[16] Born to Edward and Margaretta (Jones) Walker of Over Hall, Gestingthorpe, Bailey was from a privileged background, while transportation largely affected working-class British people, predominantly men. While Bailey's essays focus on arguments for reform to the laws around imprisonment for debt, this may be understood as one approach within broader understandings of resistance to imprisonment, anti-slavery discourses and the economic relationships of transportation to colonialism. Certainly, she did not accept this practice as natural, just or reasonable and was assured in challenging it publicly through her writing in the *Colonial Times*.

Women such as Bailey writing in colonial Tasmania were highly engaged with periodical publishing, a medium that was often both quickly and broadly distributed. In *Early Australian Poetry: An Annotated Bibliography* scores of Mary Bailey's poems are listed. In addition to over 80 poems contributed to the *Colonial Times*, as well as prose articles, Mary Bailey's literary presence sparked much correspondence from both herself and others on the topics of her poetry, poetry generally, Grecian and Roman antiquity, and local politics. The newspapers saw a foregrounding of ongoing dialogues in which poets and their critics often actively exchanged their views on the poems, as well as the communal and political contexts in which these poems were first published. While that 'community' has tended to be treated as both literally and metaphorically distanced from literary Romanticism, these dialogues demonstrate the lines of communication within colonial and imperial networks and the continued transposition of Romanticism to the colonies of Australia in the print media. The *Colonial Times* printed the following advertisement in 1847:

> The Colonial Times; the Tasmanian: Open to all – Influenced by none. This Journal is published on the evening of every Tuesday and Friday, and circulates extensively throughout the Australian Colonies, India, China, Europe and America. It is regularly filed at the office of Messrs. Simmonds and Ward, General Agents, Barge-yard, Bucklersbury, London, and at the Jerusalem Coffee House.[17]

This shows the extensive colonial, imperial and transnational networks of the paper.

Bailey published weekly in the *Colonial Times* under her initials M.B. and her poems were often accompanied by long prose explanations. On more than one occasion, the editors of the *Colonial Times* requested that the author refrain from submitting such long passages. John Campbell Macdougall was the editor and owner of the *Colonial Times*, and E. Flinn notes that the journalist Thomas Richards may have undertaken editorial work until 1847. However, Macdougall's second wife, Mary Ann, carried on the printing business, managing the *Colonial Times* from Macdougall's death in 1848 until February of 1855,[18] when Bailey was frequently publishing poetry in it. Stephen Behrendt notes of the study of British Romantic periodicals that 'in the long view, perhaps the most important contribution of Romantic periodicals, and the one that has escaped serious notice for so long, was their unmistakable contribution to the "conversation in print" that is the distinguishing hallmark of British Romantic writing'.[19]

Bailey's negotiation with British Romanticism and Romantic Hellenism is similarly evident in the numbers of her poems on classical subjects and Grecian antiquity, as well as translations from the Latin and Greek, which she published in the *Colonial Times* in Hobart (known as nipaluna in palawa kani) in the late 1840s. Bailey's use of classical knowledge and anti-slavery discourse informs much of her writing against imprisonment and this has important implications for questions of rights and the development of a colonial Tasmanian Romanticism.

As a category, Tasmanian Romanticism involved both the reproduction and adaptation of Romantic literary models, styles and tropes to specifically Tasmanian contexts, which played out in modes conceptualized in gendered ways as well as those specific to periodical culture. Bailey's poetic practice in Tasmania was concerned with intellect, emotions and rights movements and their significance within translation and broader European cultural inheritance, which manifests in both her poetry and prose in the *Colonial Times*. Kim Wheatley notes of British Romantic culture and periodicals that a 'major development was the heightening of literary pretensions of the miscellaneous magazine through the arrival on the scene of *Blackwood's Edinburgh Magazine* in 1817'.[20] This was a magazine to which both Eliza Hamilton Dunlop and Mary Bailey contributed. A strong literary presence is also in evidence in colonial Australian newspapers, which published both settler colonial and British Romantic poetry. The significance of British Romantic periodicals and Romantic poetry to the print media in Tasmania is exemplified by Bailey's contributions. Moreover, as Stuart Curran has observed of the British context, the women poets of the late Romantic period were dominant on the literary scene and later into the nineteenth century as their writings transitioned into the preoccupations of Victorian verse, a connection which is absent when only canonical male poets are considered. Bailey's poetry, like Dunlop's, reflects the significance of the anti-slavery literature as a context informing much Romantic women's writing, although it is Hellenism which functions as an access point for Bailey's political poetry.

Romantic Hellenism

Bailey's Tasmanian newspaper verses are characteristically engaged with classical subjects, including translations from the Greek Odes of Anacreon. In 1833, Bailey's translations appeared in *Blackwood's Edinburgh Magazine*. Bailey's classical subjects and her emphasis on intellectual equality reflect the influence of earlier bluestocking women. These included Elizabeth Carter, an English lesbian poet, scholar, classicist, translator and writer who was part of the bluestocking circle and translated Epictetus into English. As examples of women who were transgressing the perception of the classics as exclusively male territory, their public visibility was important. Bailey frequently cited Romantic figures, including Germaine de Staël and Lord Byron, who she describes as having 'penetrating genius'[21] and is drawn on as a major practitioner of Romantic Hellenism. Her poems from the *Colonial Times* cite passages from *Childe Harold's Pilgrimage* (1812) and the satiric *Don Juan* (1819).

Bailey, 'educated at home, was encouraged to study Greek and Latin as well as modern languages by her maternal grandfather, the Rev. William Jones, an eminent scholar'.[22] Timothy Webb notes that Romantic Hellenism

> informed a number of major creative works: the mythological poems of Keats, especially *Endymion*, 'Hyperion', 'Lamia' and some of the odes; the second cantos of Byron's *Childe Harold's Pilgrimage* and *Don Juan*, and some of his Turkish tales; Shelley's *Prometheus Unbound* and *Hellas* [...] The common factor to all these varieties of Romantic Hellenism is an interest in Greece or the Grecian model and a desire to appropriate it for present purposes.[23]

Bailey makes several references to Germaine de Staël in her later writing in the *Colonial Times*, and the significance of de Staël to Romantic Hellenism is seen through *Corinne, or, Italy* (1807) (Figure 2.2). Susan Brown notes that 'Victorian critics constantly invoked Sappho as a precedent for the poetess' and that major Romantic women's poetry like Letitia Elizabeth Landon's *The Improvisatrice* from 1824 derives from *Corinne*,[24] which also inspired verse responses from Hemans and Byron's *Childe Harold's Pilgrimage*. *Corinne* and the 'Sappho-Corinne myth' as a Romantic reworking is an overt celebration of the woman poet and was a model for many later poets, including Bailey.

White women's social, political and intellectual equality, particularly within public political debate, is approached through classical literature in Bailey's 'A Voice from Ass-Mania, or Neddy's Bray' (1847). Her poem uses Aesop's fable of the ass dressed as a wolf to critique Edward Kemp's poem, 'A Voice from Tasmania' (1846). Kemp's *A Voice from Tasmania* was published in Hobart Town by John Moore in 1846 and is listed in the National Library of Australia catalogue as the first book of verse published in Tasmania by a native-born writer, although Kemp, unlike Charles Harpur in New South Wales, is not now regarded as a canonical poet. Bailey's 'A Voice, from Ass-Mania!! Or Neddy's Bray' clearly demonstrates how she and others were using the shared knowledge of Hellenism and classical literature to comment on contemporary political situations. The poem demonstrates as well that a poetic rivalry between Bailey and Kemp was bound up in satire, politics and legislature around the policies affecting convicts in Tasmania in the 1840s.

Like Bailey, Kemp makes frequent allusions to classical antiquity, references Pope and satirizes colonial politics. The volume, Kemp notes, was 'to be merely a playful satire upon the members of the Legislative Council'[25] and reflects public dissatisfaction among colonists with Probationism. The Probation system for convicts was introduced from 1840 and administered by Lieutenant Governor John Eardley-Wilmot from 1843. It replaced the earlier Assignment system under which convict labour was assigned to colonists. Under the Probation system convicts could attain a 'Ticket of Leave' allowing certain freedoms, and Bailey's husband received one in 1847, the same year her poem was published. As Michael Roe notes,

> Early in their sentence convicts would remain in gangs, preferably employed so as to defray their upkeep; later they would enter the labour market as wage-earners. Settled colonists thus reaped no benefit of cheap assigned labour, and therefore abhorred the new system.[26]

Kemp's poem expressed such views through an attack on the unpopular Eardley-Wilmot.

Figure 2.2 Vigée-Le Brun, Elisabeth, *Portrait of Madame de Staël as Corinne*, 1809.

He noted in the volume that 'Since the foregoing was written [...] news of Sir Eardley Wilmot's recall (thank God) have arrived' (vii) and in *A Voice from Tasmania* writes:

> Sir Eardley Wilmot mourned when Forster died
> Stared at his corpse, and as he stared he sigh'd:
> These ominous words betrayed his faltering voice –
> Thou Convict Chief, Probationism's choice,
> My salary's gone, I have no friend to-morrow
> To screen another Sodom and Gomorrah. (51–52)

These lines suggest rumours of Eardley-Wilmot's homosexual relationships, which were used as the reason to recall him from colonial service.[27]

Morris Miller has pointed out that 'Bailey's [...] point of view was that of Eardley-Wilmot's friends and supporters.'[28] Bailey's 'A Voice, from Ass-Mania!! Or Neddy's Bray' reads:

> Suggested by a perusal of a poem entitled 'A Voice From Tasmania' by
>   Edward Kemp, Esq.
>   Ass intones to Ass
> Harmonic twang
>   POPE; Dunciad, Book II
>   By good master Aesop we're told of an Ass,
>   Who in impudence did all his fellows surpass; –
>   He'd fain be a Lion; but how this could be,
>   The aspiring young jackass was unable to see;
>   So he shook his long ears and in sorrowing mood,
>   Traversed slowly and sadly the skirts of a wood.
>   Not '*The sun up above, nor the fresh flowers below*'
>   Afforded to him the least solace for woe –
>   So sad was his heart while he lifted his eyes,
>   Which 'searched' long 'in vain for their own bright skies!!!'
>   It chanced that he found the old skin of a Lion,
>   Which the asinine beast thought at once he would try on.
>   The beasts of the forest, in terrible fright,
>   When they saw this strange monster, at once took to flight;
>   Till a cunning old Fox chanced to pass by that way,
>   As this Lion-that-wou'd-be; 'gan loudly to bray;
>   Says the Fox – 'as a Lion you wish to appear,
>   But I know what you are now your braying I hear,
>   Could you keep your own counsel, conceited young Ass,
>   For a Lion, with some, *perhaps* you might pass,
>   But that voice, so disgusting, so brazen, so loud,
>   Would dub you an Ass – If you're ever so proud!'[29]

Bailey likens Kemp's poetic voice to the Ass's bray, and perhaps herself to the Fox. In her accompanying note, Bailey sarcastically describes the borrowed lines from Kemp on 'fresh flowers' and 'bright skies' as possessing 'the Miltonic grandeur, the Byronic pathos and the Shelleyan soarings, which everywhere mark this exceedingly and attractively young Gentleman's muse'.

As a supporter of Eardley-Wilmot, Bailey had also commemorated him in her 'Monody on Sir John Eardley-Wilmot'.[30] This led to attacks on Bailey in the *Colonial Times*, with correspondents demanding the paper 'Keep Down the Poets'. Eardley-Wilmot's death in 1847 did little to alter his unpopularity among those colonists who 'objected [...] to paying all local police and judicial expenses insisting that these largely arose from Britain's use of the island as a convict dump'.[31] Roe points out that while Wilmot was in fact sympathetic to the plight of the colonists, 'he nevertheless had to bear the odium of representing Whitehall'.[32] Upon her husband's conviction and transportation, E. D. Daw states that 'Mary Bailey at once resolved to join him'; however, when Eardley-Wilmot 'undertook to assist her [...] He was rewarded for this with a rebuke from the Colonial Office'.[33]

Bailey's poem, 'The Exile's Wife to her Husband', is a personal reflection on her decision to follow her husband from Britain to Van Diemen's Land and an emotional account in common metre ballad form which emphasizes her own devotion to her husband:

> Urge me no more: I could not bear
> Thee to go forth alone.
> Thou wert indeed an exile then
> A hopeless friendless one.
>
> I *will* go with thee, I have weighed
> The dangers that betide;
> And I am sure the safest place
> Is by my husband's side.
>
> Oh! There are other skies as bright,
> And other lands as fair;
> Where yet thou mayest dwell in peace,
> Although an exile there.
>
> Exile! I had not thought to hear,
> *That* coupled with thy name;
> Yet, Dearest, it can never be,
> To thee the brand of shame.[34]

Devotion is a strong theme in Bailey's poetry, and she had also published a poem entitled 'Woman's Love', one of her earliest to appear in the *Colonial Times*.[35] Debates on the sexual nature of men and women proliferated in the poetry sections of newspapers in colonial Australia, with numerous poems on the topic of 'Woman's Love' appearing to support (and sometimes disagree with) the representation of women's lasting devotion (and men's implied sexual license) by poets as chronologically distanced as Mary Bailey and Louisa Lawson.

The significance of ideas of so-called sexual purity and devotion as aspects of arguments for the moral equality of women within imperial feminist discourses is evident in Bailey's earlier volume, *Palmyra*, published in Britain in 1833. The volume reflects feminist uses of Zenobia, the queen of Palmyra, who led a rebellion against Rome in the third century and was said to have been contained with golden chains upon her capture by Aurelian. In Bailey's volume Zenobia is criticized for her betrayal of Longinus, an intellectual of her court, to the Roman army of Aurelian:

> Alas! alas! behold she sorrowing stands
> A captive queen amid the Roman bands:
> Oh false Zenobia, couldst thou then betray
> Those who had shar'd with thee the stormy day?
> Couldst thou betray Longinus, Grecia's boast?
> To glut the fury of a savage host?[36]

Similarly, the representation of men as associated with war, through the Roman emperor Aurelian (the 'savage host'), and women with philosophy, through Zenobia of Palmyra, reflects Bailey's ongoing concern with constructions of gender and antiquity. These examples from antiquity are used to demonstrate historical evidence of women's involvement in philosophical, political and poetic culture and to emphasize moral claims to equality through essentialist perceptions of women as being naturally sympathetic rather than war-like. Antiquity is presented as a positive counterpoint to various aspects of women's exclusions from intellectual, public and political participation in the nineteenth century.

Bailey's translations of the 'Odes of Anacreon' (1849) are likewise positioned in terms of imperial feminist thought. In the article accompanying the first ode, she overtly states that

> I believe that once the rights and superiority of women are allowed to have their just place, on an equal footing with men, in the social institutions of the world, and that an equally impartial provision is made to effect such objects, then, and not until then, will the human race enjoy, un-beclouded, undiminished splendours of moral and intellectual enlightenment.[37]

She proposes a supposedly global approach to women's rights framed through European Enlightenment values, though considerations of race and non-European cultures are absent. In her first translation of the 'Odes of Anacreon', Bailey writes:

Oft when we tell of war's alarms,
I tune my harp to deeds of arms:
And strive some warrior's praise to sing
Love sounds alone upon the string!
Lately I changed my harp entire,
And put new strings upon my lyre;
To sing for Hercules I strove,
My harp responded *only love*
Farewell, ye warriors! – farewell all
Whom poets mighty heroes call!
While life remains, my strings shall move
Only to gentler themes of love.[38]

This recalls Pope's 'Sappho to Phaon from the fifteenth of Ovid's epistles': 'Love taught my tears in sadder notes to flow / And tun'd my heart to elegies of woe', which was also included in Mary Robinson's *Sappho and Phaon* (1796) as an epigraph. Likewise, Landon linked Sappho and women's poetry to the theme of woman's love. Landon's 'Sappho's Song' expressed this in the lines 'It was not song that taught me love / But it was love that taught me song'.[39]

Bailey fashions the Greek model as poetic and peaceful. Webb points out that Romantic Hellenist 'poets became increasingly troubled by the battle scenes in the *Iliad* and some tried to subvert the traditional connection between war and epic [...] This response [...] must have been sharpened by the long course of the Napoleonic wars'.[40] Bailey's translation takes this subversion as its central theme, in a way that is reiterated consistently throughout the poem. It also uses stronger language than Thomas Moore's translation, which reads:

Give me the harp of epic song
Which Homer's finger thrilled along;
But tear away the sanguine string,
For war is not the theme I sing.
Proclaim the laws of festal rite,
I'm monarch of the board to-night;
And all around shall brim as high,
And quaff the tide as deep as I.
And when the cluster's mellowing dews
Their warm enchanting balm infuse,
Our feet shall catch the elastic bound,
And reel us through the dance's round.
Great Bacchus, we shall sing to thee,
In wild but sweet ebriety;

> Flashing around such sparks of thought,
> As Bacchus could alone have taught.
> Then, give the harp of epic song
> Which Homer's finger thrilled along;
> But tear away the sanguine string,
> For war is not the theme I sing.[41]

In Bailey's translation, the lyre as a symbol of poetry is simply incapable of praise of war, even when the speaker 'changed my harp entire / And put new strings upon my lyre' (4). This approach to war is not conveyed so concretely by Moore's translation, which engages with Bacchanalian festivity. Bailey's lyre instead reflects a sense of integrity to a system of values which privileges the poetic and philosophical above the war-like.

Bailey's representation of women's intellectual equality and poetic tradition through antiquity is grounded in the European philosophical conceptualizations of gender they also contest. Her poetic themes address inequality in terms of a need to disprove the presumed inferiority of women through intellectual and moral arguments. Philosophical discourses held up a false gender binary within which women were understood as not tainted by association with wars in the way that men were, and it was presumed that this was due to a natural inclination of women to sympathy. Voltaire expressed in the *Dictionnaire Philosophique* (1764) that 'women, incessantly occupied with the education of their children, and shut up in their domestic cares, are excluded from all these professions, which pervert human nature and render it atrocious. They are everywhere less barbarous than men'.[42] Such representations of women are reflected on in Bailey's poem 'The Death of Pompey' (1848) in which Sappho as a signifier of women's poetry is contrasted with Pompey the Great, a Roman military and political leader associated with aristocracy, greed and military ruthlessness. The title is followed by the explanatory subheading: 'Upon occasion of a friend's dog, called POMPEY, being accidentally strangled to death by the chain of another canine playmate, SAPPHO'.[43] Indicative of Bailey's dark humour, the poem is more a reflection on politics, gender and poetry than on the 'canine playmates' she purports to be elegizing. Bailey opens it by playfully asking

> Shall I in Sapphic verse relate
> Poor curly Pompey's wretched fate?
> Or shall my plainer verses tell
> The awful fate which him befell? (4)

signalling her own authorial identification as a woman in published form. This connection to Sappho is significant in terms of its relationship to fragment in a women's poetic tradition, especially given that the poem was signed only with her initials. Even as she asks this, she has already opted for 'plainer verse', and not what is typically known as Sapphic verse (which consists of three hendecasyllabic lines and a fourth adonic. Bailey employs six four-line stanzas of rhyming couplets in iambic tetrameter). The use of 'plainer verses' signals that Bailey's poetic concern with Sappho is contemporary and symbolic, aligned with the Romantic tradition and Victorian women's tradition signified by Sappho, rather than being imitative of ancient Greek poetry.

'The Death of Pompey' (1848) recasts Pompey and Sappho as dogs in an allegorical contest, revealing a feminist approach to poetry and war as gendered concepts. It concludes:

SAPPHO and POMPEY – mighty names!
They each have set the world in flames!
POMPEY THE GREAT by wars and arms;
But SAPPHO by poetic charms!![44]

Bailey repeatedly aligns the Grecian and other cultures in antiquity with the poetic and with women, and the Roman with war and men. Susan C. Jarratt points out that Sappho's fragments when compared with those of the poet Alcaeus, who lived during the same period in Mytilene, suggest war and love as particularly gendered subjects in Grecian antiquity. She notes that Alcaeus was writing 'elaborate descriptions of armour, of the pain and strife of battle, and of fathers, shame and honor' although, she adds, this is 'not meant to be a comprehensive account of their achievements. Nor do the interpretations add up to a simple binary formula of gender difference'.[45] Nonetheless, Bailey's alignment of the poetic with Sappho articulates women's poetic and intellectual equality and promotes pacifism.

Bailey, like feminist Saint Simonians of the early nineteenth century, equates women with pacifism and calls on alternatives to patriarchal war heroism through her representations of antiquity. Claire Goldberg Moses notes that

> The Feminism of Saint-Simonism was developed in conjunction with the movement's Pacifism and Socialism [...] his followers based their Feminism on an interpretation of Saint-Simon's project to reorganise the globe by replacing the rule of 'Brute force' with the rule of 'Spiritual powers' [...] Sexual equality, they sometimes added for further

justification, would reward woman whose character had served as an example for a superior way of life and thus 'won man over to peace and love'.[46]

Goldberg Moses further maintains that the French utopian socialist feminists 'were Romantics [...] spiritual, mystical and visionary [...] they were internationalists and pacifists, opposed not only to war but even to national boundaries'.[47] In the article accompanying her translation of the ode of Anacreon, Bailey indicates her familiarity with the French feminism of the 1830s, and the positions of her poems clearly reflect those of the Saint Simonian utopian socialist feminists.

Bailey's approach to feminist transnationalism and cosmopolitanism is Eurocentric, apparent as much from the representation of various geographical locations in her poetry as it is from her prose discussions of contemporary French ideas on women's education, or the 'Odes of Anacreon' as universally applicable. She quotes and paraphrases various passages from *Woman's Mission*, a well-known moderate work published in 1839 by Sarah Lewis, in which questions around women's involvement in political activities such as abolitionism and prison reform are considered in terms of women's so-called proper mission, with an emphasis on morality and the domestic sphere. Related questions around women's education are discussed in Bailey's article published with her translation of the ode of Anacreon. She includes an anecdote about Madame Campan and Napoleon regarding mothers' educative role, from the title page of *Woman's Mission* (the popular English translation of the original French from Aimé Martin) and a quotation of the phrase 'woman's physical inferiority – the only inferiority which we acknowledge'.[48] Likewise, Bailey's assertion that Anacreon was 'for all times – for all climes' (4) clearly echoes the sentiment voiced in the preface of *Woman's Mission* that in this translation of Aimé Martin's ideas for English women, 'the reader might perhaps fail to discover that these were of *universal* application, equally sound and true in all ages and in all countries'.[49] Such universalizing presumes a global applicability of particular European world views about gender rather than universal equality.

'The Death of Pompey', as an example of Bailey's Romantic Hellenism, articulates a feminism which is gender-conscious but does not consider race. Bailey's description of 'dark Sappho' explicitly references Byron's stanza (canto II, stanza XXXIX) on Sappho in *Childe Harold's Pilgrimage*:

> And onward viewed the mount, not yet forgot
> The lover's refuge and the Lesbian's grave.
> Dark Sappho! Could not verse immortal save
> That breast imbued with such immortal fire?[50]

Likewise, Bailey's later reference to 'mighty names! / They each have set the world in flames!' (*Pompey* 4) suggests Byron's line on the 'immortal fire' in Sappho as a metaphoric equivalent of immortality through verse to that of elite male constructions of Western culture and war heroism.

Felicia Hemans's 'The Image in Lava' is similarly concerned with a gender-conscious approach to ancient culture, in line with philosophical arguments for women's virtue through maternal sympathy. Her footnote to the poem describes the 'impression of a woman's form, with an infant clasped to the bosom, found at the uncovering of Herculaneum', linking women's sympathy and love with nature as in the lines:

> Temple and tower have moulder'd,
> Empires from earth have pass'd,
> And woman's heart hath left a trace
> These glories to outlast![51]

Romantic poets had increasingly shown interest in ancient Greece and classical culture, which was understood as signifying connection to Western civilization and empire, both a philosophical and political basis. These connected understandings of the philosophical relationship of culture to nature were significant to questions of women's rights.

Bailey's 'The death of Pompey', even as a satirical elegy supposedly for a dog, is concerned with ideas of gender and culture, immortality through verse and anti-war sentiments. But the seriousness of Bailey's early poetry is often replaced with a satirical edge in her colonial poetry. The pacifism and poetic achievement of women is depicted as triumphing over war through the accidental strangulation of a dog, an irony that is far removed from both the seriousness and the separateness of women's domestic and emotional roles as presented in Hemans' poem. Bailey's use of satirical voice reveals a more scornful politics, with the expectation of peaceful submission within the domestic ideal transgressed in an imagined violent, though accidental, destruction of both women's subordination and men's violence within that binary. As Andrew Stauffer suggests,

> like irony, anger often acts as an instrument of truth, pointing out injustices, betrayals and false states of affairs. So for the Romantic poets, angry satire was a highly rhetorical art and also a test of sincerity, a theatrical performance aimed at stripping away masks, an antithetical charade in the service of truth.[52]

Bailey's satirical poetry remains highly intellectually engaged with both Romantic Hellenism and Victorian modes of political poetic voice.

Feminist discourse and Romantic women's poetry

Mary Bailey links women and the intellect through Romantic Hellenism, which she uses to give weight to ongoing debates on women's intellectual equality, a central aspect of arguments around women's inclusion in citizenship and democracy. As Geneviève Fraisse notes of the debate around French women's exclusion from democracy, from 'around 1800, at the birth of modern democracy [...] woman's reason, rather than her body, was at the centre of the debate. Since the reasonable individual was the centrepiece of democratic process, reason was the most logical criterion for sexual equality'.[53] As Fraisse further argues, 'this systematic desire to exclude is undoubtedly democracy's (it is also Christianity's) inevitable lie: an affirmation of an equality that is too abstract to be concretely true'.[54] Bailey was engaged in these ongoing 'debates' around reason and women's intellectual equality. In 1834, a reviewer in the *Gentlemen's Magazine* made a lengthy discussion of Bailey's volume *Palmyra*, then in its second edition. The reviewer noted that Bailey 'launches out in praise of Zenobia'.[55] Zenobia is also represented in Shelley's *Queen Mab* (1813), and Shelley's friend, Thomas Love Peacock, published *Palmyra and Other Poems* (1805). Charlotte Bronte's juvenilia refers to Zenobia in 'Marian v. Zenobia'.[56]

Bailey's poems are highly conscious of approaches to intellectual equality within Romantic women's poetic discourses. This is clear in Bailey's volume *Palmyra* (1833), especially in relation to Zenobia and her capture by Aurelian. *The Oxford Companion to Classical Literature* notes that 'Palmyra was utterly destroyed, but the queen, having probably been exhibited in Aurelian's triumph, was granted a pension and a villa at Tibur.'[57] Other representations of Zenobia also utilize imagery of her being exhibited in chains, as in the 1780 painting by Guy Head, 'Zenobia, Queen of Palmyra in chains', and Harriet Hosmer's sculpture, 'Zenobia in Chains' (c.1859) (Figure 2.3). However, Bailey's *Palmyra* is particularly concerned with women's political equality and associates war with the decay of ancient civilization:

> How art thou sunk, Arabia's mighty queen,
> Fall'n from thy height as if thou ne'er had been!
> Thy broken shafts, and columns peering high,
> Speak but the loss of ancient majesty;
> Thy batter'd walls, and ruins stretching wide,
> Declare the nothingness of human pride:
> The angry Sun looks down, with scornful ray,
> On glory lost, and grandeur in decay. (5)

Figure 2.3 Hosmer, Harriet, *Zenobia in Chains*, c.1859.

Zenobia, as a figure of power, is addressed from a nineteenth-century future in which her 'glory' has become 'decay', amid current anxieties around women's political exclusion and voice: 'How art thou sunk, Arabia's mighty queen, / Fall'n from thy height as if thou ne'er had been!' This fall is similarly positioned in the later passage: 'Alas! For Tadmor though she long withstood / The cruel soldier thirsting for her blood, / At length o'ercome by still increasing foes / Which like a gathering storm, around her rose.'[58] These lines again cast war, political power and imperial expansion as masculine, with 'the cruel soldier thirsting for her blood'. Criticism of Zenobia is centred primarily on her moral weakness in betraying Longinus.

Bailey uses figures such as Zenobia in *Palmyra* and Sappho in 'The Death of Pompey' as emblems of women's intellectual, poetic and political voice. Feminist writer Anna Jameson had also discussed Zenobia as a feminist figure in *Memoirs of Celebrated Female Sovereigns* (1831), and the American neoclassical sculptor Harriet Hosmer produced her sculpture of Zenobia, depicted in chains in 1859. In both *Palmyra* and 'The Death of Pompey' Bailey presents Zenobia and Sappho in contrast to masculine symbols, like Aurelian and Pompey the Great, that lack intellectual associations.

Bailey uses classical models of women's intellect, to signal her own, in order to contest oppressive nineteenth-century views about women's rights to education and political participation. Her article on her translation of an ode of Anacreon in the *Colonial Times* mentions her rivalry with Thomas Moore in producing translations in *Blackwood's Edinburgh Magazine*.[59] Bailey's translation of Ariphron from the Greek appeared in *Blackwood's* in October of 1832.[60] *Blackwood's* gave a positive review, stating that 'Mrs Bailey's version is excellent – far superior to some sent us by "bearded men"' (Bailey, *Greek*, 423), in response to her letter and translation of 'Hymn to Health' (a poem she later republished in the *Colonial Times* and later still in the *Sydney Freeman's Journal* (1860)).[61] The comments were perhaps by John Wilson (Christopher North), who was particularly active as a writer for *Blackwood's* at this time. Two versions, one line for line, and one in verse, of 'Ariphron's Hymn to Health' by 'Christopher North' are included in the editor's reply to Bailey's letter and version.

The comment relates to the mocking of intellectual pursuits by bluestocking women as unfeminine. Jane Rendall notes that

> the recurrent figure of the bluestocking reflected the high levels of anxiety and tension surrounding the claims of literary women. There has been little systematic discussion of early nineteenth-century uses of this term [...] from the late 1770s, though the term could be either complimentary or, more often, pejorative, it described women with intellectual interests.[62]

Rendall points to the differing attitudes to bluestockings of leading periodicals like *Blackwood's* and the *Edinburgh Review*, noting that John Wilson, in an issue of *Blackwood's* in 1820, had 'claimed a victory for *Blackwood's* in the defeat of all pretensions to knowledge of politics and political economy among women' (355).

Bailey's comment in the letter accompanying her poem in *Blackwood's* suggests her familiarity with attitudes to bluestockings in that particular periodical:

> Certainly the ladies now-a-days have to congratulate themselves, that the Popish qualification of sustaining a long beard is not indispensable for the character of being truly learned; for the Papist doctors inform us, that before they admitted St Theresa de Jesus to the doctorate, the doctors of the university of Salamanca required such a distinction [...] I am satisfied, sir, that you require no such qualification from your female correspondents.[63]

Bailey's resistance to this idea appears to be a reference to Wilson's words in an article in *Blackwood's* from 1820:

> Every female leg was azure – absolutely painted blue like a post. A slight beard was becoming visible even on women still marriageable – a certain consequence of incipient literary habits.[64]

The tensions apparent in Wilson's editorial and Bailey's comments, as Rendall suggests of the intellectual contexts of the various periodicals, must 'be understood in terms of the practices of sociability of which they were part [...] the sociability of early nineteenth-century Edinburgh meant that the Republic of Letters was not only for gentlemen, though its spaces were undoubtedly contested'.[65] Points of disagreement between poets and correspondents or editors are in evidence in various colonial periodicals as well. These tensions between literary production and criticism in periodicals and newspapers reveal these forums to be contestable spaces in which these women's poetry, particularly that which was of a politically astute nature, could be reproduced.

The symbolism of Zenobia is only one example showing Bailey's feminist reading of classical history and literature, and this continues in the poetry produced after she arrived in Tasmania. As Noah Comet suggests, Romantic women poets including Felicia Hemans, Letitia Landon, Lucy Aikin and Mary Robinson were engaged with Romantic Hellenism in unique and distinctly gender-conscious ways. Comet suggests that Landon 'struggles with a Hellenism of second thoughts. Like Keats, Byron and Shelley, she finds in the idea of Greece an appealing range of aesthetic and political values, but unlike her male predecessors, she cannot identify with them, not in the 1830s, not as a woman poet with an acute sense of women's history.'[66]

Colonial newspaper poetry and British periodicals

It is likely that Bailey did not receive payment for her publications in newspapers and she certainly met with animosity as a woman contributor in this public space. One of Bailey's poems, entitled 'Keep Down the Poets', was published in the *Colonial Times* on 2 March 1847.[67] It specifically addresses a previous letter to the editor complaining about poetry appearing in the newspapers. Webby notes that 'from almost the first issues of the *Sydney Gazette* in 1803 [...] most early Australian newspapers featured a "Poets Corner" '.[68] Bailey's poem satirically attacks the correspondent:

> Pooh! What have news supplying papers
> To do with poet's silly capers?
> 'Keep down the poets', they're so airy,
> Companions fit for witch or fairy;
> But we, ensconced in bodies bluff,
> Think poets ravings arrant stuff!
> We love to hear of prime fed beasts
> Of markets, pastry cooks, and feasts,
> Where every sort of food we find,
> Save that which nourishes the mind! (*Keep*, 4)

In the accompanying note, Bailey asserts (of the letter to which she was responding) that

> The said communication wages war against the whole brotherhood of rhymesters [...] Newspaper devotees of song are more specially doomed to extirpation. The poets, then, it now seems, who have published many volumes in sturdy octavos, in this writer's opinion offend against the majesty of literature if they haply pen any of their superabundant thoughts for the Daily Press! (*Keep*, 4)

The criticism of poets had in fact been aimed squarely at Bailey following her 'Monody on Sir John Eardley-Wilmot'. The critic signed themselves 'C.D.', and Morris Miller speculates this may have been Cornelius Driscoll, a member of the upper house, banker and convict administrator in Tasmania.[69] 'C.D.' responded to Bailey's counter-attack with the comment: ' "M.B." mentions Byron: does he recollect the noble poet's loss of temper at the chastisement his "Childe Harold" received from Jeffrey in the *Edinburgh Review*?'.[70] This comment demonstrates the level of familiarity with British periodical literature as applicable to debates between colonial newspaper contributors, as well as presumes M.B. to be a man.

The exchange outlines the animosity settler women poets publishing in newspapers could meet with from both readers and editors. While the editors of the *Colonial Times* had as their motto 'open to all; influenced by none', a specific case of editorial opposition was the demonstrated animosity of the editors of the *Sydney Morning Herald*, as Webby notes, towards Eliza Hamilton Dunlop for many years. Particularly, as Webby discerns, for settler colonial readers

> the most important influence on the production of literature was the relationship with the parent culture [...] Imported books and magazines were preferred to the local product, partly because they were cheaper [...] English publications also had the charm of the known amidst the unknown. A favourite vignette of writers describing life in mid-century Australia was the squatter's table with its copies of *Punch* and the *Illustrated London News*. And, of course, imported books were believed to be of superior quality.[71]

However, there were also readers who praised Bailey's contributions.

A letter in the *Colonial Times* entitled 'M.B. and Sacred poetry' and signed 'COSMOPOLITE' states that 'In reading some articles in your pages, I am often reminded of the higher toned metropolitan journals, especially of the periodical press of the Continent of Europe [...] I am most willing to award much praise to your correspondent, signed "M.B.," for the distinguished part he so ably performs.'[72] This presumption that M.B. was a man is later addressed in the same letter: 'It is hinted that your correspondent is an amiable lady [...] I beg to submit to your correspondent's future imitation, as *models*, the truly illustrious female names of More, Landon and Hemans, and forever to leave buried in their merited dust, the moth-eaten tomes of monks, friars, and abbots.'[73] The suggestions of More, Landon and Hemans to Bailey's 'future imitation' may be seen to imply that she might, if she is a she, model herself more in the feminine space of the figure of the 'poetess'. Bailey's gender was eventually established to her readers in the *Colonial Times*, and, although she does not appear to have mentioned Hemans, Landon or More specifically, her poetry reflects an awareness of these poets. Her work was highly regarded by many contributors. One letter to the editor, signed 'A Catholic, But not Bigotted [sic]', notes that 'a literary friend has just put in to my hands a criticism of the noted *John Bull* journal of London, on a publication, it is conjectured of M.B. This review says that M.B. is gifted, with no less than "the profound learning of an Usher, and the piercing indignant invective of a Junius and a Pascal"'.[74]

A correspondent signing themselves 'Philalethes' writes, with presumptions of Western superiority, in the aftermath of the 'Keep down the poets' exchange, a letter entitled 'M.B. and Colonial poet-haters':

> I had thought that even at our great distance from the focus of the world's intelligence, it was impossible that any individual would be hardy enough to stigmatise with lunacy the celestial boon of poetry.[75]

When correspondence is taken into account, there were often whole pages dedicated to poetry and its discussion, and even specifically to 'M.B.' Poetry, articles and correspondence appeared on pages three and four of a four-page paper. Often up to half of its pages were somewhat in the style of a literary journal. Although not exclusively on literary topics, this does significantly alter the idea of the poetic presence in newspapers such as the *Colonial Times* as being limited to a small poet's corner.

While newspapers tend to be regarded as ephemeral, in opposition to ideas of poetry as immortal, there is evidence of the significance and ongoing legacy of newspaper poets in Australia. Miller states that 'it is without doubt that Mary Bailey's creative writings and scholarship have left traces in the literary heritage of the island'.[76] And poems were often reprinted in various newspapers around the colonies, extending their readership beyond just the original publication. It is probable that a similar situation may have played out to that noted by Stephen Behrendt of Britain in the Romantic period:

> We know from the historical record and from modern scholarly studies that the contents of periodicals of all sorts reached a far greater number of citizens than is indicated merely by the number of copies printed, for in addition to their presence in circulating libraries, their contents were read out in coffee houses, pubs, and other meeting places, so that one single copy might have served literally dozens of readers.[77]

Articles on British women's literary topics also appeared in the *Sydney Gazette* (1803–42), such as one entitled 'Literary Women'.[78] This was taken from the London *Quarterly Review* and was a review of 'The Letters of Mrs Elizabeth Montagu. Part the second, Published by Matthew Montagu Esq. Volumes III and IV'. The article also appeared in a Florida-based publication, the *Analectic Magazine*, demonstrating the transnational flows of British periodical items.

It is worth quoting from this article for its relevance and similarity to articles by Bailey, as it is probable that she would have been familiar in Britain with such articles, if not with this particular one. Bailey, it is known, wrote for the London reviews, and she would have been 22 at the time it was originally published. The article is certainly in Bailey's area of interest, mentioning several of the same women writers as did articles attributed to Bailey, such as Madame de Staël, Madame D'Acier, Mrs. Carter and Maria Edgeworth, as well as highlighting classical scholarship and women's poetic tradition through Sappho:

> Whatever doubts may be entertained as to the advances toward knowledge that have been lately made by the male part of our species, it is, we think, impossible to deny that the female have made a great and rapid progress [...] There are now alive, or at least, there have lived within the last twenty years, more women distinguished for their literary talents, and whose works are likely to immortalize their names, than in the twenty centuries that had elapsed, from the time of Sappho to that of the ingenious lady whose letters are now before us.[79]

This article further indicates the literary predominance of British women during the early nineteenth century, noted by Stuart Curran and others as being particularly the case in the late Romantic period. The abridged version of this review, published in the *Sydney Gazette*, omits the references to the text of Elizabeth Montagu's letters, and consequently decontextualizes the piece from the bluestockings, perhaps in order not to draw attention to the 14 years that had elapsed since its original publication. However, its sentiment was still highly relevant, with the emergence of popular women poets including Hemans and Landon following the deaths of most canonical male Romantic poets.

This is a significant point that has been overlooked in studies of Romanticism in Australia, such as Paul Kane's. These studies have tended to perpetuate a false impression, through exclusively discussing male canonical writers, that poetry by settler women was non-existent or apolitical. Women's poetry, which most frequently appeared in newspapers and not printed volumes, represents a major challenge to these assumptions. Mary Bailey's writing was highly politically engaged with major concerns of the day and with imperial and cosmopolitan feminist arguments and transnational networks of literary women. The introduction to Caroline May's anthology *The American Female Poets* (1848) likewise suggests women's dominance of these literary scenes at the time:

> One of the most striking characteristics of the present age is the number of female writers, especially in the department of belles-lettres. This is even more true of the United States than of the Old World; and poetry,

which is the language of the affections, has been freely employed among us to express the emotions of woman's heart [...] fugitive pieces of various merit have been poured forth through our newspapers and other periodicals, with the utmost profusion.[80]

May's account of the proliferation of settler women's poetry in American periodicals reiterates the role of the press as a space for local, imperial and transnational exchange. Likewise, in colonial Australian newspapers, women poets like Mary Bailey were highly visible, expressing dissent and strongly advocating for their rights through their literary presence.

Separate spheres, newspapers and reading rooms

Bailey notes that at the time of producing her Greek translations in *Blackwood's* in the 1830s, she had been 'delighted by literary circles and sided by the noble libraries of the first capitals of Europe'.[81] The physical presence of women in spaces such as the British Museum Reading Room, Ruth Hoberman argues, was 'a public stage, an opportunity for women to dramatize their entry into – or rejection of – public life [...] The reading room emerges, finally, as a contested space in which women use both their literal visibility in the room and the writing that resulted from their work there to lay claim to public life'.[82] Hoberman notes that these women refused to sit in the limited space designated for ladies and caused angry responses in the media. Although Hoberman's study focuses specifically on women in the British Museum Reading Rooms in the late nineteenth century, Bailey's presence in the 'noble libraries of the first capitals of Europe' was similarly a disruption to the increasing expectation that women should not transgress from the feminine domestic 'proper sphere'. Bailey clearly contests the conflation of knowledge with men and engages in the 'public sphere'. Mary Robinson was an important precursor to Mary Bailey, not only as a woman poet but also as a Romantic Hellenist, a feminist and a regular contributor to the press. Robinson was acquainted with Mary Wollstonecraft through William Godwin, and both argued for the education of women and against the sexual double standard. Much as Bailey's usage of classical mythology does, Sharon M. Setzer notes that Robinson's 'Letter to the Women of England' [...] 'devotes much of her Letter to examples of such heroic *women* from antiquity to her own day'.[83] The push for women's education and intellectual equality suggested by the works of Wollstonecraft and Robinson is continued through later writers, including Bailey, across the nineteenth century.

Bailey's political uses of Romantic Hellenism and her views on women's rights, prisoner's rights and education were no doubt augmented by the medium of the newspaper, arguably a more communal space for disseminating and receiving information than book publications. As Adriana Craciun has noted of Mary Robinson, there is a 'vision of metropolitan print culture as fundamentally democratizing'.[84] In the prose article Bailey published in the *Colonial Times* along with her first 'Ode of Anacreon', she refers to 'the educated classes', adding, 'for mind alone confers essential greatness'. Class and culture have important implications for education, though Bailey's comments may indicate an understanding that despite class-condescension, education and access could help address inequality. She is overtly and highly critical of presumptions of superiority connected to wealth and states that

> In the regions of the intellectual or moral world, a fellow-worm there *aristocratically* pluming himself in a fancied superior greatness over a less fortunate fellow-being, because of the mere outward appendage of possessing more bread, more loaves, that is wealth – this is indeed a monstrosity.[85]

Bailey here frames the question of education and gender in a particularly class-conscious way, as analogous and connected with other forms of inequality.

Bailey's problematization of wealth and appearance as metaphors for intellectual greatness can also be seen to critique both gender and class-condescension beyond 'the regions of the intellectual or moral world'.[86] Her metaphor of knowledge as wealth is transformed into a highly political act of breaking down hierarchies of class and gender by publishing her translation of a Greek author in a colonial Australian newspaper.

Bailey was conscious of the medium of the newspaper as having this potential impact on readers in Tasmania. As Webb points out, 'knowledge of classical literature, and in particular the Greek language, was a widely recognized badge of exclusivity both among those who possessed it and those who did not. The classical languages were associated with the privileges of the ruling class.'[87] Bailey, in her prose accompanying her poems, explains in plain language her various allusions, in some ways undermining this exclusivity and the inequality of education. Bailey was also an educator and, with her husband, later opened separate schools for girls and boys in Tasmania. Bailey, like Hemans and other successful Romantic writers, appears to have sought economic independence through teaching and the sale of her writing. As Claire Goldberg Moses notes, Saint Simonian feminists wanted to be economically independent of men, so they 'needed the educational opportunities still reserved for men alone'.[88] As an educator, Bailey advertised in the *Courier* a course of learning for young ladies to whom she offered drawing, theory and practice of music, French and Italian, as well as Hebrew, Greek and Latin, with the elements of science. Also, she would take young gentlemen, to be schooled along with her own son, in studies preparatory for English universities.[89]

Gender is particularly significant in the translation of scholarship to periodicals as these were more widely available, and Fiske argues that 'quite often, as in the case of Charlotte Brontë, women's exposure to the classics came from articles, translations and reviews in popular journals and periodicals' (5). Tasmanian Romanticism is exemplified in Bailey's poetry and in its connections with women's Romantic traditions including Hellenism. The reading rooms, like the publication of scholarship and poetry in newspapers, related to these women's education and intellectual equality exemplifying women's public political presence and voice.

Adriana Craciun describes the little-known essay on the 'Present state of the manners and society of the Metropolis' Robinson published in *The Monthly Magazine* as a 'vitriolic attack on the leisured classes' hypocritical relationship to public culture and its democratizing potential' and notes that Robinson was increasingly a political radical.[90] Bailey was likely aware of Robinson, who had appeared in Gillray's cartoons and was a notable celebrity. Craciun further notes that

> Robinson's poetic practice has been put forward by Stuart Curran, Jerome McGann, Judith Pascoe and others as a significant alternative to the Wordsworthian model under which Romantic studies have so long labored. Thus McGann, referring to Robinson's preface to *Sappho and Phaon* (1796), in which she elevates feminine sensibility to the highest poetic calling, persuasively argues: 'Well might Wordsworth, in the face of such a consciously feminized prophecy, step slightly back and try to re-establish poetry as the discourse of a "man speaking to men"'.[91]

Charlotte Smith was an influence on both Bailey and Robinson, and Bailey refers to earlier Romantic women poets such as Barbauld and Smith rather than later poets like Hemans.

But Bailey was no doubt also influenced by Hemans, who wrote on Greece and, like Bailey, included long prose explanations. Yet in overtly referencing male poets like Byron as well as earlier British women poets linked to the bluestockings, the Wollstonecraft circle and the Della Cruscans, she perhaps suggests a desire for distance from a restrictive idea of Hemans as the epitome of the feminine 'poetess'. The ideas associated with these poets all relate to Bailey's own negotiation with the constraints of gender through arguments for women's intellectual equality and citizenship. Amanda Gilroy argues that 'a more direct constraint on women poets was the image of the "poetess" cultivated by influential reviewers' and quotes from a review of Hemans' work by George Gilfillan in *Tait's Edinburgh Magazine* from June 1847:

> We have selected Mrs Hemans as our first specimen of Female Authors, not because we consider her the best, but because we consider her by far the most feminine writer of the age [...] You are saved the ludicrous image of a double-dyed Blue, in papers and morning wrapper, sweating at some stupendous treatise or tragedy from morn to noon, and from noon to dewy eve.[92]

As Gilroy notes, the 'double-dyed Blue' refers to bluestockings. Gilroy has also pointed out that Hemans was publishing political poetry, despite her continued characterization as belonging to the so-called 'proper sphere and mission of woman'.[93] Yet this review demonstrates the increasing constraints on British women poets through the imposition of the domestic ideal in the nineteenth century.

The prolific poetic contributions by Bailey, like Dunlop, to newspapers and periodicals suggest that these formed a particularly significant space for settler women poets, whose work exemplifies a significant transposition of British Romantic poetry to colonial Australia, as an access point for political voice. Mary Bailey's engagements with both British Romanticism and Romantic Hellenism in the poetry she produced in Tasmania challenge injustices relating to the penal system and to white women's rights, particularly through ideas of intellectual equality. While women poets in Britain can be said to have dominated in the literary markets in what Behrendt has called 'the gap that is not a gap'[94] between the male canons of British Romantic and Victorian poetry, those late Romantic women poets who came to the Australian colonies would appear to have found that their gender worked against the likelihood of being published, particularly in volumes, due to both the expense and a colonial preference for Australian-born, white male poets in the 1840s.

By including settler women's newspaper poetry, the significant presence and political contexts of these women poets become much clearer than when published volumes alone are taken into account. Fidelia Hill was the first settler woman to publish a volume of verse in Australia – *Poems and Recollections of the Past* – which published in 1844, by T. Trood in Sydney. It appears that she was able to do this by obtaining an extensive list of subscribers, including Lady Gipps. This was the year Bailey arrived in Tasmania and her poetry began appearing in colonial newspapers around this time. In these newspapers, Mary Bailey was publishing highly politically engaged poetry. She was actively critical of imprisonment, slavery, class and gender inequality, and the exclusion of women from intellectual, democratic and public spheres. Her newspaper poems also included robust criticism of conservative colonialist literature such as Kemp's *A Voice from Tasmania* published in 1846, which was 'the first book of verse which, written by a writer born in Tasmania, was published there'.[95] Bailey's poem, 'A Voice, from Ass-Mania!! Or Neddy's Bray', published in the *Hobarton Guardian*, signals her strong disagreement with his position against the legislative changes to the convict system that had assigned colonists convict labour. In doing so, she also demonstrates alternative positioning in terms of gender and medium of publication, critiquing the prioritization of an ideal of the Australian-born white male poet in the publication of volumes. Her publication in newspapers reveals awareness of how these could be understood as more democratic and communal spaces than that of the printed volume. Her publications in these spaces operate on multiple levels as challenges to women's exclusions from democratic processes and more broadly from the political and public sphere. As a major aspect of her writing, Bailey's uses of Romantic Hellenism are crucial to her political voice, as they relate to questions of liberty, political inclusion, access to education and spaces for women's poetic, political and physical presence. Earlier women's literary Romanticism and Romantic Hellenism are drawn on politically in her expression of poetic voice. As literary models looking to the past and a more radical historical moment, their uses in her poetry function to signify a reaction away from increasing conservatism and constraints on women through the imposition of the domestic ideal in the nineteenth century. Likewise, Classical and Roman antiquity were constructed in Bailey's poetry, like much of these earlier women's poetry, as feminist contestations of elite male power and violence. However, these constructions, as appeals to intellectual equality, democratic inclusion and legal reforms, did not consider or acknowledge the extreme and inherent violence of settler colonialism. Rather they position white women's rights through imperial expansion in colonial Tasmania, in terms of exile and moral differentiation from English laws. As both Bailey and Caroline Leakey were writing in Tasmania during the late 1840s, British and European ideas around natural rights, gender, imprisonment and transportation are highly significant to both poets. Leakey is notable as also writing poetry engaged in feminist discourses that centre white women's concerns, particularly about women's sexuality and transportation, as part of developing challenges to the restrictions of the domestic ideal, capitalism and women's subjugation through the law.

Chapter 3

CAROLINE LEAKEY: THE EMBOWERED WOMAN AND TASMANIA: 1850–60

Caroline Leakey's *Lyra Australis: Or Attempts to Sing in a Strange Land* (1854) is closely connected with feminist representations of women's sexuality and the legacy of the Romantic women's tradition in Britain. While Leakey's novel, *The Broad Arrow, Being Passages from the Life of Maida Gwynnham, a Lifer* (1859), relating to the brutalities of the penal system in Tasmania has been critically noted as part of a growing concern with ideas of an emergent Australian national identity, the more broadly feminist aspects of her poetry linking Tasmania symbolically with women's sexuality are significant to developments in transnational women's poetry of the period. Leakey's poetry is engaged with a tradition of British poetic works, including those of Caroline Norton and Caroline Bowles (later Southey), which were exemplars of the narrative poem on the fallen woman and the imprisoned woman. Leakey's poetry constitutes a strong rejection of the increasing restrictions placed on these sympathetic narratives. When viewed in the context of Victorian shifts away from earlier works by Charlotte Smith, Felicia Hemans, Letitia Elizabeth Landon and Elizabeth Barrett Browning, Leakey's poetry is more radical by the standards of British women's poetry than has been previously recognized.

The trope of the fallen woman, so prevalent in *Lyra Australis*, should also be recognized as a transnational narrative. This attracted localized colonial and emergent nationalist responses and was altered with increasing evangelical religious fervour, as in American examples such as Emily Chubbuck Judson's short story 'Lucy Dutton', published in *Alderbrook: A Collection of Fanny Forester's Village Sketches, Poems etc* (1847). The narrative of the fallen woman was employed in works by British Romantic women poets, including Norton's *The Sorrows of Rosalie* (1829) and Bowles' *Ellen Fitzarthur* (1820), as a feminist trope speaking to the sexual double standard, inequality and the need for financial independence. Similarly, the metaphoric use of flowers in Leakey's poetry reflects a strategy to articulate concerns over the fallen woman and the sexual double standard. While Leakey's novel has been recognized as a feminist text, her volume of poetry has been read as disconnected from the

Romantic women's tradition. Yet the use of the figure of the fallen woman is also important for representations of both the woman as poet and class, challenging aspects of the domestic ideal. Religion, however, as a significant aspect of ideal womanhood, is important to Leakey's poetry. Religiosity is used to promote feminist arguments, as well as to defend the view that women should write, by presenting her writing as a moral and sacred duty. Leakey's approach must be situated within recognition that Christianity was broadly a significant aspect of imperial and settler colonial presumptions of superiority and colonization.

Leakey's volume does not acknowledge any Indigenous people. Her sidelining of any question of Indigenous peoples produces an ordering of the volume limited to white settler and imperial feminist understandings of questions of justice and 'progress'. Such representations in settler women's poetry of colonial spaces in which Indigenous peoples are entirely absent functioned to reinforce the imperialist falsity of terra nullius. For settler women poets engaging with women's rights discourse conceptually tied up with Christianity and the imperial idea of 'progress', this meant that colonial spaces were often framed in terms of potential to expand white women's rights. While Leakey's novel has been seen as a feminist precursor to Marcus Clarke's *His Natural Life* (1874), her volume of poetry has received very little critical attention.

The novel's title *The Broad Arrow* refers to the pattern of broad arrows on convict uniforms, a symbol of government ownership. This reflects Leakey's heavy use of symbolism in her poetry and novel. As Jenna Mead, Shirley Walker and Dale Spender suggest, themes of women's oppression and sexuality are apparent already in the poem 'Dora' in *Lyra Australis*, and 'Dora' is certainly not the only poem related to the novel, the figure of the fallen woman or the convict system. While the third section of Leakey's *Lyra Australis*, 'Blanche and Other Tales', is particularly concerned with the fallen woman, this trope is consistently addressed throughout the volume. Many others than 'Dora' have this theme as a preoccupation, such as 'XIII', many of the 'shadows of death' poems, 'To the Evening Star' and 'The Fallen Jasmine Blossom', in which there is repeated imagery of stars, falling autumn leaves and flowers as women. In 'The Fallen Jasmine Blossom', the blossoms are in turn presented as stars, fairies and fallen women:

FALL'N, Fall'n, thou little silvery star
Fall'n from thy happy skies;
Left the fairy multitude,
And thy starry sisterhood
With bright and loving eyes
Innocents sin may never mar.[1]

Walker asserts that 'to the modern reader the poems suggest an almost pathological concern with sin (usually illicit sex) and its consequences (unwanted babies)'.² Emily Leakey refers to 'discreet rather than blameworthy' omissions in her biography of her sister, *Clear Shining Light: A Memoir of C.W. Leakey* (1882), hinting obviously at sexual relationships and pregnancy outside of marriage.³

She also replicates a letter and poem Caroline Leakey sent to her father around 1851, which begins 'My Beloved Father, – [...] were you never to send me even a message I should be in peace on the subject, being still sure of dwelling in a snug corner of your fond heart'. The verses enclosed with this letter, otherwise unpublished, begin:

> Strength, Lord, Thy strength is all I seek
> To bear this heavy load
> Lest my poor frame, so passing weak
> Should sink upon the road
> Light, Lord, let light revealed be
> Below, around, above,
> That knowing, I may also see
> I love-encompassed move.
> Nor yet release from pain's unrest
> I ask Thee, O my God,
> But that this failing arm may rest
> On Thy supporting rod.
> Not one pain gone, not one drop less
> Within this bitter cup,
> But that the pouring hand I bless,
> And while I drink, look up.
> What would a Marah'd ocean be
> That blood-red stream beside?
> Lord, one dear drop from Calvary
> Would drown a world's grief-tide.⁴

This poem articulates fear and establishes the religious and exilic basis of her later framing of the fallen woman in her volume through its reference to Marah, a region through which the Torah describes the Israelites travelling. The Orlando project entry for Caroline Leakey notes that the title *Lyra Australis: Or Attempts to Sing in a Strange Land* 'identifies her sojourn in Tasmania as exile, since it comes from Psalm 137, in which the exiled Israelites demand, "How can we sing the Lord's song in a strange land?"'⁵ The poem sent to her father as a precursor also frames her poetic expression through musicality and lyric in its employment of common meter ballad form.

Lyra Australis is similarly concerned to reframe the figure of the fallen woman in terms of sympathy rather than sin. She urges readers to acknowledge a deeper understanding and compassion, as in the lines 'And in thy fall I see / Truths which wisdom cannot teach – / Truths which deeper lie than speech'.[6] The imagery of flowers, reimagined as stars and fairies, situates the figure of the fallen woman within discourses of sexuality and nature, with a 'sisterhood' emphasized and presented as a resolution to these concerns in the final stanza of the poem:

> Set, set, thou little silvery star;
> Set, never more to rise!
> And, one by one, each sister thine
> Will cease in yonder light to shine,
> And from her happy skies
> Fall down to thee, sweet fairy star. (272)

Poems such as 'English Wild Flowers' engage in a wider European literary culture in which botanical language, and especially the 'bloom' of flowers, represents various aspects of sexuality and courtship:

> Oh! Dearer to me are the sweet wild flowers
> A hand unseen on England showers;
> They are born unknown and all unknown fade,
> Far and away in woodland shade;
> And dearer to me are those lesser gems,
> Peeping from earth on tiny stems,
> Than the vaunting glow of rare Eastern lands,
> And the gorgeous show which in proud pomp stands
> For they have a voice and they speak to me,
> With their eyes so full of Love's mystery! (119)

As Sam George suggests, 'Flowers are traditionally emblematic of the female sex in literary texts; however, a particular, complex refinement is taking place [...] botany becomes a discourse of female sexuality in eighteenth century literature.'[7] In this poem, Leakey articulates a clear preference and desire for English wild flowers over 'the gorgeous show' of 'Eastern lands' which 'in proud pomp stands', stating 'But oh! Give me from England again / The wild red rose, as it used to bloom / Round my father's door with its sweet perfume' (117). Her preferencing English flowers over colonial landscapes is an assertive imperial nostalgia that functions to temporally and spatially link England with 'virginity' and the guardianship of the father.

The 'wild' floral imagery however suggests women's sexuality preceding, or otherwise outside of, the parameters and legality of marriage and marriageability. As settler literature, the preferencing of English flowers may be read as a refusal of ideas of emergent settler nationalist difference. Yet Leakey's connected linking of Tasmania with fallen womanhood is not consistently negatively accented. Rather, the question of women's so-called deviant sexuality is problematized and challenged through the imperial relationship of England to colonial Tasmania. The final lines of the poem reiterate the sense of community and affinity expressed in 'The Fallen Jasmine Blossom', for the English wild flowers 'have a voice and they speak to me / With their eyes so full of Love's mystery' (119). These key themes locate Leakey's poetry as politically connected to an earlier Romantic women's tradition, in which the figures of the fallen woman and the embowered woman were increasingly significant. Jenna Mead points out the connection of Leakey's poems to the work of Tennyson and Wordsworth.[8] British women poets like Caroline Norton also took up these concerns.[9]

Caroline Norton and Caroline Bowles, as well as Hemans, Landon and others, were dealing with themes of women and the law, as well as the sympathetic portrayal of the fallen woman, and these feminist connections are crucial to Leakey's poetry. However, within masculine nationalist interpretive frameworks, we find settler and traveller women poets such as Leakey criticized in terms of a perceived failure to engage in the emergent nationalist poetic discourse of landscape. Richard Davis writes of Leakey that

> She too ignores what is in front of her, refusing to look at any flowers other than the English wild-flowers that grew in the landscape of memory, and dismissing the 'vaunting' blooms of Eastern lands (including, presumably, the exquisite little wild-flowers of Tasmania).[10]

The metaphoric use of flowers in Leakey's poetry reflects a strategy by women poets to articulate concerns over the fallen woman and the sexual double standard.

Leakey's volume of poems was published in 1854, and as Isobel Armstrong asserts of the British context, the sympathetic portrayal of the fallen woman was by then no longer considered as acceptable as it had been in the earlier decades of the nineteenth century:

> Numerous poems on the 'fallen woman' and prostitute are all part of this ceaseless dialectic on marriage. But it is important to note that the mood and approach to these writings alter as social attitudes to such women begin to harden, notably with the increasing influence of

evangelical morality and rigorous codes of moral respectability. In the early part of the period, compassionate narratives of betrayal are permissible. Consider, for example, Caroline Bowles's *Ellen Fitzarthur* (1820) and Caroline Norton's 'The Sorrows of Rosalie' (1829). By the time of Elizabeth Barrett Browning's *Aurora Leigh* (1856) and Christina Rossetti's 'Under the Rose' (1865), a far more intense politics has emerged. One only has to recall the vociferous attacks on the prostitute, such as those by William Acton, to see how decisively women poets felt they had to resist hypocrisy.[11]

It is significant that the narratives of Leakey's fallen woman protagonists, including Dora and Maida Gwynnham, are so closely based on Norton's much earlier *The Sorrows of Rosalie* (1829). The main point of difference between the plot of Norton's *Rosalie* and Leakey's 'Dora' is the connection to Tasmania.

Leakey's narrative poem 'Dora' closely reworks both Norton's *The Sorrows of Rosalie* (1829) and Bowles' *Ellen Fitzarthur* (1820). There is a focus in these narratives on the figure of the father who is abandoned at the demand of his daughter's lover, the father's support denied due to his recognition of the lover's falseness. These relationships are explored in *Lyra Australis*, as in *Rosalie*, where Dora returns to her father in shame to beg for his forgiveness and assistance: 'Thus time went on – / Till Dora's hope of reconcilement gone. / Still the proud father kept his sullen grief / Within himself, scorning to seek relief' (209). Jenna Mead treats the poem 'Dora' as an intertext of *The Broad Arrow* and describes 'the difference in the texts, from neat, controlled poetic song to a two-volume, sometimes anarchic, and often transgressive, text that continued to outstep its various editors' attempts at containment'.[12] However, this appraisal does not take into account Leakey's overarching feminist resistance in the poems, perhaps because they have been read outside the contexts of Romantic and Victorian women's poetry. Mead discerns that 'Dora' is a poem which presents 'a woman whose life reproduces the same story as Maida's'.[13] Dora loves a man, becomes pregnant and is abandoned. The baby dies, her father will not forgive her and he eventually dies by suicide after becoming 'worn to a shadow, ghastly and most wan' (Leakey, *Lyra*, 209).

While 'Dora' is focused on the relationship between Dora and her father, as are the first parts of Norton's *The Sorrows of Rosalie* (1829), *The Broad Arrow* takes its focus from the later parts, in which Rosalie steals bread for her baby and is imprisoned. The narratives of Leakey's Dora and Maida echo details of Norton's Rosalie very closely: the fear of and death of the father; the betrayal by a lover who too later repents; the death of the infant son; the proud refusal of the gold of her deceiver; and even the stealing of bread for the dying infant: ' "Food for my child!" I could no more restrain / My weakness and my woe – I snatched the bread'.¹⁴ There is also the imprisonment of Rosalie and an emphasis on redemption through religion.¹⁵ These narrative features are common to Caroline Bowles' earlier narrative of *Ellen Fitzarthur* as well. In the fifth stanza of *Rosalie*, the speaker exclaims:

> Oh, woman! In this hour of agony
> Trample not rudely on the fallen one;
> I have been weak, been guilty, but I die,
> Spurned at, forgotten, friendless and alone:
> All that I had, save hope of heaven, is gone;
> From *that* safe port no wand'rer shall be driven;
> God, before whom I bow, will hear my moan;
> For there's no sin too great to be forgiven
> By him who pities all – th' Omnipotent of Heaven.¹⁶

A call to the sympathies of other women, reflecting those of God, is strongly articulated in Leakey's volume, where Dora's 'thoughts grow wild / And rave of mercy shown by all beside / Yea, e'en by God!' and leads to the question for readers, 'Where God forgives, shall you your anger keep?' (203). In its version, sympathy and forgiveness are framed in religious terms, significantly as morally superior positions to judgement and shaming.

While there can be little doubt that Leakey was familiar with *Rosalie*, her 'Dora' includes an epigraph from Shakespeare rather than Norton. Norton's poem 'The Name' (1830) also used Shakespeare in this way. A possible reason for Leakey's lack of overt acknowledgement of Norton through epigraphs might have been the increased unacceptability of Norton's sympathetic approach. Alternatively, the inclusion of the epigraph from Shakespeare's *Hamlet*, 'Oh Gertrude, Gertrude, when sorrows come, they come / Not single spies, but in battalions' provides a greater ambiguity.¹⁷ Gail Marshall suggests that as 'both establishment bard and a voice adopted by radicals, Shakespeare's sheer variety made him peculiarly suitable for adoption by politically various Victorian women in need of a mouthpiece'.¹⁸ In the same year that *Lyra Australis* was published, Caroline Norton published *English Laws for Women in the Nineteenth Century* (1854) and was instrumental in campaigning for reforms of the legal status of women as 'femme covert'. Coverture was the legal principle by which a married woman's legal rights were subsumed by her husband. This followed the breakdown of Norton's marriage and her subsequent discovery that her husband had the legal right to deny her access to her children and to claim the earnings from her writing.¹⁹

The celebrity of Norton was taken up in women's poetry during this period. Landon's poem 'To the Author of the Sorrows of Rosalie', published in

The Lyre; Fugitive Poetry (1840), incorporated the life of Norton into a poetic mythologizing of the fallen or imprisoned woman, and appealed to readers for compassion:

> The stern, the selfish and the cold,
> With feelings all repressed –
> The many cast in one base mould,
> For them life yields her best:
> They plod upon one even way
> Till time, not life, is o'er;
> Death cannot make them colder clay
> Than what they were before
>
> But thou – go ask thy lute what fate
> May for thy future be,
> And it will tell thee tears await
> The path of one like thee.[20]

Landon's poem, like Leakey's 'Dora', is damning of 'the stern, the selfish and the cold'[21] and further attests to the celebrity of Norton, whom contemporary sources had 'styled the Byron of her sex [...] more widely read than the works of any poetess except Mrs. Hemans'.[22] Norton herself had begun *Rosalie* by addressing 'Ye marble-hearted ones': 'To such I would not speak / But oh to *you* / Whose generous hearts can feel another's grief [...] to those alone I call, for *they* can feel for me' (3–4). Both Norton's original poem and Landon's to Norton about her life base their appeal for sympathy on the notion of a sisterhood.

Leakey was born in 1827 in Exeter and was writing among the newer generation of women poets, such as Elizabeth Barrett Browning. The dedication of the third chapter 'Blanche, and Other tales' to Caroline Kindersley 'with grateful regard' in *Lyra Australis* suggests that Leakey may even have been introduced to Barrett. Caroline Kindersley lived next door to Elizabeth Barrett on Wimpole Street and had notably introduced Anna Jameson to Barrett.[23] Emily Leakey in *Clear Shining Light* notes that Leakey had been introduced to London literary society, although she does not give any indication of whom she met. Poets including Elizabeth Barrett Browning and Leakey were mounting a strong resistance to the increasing attacks on women's sexuality. This growing hostility goes some way to explaining the equivocality with which these poems were excused by Leakey in her preface as the products of a woman suffering through a period of illness:

There, perhaps, may be due to my readers some explanation of the titles chosen for the first and second chapters of this volume. 'Shadows of Death' were a series of thoughts which were presented to my mind during a long illness in Tasmania. Some of the poems perhaps are – or rather appear – of a wild and wilful nature; but I give them a place here, in order to show to greater advantage those which breathe the better spirit of resignation and trustfulness. (3)

While Armstrong suggests that in her 1856 verse novel, *Aurora Leigh*, Elizabeth Barrett Browning felt she needed to have Marian Erle's status as a single mother explained by her being a victim of rape rather than seduction, the poems in Leakey's *Lyra Australis* present the earlier sympathetic approach of Norton and Bowles to seduction, in which these women are to be sympathized with rather than condemned. Nonetheless, Leakey's approach demonstrates that poetry produced in the colonies often paralleled the thematic and stylistic developments in the work of British women poets. Rather than reflecting a delayed relationship to transnational and British literary movements, this poetry could also take radical approaches to these themes by British standards. Reading *Lyra Australis* within the contexts of British women's poetry and earlier Romantic women's poetry illuminates how topical and politically engaged with the representation of white women's sexuality was Leakey's poetry. By the standards of the 1850s, Leakey's volume was defiant in its use of Norton's *Rosalie's* compassionate narrative, and Leakey's use of both her Tasmanian colonial experience and religious language appears to have masked the resistance of her feminist approach.

Tasmania and the fallen woman

Leakey's poetry is engaged in the work of resisting and countering the increasingly unsympathetic representation of the fallen woman, with important implications. Her self-positioning as an 'exile' to colonial Tasmania relates to the signification of her incompatibility with British laws, the middle-class British domestic ideal, approaches to women's sexuality and the woman poet's ability to address political and sexual topics. It is noted in Edward E. Morris' *A Dictionary of Austral English* (1898) that the term 'exile' was used euphemistically to refer to convicts.[24] Ken Buckley and Ted Wheelwright argue that because convicts were mainly working-class British with far larger numbers of men transported, 'female convicts in the colonies were widely regarded as prostitutes'.[25] They suggest that out of a total of about 160 000 convicts transported to Australia between 1788 and 1868, only 15 per cent were female. Employers and masters deplored the 'moral evils' – homosexuality and prostitution – associated with the disparity [...] Female convicts were desired mainly as domestic servants and for sexual purposes.[26]

Leakey's use of the term 'exile', given this context, would have clearly signified 'sexual deviance' to many British, transnational and colonial readers. It could also relate to women's poetic tradition through the exile of Sappho.

The identification with the exile can be read as revealing a challenge to the restrictions of the domestic ideal and purity discourse through its differentiation from British law and the middle-class ideal of womanhood. As Patricia Ingham has shown of the British context, this ideal was crucial to the nineteenth-century coding of class and gender as interlocked, with all working-class women already coded as impure:

Female sexuality [...] was deviant and its natural location was amongst the class which in practice provided the prostitutes [...] Clearly, though one task of ideology is to conceal its own illogicalities, not all working-class women could be categorised as sexually 'deviant' just because some of them were. Instead, those who were not became invisible.[27]

This was a significant part of the supposed justification of the subordination of the working class. Similarly, middle-class women were presumed never to 'fall' within this ideological framework. The popular idealization of white middle-class women's so-called purity was deeply damaging and oppressive. In this way, literary 'attempts to reaccent the signs of both the *womanly* woman and the *fallen* woman succeeded in rewriting their significance and what this meant for the treatment of class and gender as a whole'.[28] Particularly, Leakey's poems advocate ways that readers might come to understand alternative conceptualizations of morality in relation to the harmful cultures of punishment, judgement and shaming around class, gender and sexuality, though with considerations of race remaining absent.

While she worked to re-accent both class and gender through her uses of British symbolism and associations of Tasmania with punishment, the brutalities of the penal system and women's sexuality, Leakey did not acknowledge the First Nations peoples at all. This omission is in line with wider colonialist erasures of Indigenous peoples in literary representations and is of greater consequence given her poetic concern with ideas of law, incarceration and her self-positioning as an exile in Tasmania.

In addition to settler violence and dispossession, policies of forced removal and incarceration had included Palawa and Tasmanian Aboriginal peoples being incarcerated at Macquarie Harbour Penal Station and at Hunter Island, Grummet Island and to Wybalenna on Flinders Island, offshore from their traditional lands. Tim Bonyhady and Greg Lehman note that the 'mortality suffered at Wybalenna was extraordinary [...] Despite such adverse conditions, the residents of Wybalenna refused to give up their language, or cultural practices such as shell-necklace making'.[29] James Boyce suggests that the belief that Christianization was beneficial to Indigenous peoples may have been one reason for the colonial government policy of 'removing *all* Aborigines[sic] from Van Diemen's Land without their consent' in the 1830s. Boyce notes that very little documentation of the policy exists and that it was 'never put to either the executive council or the Colonial Office', adding that the 'deportation of most of the Aborigines[sic] proceeded in circumstances that were in direct contravention of official government policy'.[30] He argues that this practice represents an enormous gap in Tasmania's colonial history beyond the more documented violence.

In 1854, the year Leakey's volume was published, Church of England Bishop Francis Nixon, the first bishop of Tasmania, who had earlier encouraged Leakey to publish her poetry, voyaged to 'the refuges of the dispossessed first peoples'. This included a visit to Wybalenna, which had been abandoned in 1847 and the surviving residents removed to 'a condemned convict probation station at Oyster Cove south of Hobart'.[31] In March of 1847, a petition signed by eight Tasmanian Aboriginal people living at Wybalenna had been presented to Queen Victoria. As Henry Reynolds notes, 'A number of factors contributed to the British government's decision to abandon Wybalenna, but there is no doubt the Aboriginal petition was the precipitating factor.'[32] Leakey's literary representations of Tasmania and her critiques do not recognize or consider their own positioning within the extreme injustices of the invasion, the Tasmanian genocide and the Black War (c.1828–32), nor removals of Indigenous peoples and colonization.

In drawing on Tasmania symbolically to emphasize suffering in white women's experiences of the sexual double standard and British law, especially given the extent of the atrocities committed against Tasmanian Aboriginal peoples, Leakey's absence of consideration is enormously significant. Lyndall Ryan describes some of the ways in which ideas around so-called purity in women were at their most extreme in the racist colonial governmental policies affecting Tasmanian Aboriginal people. She states that Lieutenant Governor Denison was perturbed that the women's sexual liaisons with sealers on the nearby islands would contaminate the remaining 'full-bloods' and that their offspring, by virtue of their Aboriginal descent would demand financial support from the government. For he was aware that the number of children born to Aboriginal women living with the sealers was more than four times the number born at Wybalenna over the previous fifteen years.[33]

As Jennifer DeVere Brody notes in the American context, of 'these convoluted constructions of pure whiteness and pure blackness in Victorian culture [...] the words are themselves always already impure, hybrid terms [...] that purity is impossible'.[34] Leakey does not consider the imposition of British law on Aboriginal lands, genocidal practices or abuses of the human rights of Palawa and Tasmanian Aboriginal peoples, in the connections she makes between Tasmania's penal system and the legal, societal and elite male control of white women's sexuality as unjust.

The varying reception of Leakey's *Lyra Australis* is illuminative of how a colonial woman poet was perceived. It is likely Leakey herself was resistant to such a casting, though at the time of writing her volume she does not seem to have known if she would return to Britain. Like many colonial poetic texts, the volume was simultaneously published in London and colonial Australia – in London by Bickers and Bush, and in Hobart by J. Walch & Son. A review in the London *Gentlemen's Magazine* (like the review in the *Dublin Magazine*) focused on colonialist misrepresentations of Australia as a 'sterile' place and as a place not associated with poetry, reflecting what Ryan notes as 'the standing in European law of possession by discovery and possession. This convenient legal fiction was based on the Roman legal principal of *terra nullius*, or empty lands.'[35] The reviewer thus values Leakey's volume as evidence of white women's so-called civilizing role:

> A sterile place, first sown broadcast with felons and afterwards occupied by struggling men essaying to become rich, and having no other object in the world, is but an unpromising locality for the minstrel. But the truth appears to be that these generalities will no longer apply to the wide continent at the antipodes. Woman, the great civiliser, has established a home there, and the sisters of song are not mute amid sounds of daily care and strife, success and failure.[36]

The review implies that Leakey's poems were understood as secondary and related to colonialist expectations of white women's roles. The resistance to gender and class-based oppression through sexuality in Leakey's poetry is invisible in this dominant critical lens. Similarly, Leakey's poems such as 'On Tasmania's Receiving the Writ of Freedom' have been viewed by later Australian critics as specifically Tasmanian, and Mead suggests that 'four poems in *Lyra Australis* are striking – "The Prisoners Hospital, Van Diemen's Land," "On Tasmania's Receiving the Writ of Freedom" and "New Light on an Illumination," also celebrating Tasmania's Writ of freedom –because they are overtly political poems, unique in Leakey's oeuvre and a type rarely written by women in the period'.[37] Neither the dominant lens nor the second wave feminist, however, recognize the significance of the relationship of Leakey's poems to Romantic and Victorian British women's traditions.

In 'The Prisoner's Hospital, Van Diemen's Land' Leakey describes the hospital with a clear emphasis on women's experiences that parallel those of the fallen woman:

> O Prison – house of sighing!
> Where the weary and the worn,
> The long-pent and the dying,
> Lie friendless and forelorn;
> Where sickness preys on weariness
> And both they prey on life,
> The mother weeps in dreariness
> And pines the lonely wife.
>
> Where tender babe and wasted child
> Look eagerly around,
> And wonder why the face that smiled,
> Can nowhere *now* be found.
> Where on the sickly little one
> Rests no kind eye of love;
> It's pleading moan there heark'neth none,
> Save God, who dwells above. (121–22)

The linking of the prisoners' hospital with the concerns of her poems on fallen women is particularly evident in the final stanza, which calls for mercy and forgiveness:

> Oh! Ere death's heavy bolt be drawn
> Upon life's gate for ever,
> And deeps of black perdition yawn
> Beneath their souls for ever,
> Thou who sweet mercy lov'st to show

> Look down! forgive – relent!
> Haste, Lord, ere sealed this worst woe
> On earth's long banishment. (123–24)

Much of the volume takes a far more imaginative, symbolic approach to British conceptions of Tasmania.

This symbolic use is particularly explored in relation to ideas of imprisonment and servitude, and women's sexual and intellectual freedoms and domestic roles. Mead points out the conflict between emergent masculine nationalism and a feminized position in relation to Leakey's poem on 'Tasmania's Writ of Freedom', stating that

> Leakey's ambitious project is to describe the movement toward nationhood within a language that is feminine, Christian and domestic. Her choices are difficult: either popular English poetic diction that is often archaic, pensive and retrospective or an emergent national Australian poetic diction that is strident, masculine and triumphant.[38]

A 'strident, masculine and triumphant' poetic voice is at odds with Leakey's overarching concern with re-accenting women's sexuality. While the women poets of this study were also often writing emergent nationalist poetry, they did so with awareness of their marginalization from that discourse and of international women's traditions which later readers would not inherit until the 1990s with the critical revaluing of British and wider Romantic women's poetry. The political charge of these fallen woman poems links Leakey's poetry to transnational and imperial women's traditions more than to emergent nationalist modes in settler Australian literature. It should also be remembered that the underlying social critiques in a women's writing tradition, as Armstrong has suggested, are perhaps even more strident in the poetry which most appears to conform to feminine conventions.[39] Certainly, Leakey's poems are enormously symbolically significant in light of these women's traditions. The resistance of the poems originates in a backwards looking connection to the earlier radical moment of British Romantic women's poetry.

The symbolic resonance with a women's tradition can also be found in Leakey's novel, as women's sexuality, domestic role, motherhood and imprisonment are presented as inter-connected. Leakey notes that a Tasmanian concern over the morality of children exposed to convict nurses led to increased vigilance of some mothers in caring for children themselves. This was given as the reason for Leakey's need to come to Tasmania, to be nurse-maid to her sister's children, who, Emily Leakey writes, would 'otherwise be dependent on the care (!) of convict nurses'.[40] Caroline Leakey herself takes a more class-conscious feminist position that is symbolically aligned with women prisoners and convicts rather than a critical one, and in *The Broad Arrow* (1859) writes, 'Such a young mother will look piteously at you, and ask "Is it to be expected, now, that I am to be shut up with these children all day long? I might as well be a prisoner at once".'[41] The idea of women's domestic role as a form of imprisonment was an already established trope. Leakey would certainly have been familiar with it as one not specific to Tasmanian convict women for whom domestic servant roles were the norm during both the Assignment and Probation periods. However, this was not Leakey's personal experience. In 'Dora', Leakey expands on tropes of women's suffering by drawing on the association of madness with the fallen woman, acknowledging the literary tradition of this figure as one 'too often told':

> Hers is a tale, alas! too often told
> To need afresh its dark records unfold, –
> Where Death and Sorrow their sad pages blend;
> A tale 'twere vain to hope might have an end,
> While there are those – Oh, mark them as they stand,
> The blasting curse – pollutions of our land!
> Who care not for the graves they early fill
> With those who trusted, for they feared no ill;
> Who care not when they drive the hoary head
> To sink in sorrow to the earth's cold bed;
> Who care not when deluded Madness sings
> Her wild unmeaning glees, nor when she rings
> Her savage laughter through the grated pane,
> Which bounds the sceptre of her fancied reign. (Leakey, *Lyra*, 204)

This passage suggests not only Leakey's encompassing of the fallen woman, 'madness' and the geographical and imprisonment symbolism of colonial Tasmania, as 'earth's cold bed', but also the tradition of writing on these topics. Leakey makes several references to imprisonment through the volume, in poem XXVII of 'Who Sweetest Sing their Songs of Home?', and in poem V of 'Shadows of Death', 'I hear their voices from afar / But only from this prison bar' (Leakey, *Lyra*, 13).

Hemans's 'Arabella Stuart', a poem concerned with the figure of the imprisoned woman and romantic love, is another intertext Leakey clearly draws on. Hemans opens her poem with the epigraph from Byron: 'And is not love in vain, / Torture enough without a living tomb?'.[42] This sentiment is a central point of Leakey's poems and suggests the way in which her use of convictism in Tasmania is heavily symbolic of the emotional state of the fallen woman. In both the opening chapter of *The Broad Arrow*, in which Norwell is at the Ball of the Assizes, and the second chapter, scenes are presented by the narrative device of a crystal ball visualization (which Leakey calls 'time's far telescope' (C. Leakey, *Broad*, 11)). This framing recalls the use of the 'magic glass' in the twelfth stanza of Hemans's poem 'Arabella Stuart':

> Thou hast forsaken me! I feel, I know,
> There would be rescue if this were not so.
> Thou'rt at the chase, thou'rt at the festive board,
> Thou'rt where the red wine free and high is pour'd,
> Thou'rt where the dancers meet! – a magic glass
> Is set within my soul, and proud shapes pass,
> Flushing it o'er with pomp from bower and hall; –
> I see one shadow, stateliest of all –
> *Thine!* What dost *thou* amidst the bright and fair,
> Whispering light words and mocking my despair?[43]

The influence of *Records of Woman* (1828) is apparent in Leakey's poems, and perhaps even more so in the novel.

Leakey's inclusion of elements of 'Arabella Stuart' reiterates the poetic significance of this figure of a woman abandoned by her lover and imprisoned, ending with her death. Landon's 'The Female Convict' published in 1825 in *The Improvisatrice* reflects a similar use of madness, in which 'her large dark eye / had the glisten of red insanity'.[44] Ann Vickery points out that this is as an embellishment on 'Nichol's already mythicised and sentimental story of the unknown girl aboard the *Lady Juliana* [...] her red eyes are not the result of weeping as in Nichol's account, but the glint of madness'.[45] Leakey was well read, particularly in poetry, and her sister Emily Leakey notes in her memoir that 'she read all standard works with avidity'.[46] While she was familiar with Shakespeare, Wordsworth, Tennyson and Byron, Leakey's poetry also reflects her close knowledge of the women poets, particularly Norton, Hemans and Landon. Vickery discusses the representations of the figure of the convict woman, both in the colonies and in Britain from 1788 to 1850, and makes the point that Landon's 'The Female Convict' might be viewed as 'an allegory of the woman poet'.[47]

Leakey's poem 'Queen Ina' likewise symbolically treats the subjects of women's supposedly deviant sexuality and poetic song. Within Victorian women's poetry Isobel Armstrong points out that 'the adoption of the mask appears to involve a displacement of feminine subjectivity, almost a travestying of femininity, in order that it can be made an object of investigation'.[48] This poem is typical of Leakey's extensive use of symbolism, as well as the use of her experience and of Tasmania in symbolic ways to revalue the fallen woman and challenge the discourse around purity. The figures of the mermaid, associated with seduction, and the Queen, associated with power, are brought together in this poem, through the mermaid Queen Ina:

> She scorneth flowers of the earth!
> Rare jewels she finds,
> And of dripping gems,
> For her hair, she binds
> Bright diadems.
> O royal and rare
> Queen Ina fair
> The Mermaid of the South! (Leakey, *Lyra*, 106)

Nina Auerbach describes 'a myth that was never quite formulated, but that recurs incessantly in literature and art, a myth crowning a disobedient woman in her many guises as heir of the ages and demonic saviour of the race'.[49]

The symbolic resonances of Leakey's mermaid Queen are interwoven with ideas of power and sexual 'disobedience' in an inversion of the cultural standing of the sexual woman in mid-Victorian England. Leakey makes this distancing explicit from the first words of the poem, 'Not here. Far away' (105). This 'far away' place is identified as not only a fantastical oceanic space but also one with a geographical location in the Southern hemisphere. It is presented as the site of Antipodean reversals, as Ina is declared to be 'The Mermaid of the South!' The line, 'Where the dolphins play', further suggests Leakey's referencing of Shakespeare's *A Midsummer Night's Dream*, in which there are connections with mermaid mythology:

> Thou rememberest since once I sat upon a promontory,
> And heard a mermaid on a dolphin's back
> Uttering such dulcet and harmonious breath
> That all the rude sea grew civil at her song
> And certain stars shot madly from their spheres to hear the sea-maid's music.[50]

In Shakespeare's work, the mermaid has been noted as a metaphor for Mary Queen of Scots, the dolphin alluding to her adultery with the Dauphin. This connection was made in nineteenth-century critical accounts of *A Midsummer Night's Dream*, such as that in *The Dramatic Works of William Shakespeare: With the Corrections and Illustrations of Dr. Johnson, G. Steevens and Others* (1817).[51]

'Queen Ina' suggests an autobiographical element, as the name Ina is a variant diminutive ending of the name Caroline. Leakey used parts of her name in the pseudonym Oliné Keese under which she published her novel. She explains in a letter to Octavian Blewitt that this name is taken from the end of her first and last names, 'because it had only Car taken off my Xtian [sic] name, and the Lea dropped from the surname, – Key being altered to Keese'.[52] Leakey also notes in this letter the other pseudonyms she had used, stating that 'Simond, Oline Keese, and K.G.G. and my own name are the names under which I have written.'[53] Leakey may also have been referring to the Queen Caroline affair of the early nineteenth century, in which the Queen was subjected to a trial for adultery by her publicly adulterous husband, King George IV, and public opinion sided with Caroline. As Tim Fulford points out, Romantic poets including Coleridge felt that the Queen Caroline trial had 'demonstrated the moral bankruptcy of the established order'.[54] Certainly, Romantic as well as Victorian women poets widely addressed these questions around the sexual double standard.

Hemans had written of the 'witching' seduction of a mermaid in 'A Tale of the Fourteenth Century':

> Is it the mermaid's distant shell
> Warbling beneath the moonlit wave
> Such witching tones might lure full well
> The seamen to his grave.[55]

Auerbach notes the opposition of mermaid mythology to nineteenth-century middle-class representations of the woman as angel, arguing that

> The mermaids, serpent–women and lamias who proliferate in the Victorian imagination suggest a triumph larger than themselves, whose roots lie in the antiquity so dear to nineteenth-century classicists. These creatures' iconographic invasion may typify the restoration of an earlier serpent woman, the Greek Medusa.[56]

Other Romantic women poets had also taken up a concern with mermaids, as in Landon's poem 'The Fairy of the Fountains' (1834). Landon's poem combines the figure of the Queen with the story of Melusine, a water spirit of European folklore often depicted as a mermaid. Landon's poem, like Leakey's, also includes a south star and an exile.

The linking of the mermaid with song is a recurring theme too, so Leakey's use of the mermaid is a representation of women's lyricism and performative poetry. This poetic voice is, in Leakey's poem, however, silenced by the death of Ina:

> All silently
> She lieth alone
> By her empty throne
> All silently. (*Lyra*, 107)

Her mermaids will resume their song for her.

In Leakey's poem, the mermaid is revered, particularly by her fellow mermaids:

> And the mermaids weep –
> They a vigil keep.
> Hark! now they sing
> And their voices ring
> A solemn dirge. (108)

As Glennis Stephenson notes, the death of the woman poet plays an important role in the poetry of Landon: 'The heroine of "The Improvisatrice", once dead, and – as is the fate of a significant number of Landon's creative female figures – safely statufied, apparently returned to a more acceptable feminine stillness', suggesting a recurrent theme within women's tradition exemplified by the ancient Greek poet Erinna.[57] Significantly, Leakey depicts death as a fate fallen women faced with lack of access to any financial or social support, as did earlier works like Bowles' *Ellen Fitzarthur*.

In utilizing a mermaid mythology and death Leakey seems to have also been referencing the Hans Christian Anderson fairy tale of *The Little Mermaid* published in 1837, in which the mermaid dies and is not united with the prince. Auerbach and U. C. Knoepflmacher note that women resisted the co-opting of women's oral fairy tales by Hans Christian Anderson and the Grimms.[58] At the poem's conclusion, rather than shamed silence the mermaids' song can be heard:

> Like a voice of love
> That weepeth a woe,
> It soundeth below,
> And riseth above
> And the sailors know,
> 'Neath that tuneful wave
> In a crystal cave

> In her ocean land
> By her mermaid band
> Queen Ina is laid to rest. (108)

The short lines of flowing couplets punctuated without full stops create a continuous chant building in intensity, as the song of the mermaids 'soundeth below, / And riseth above' (108), proclaiming Ina's death not only to 'her ocean land' but to a masculinized and responsible world above. Leakey's Queen Ina is not only about re-accenting women's sexuality positively but speaking the experience and evoking women's communal poetic traditions and ideas of a sisterhood as crucial to being heard.

Religion and the woman poet

For transnational and settler women poets such as Leakey, religious content could function to excuse the writing of poetry, perceived as a 'masculine' activity. Bishop Nixon of Tasmania was instrumental in encouraging Leakey to publish her poems, reflecting the close connections between religion and imperial feminism in much women's poetry in the period. Individual poems of Leakey's were published in the *Hobart Town Courier and Van Diemen's Land Gazette*, later known as the *Courier*, and these were sent in by her doctor, Dr. Agnew.[59] Leakey also had some poems, 'The Rock of Martin Vaz' and 'The Muezzin's Cry' from *Lyra Australis*, republished in American magazines.[60] Her religious tracts appear to have also been somewhat popular in America. An extract from 'God's Tenth' appeared in the American Sunday School Union publication, *The Sunday-School World* (1899).[61]

Leakey dedicates the second chapter of Lyra Australis, 'Boa Vista' (Figure 3.1) to Lady Denison, the wife of Tasmanian Governor William Denison. It was a common practice in settler colonial women's poetry to dedicate poetry to the wives of prominent political figures. The following account by G. W. Walker, a Tasmanian Quaker, gives some detail of 'Lady Denison, the Governor's wife, who enlisted [...] assistance in the revival of a scheme to found a refuge for prostitutes'.[62] The involvement of both Lady Denison and Leakey herself in homes for fallen women reflects the ongoing ways in which religiosity intersected with some arguments for women's increased participation in social issues beyond their own domestic roles.

Leakey clearly conceived of herself as a writer and, like many women poets including Charlotte Smith and Felicia Hemans, earned a living by writing. She stands apart from the other women poets of this study as the only one to have returned permanently to England as well as being the only one to

Figure 3.1 Bruce, Charles, *Miss Debney's Establishment for Young Ladies*, 1831.

have never married. Certainly, she was not as financially successful as either Smith or Hemans. After returning to Britain, as her application in 1871 to the Royal Literary Fund attests, she did write for a living. This application was unsuccessful, no doubt hindered by W. Forsyth, who wrote in his report on the literary merit of Leakey's *Broad Arrow* that 'I have accordingly looked through the two volumes [...] and my verdict is that they are nothing but contemptible trash. I think that the book is one of the very worst novels I ever read.'[63] Leakey notes in her application that she was receiving '50 to 80 £'s per an. and state of £30 to support of insane sister'.[64] This income, she notes, was from a small property she owned. Leakey writes that 'I could obtain a good living by writing if I had strength, but, as it is, I only get £1 where I might get £50!' While it has been suggested that novel writing was both more profitable and more acceptable for women than the writing of poetry, Jenna Mead has pointed out that although *The Broad Arrow* 'was extremely popular (running to at least twelve reprintings of two editions) [...] Richard Bentley and Son's archives show that little commercial success returned to the author'.[65] Of the profits from her poetry, Emily Leakey writes of her sister's generosity, stating that 'She gave the WHOLE profits of her poems to one in need, never spending one penny of it on herself.'[66] Emily Leakey's emphasis on piety and unselfishness frequently functions to both overshadow and justify Leakey's writing.

In addition to supposedly legitimizing writing as an activity, the increased religiosity in women's poetry during this period was recognized as a resolution to problems associated with women's affectional poetry, often dismissed as sentimental. Leakey's use of the trope of the fallen woman combines the earlier affectional Romantic women's use of emotional pain, while emphasizing the religious in such suffering. Julie Melnyk argues that Hemans' later poetry was in fact important to this shift, in which the divide between 'domestic' women's poetry and the 'high nature' poetry of male Romantics is suggested to have been bridged by the claims of religious transcendence for women's poetry.[67] Leakey's poetry shows that she evidently felt a strong connection to earlier Romantic poets, which she expresses in the poem 'Romantic' in *Lyra Australis*:

> AND if to be romantic is to gaze,
> With throbbing heart and tearful eye, intent
> On oceans breast, where, tremulously bent,
> The moon in liquid glory hides her rays
> And see in each soft ray another string
> On which, in silvery tone, God's praise to sound
> Till every beam with His high name resound
> And the calm air one peal of gladness ring, –
>
> I only ask to be romantic still! (276)

This poem also suggests the shifts occurring in women's poetry during this time to a heightened religiosity. Leakey links women's poetry both to a religious calling and to the Romantic tradition. Her desire 'to be romantic still' perhaps suggests Leakey's own sense of the increasing restrictions on women poets occurring in the nineteenth century. *Lyra Australis* stands as a rejection of these restrictions, particularly through its engagement with the trope of the fallen woman.

The legitimacy of the woman poet is particularly significant to Leakey's use of these tropes as well as shifts in Victorian approaches. Both the Tasmanian symbolism and the heightened religiosity of Leakey's volume reflect changes occurring in women's poetry in this period. Emma Mason has argued that the British poet and Anglican priest John Keble's

> shaping of an at once restrained and intensely emotional poetics is [...] fundamentally central to the poetry of several nineteenth-century women poets – Dora Greenwell, Cecil Frances Alexander, Caroline Leakey, Bessie Parkes, Adelaide Anne Procter – wary of their assumed proclivity to extreme sentimentalism.[68]

Mason suggests that the religious poetic theory of Keble operates, in the mid-Victorian period, as a means of disassociation from the heavy emotive voice of the earlier Romantic poetesses such as Hemans and also notes Christina Rossetti as one of the best-known heirs of Keble. However, as Julie Melnyk argues, the later work of Romantic poets like Hemans had also turned 'to religious inspiration as a way of vindicating women's poetry and freeing it from the confines of affectional tradition'. Melnyk makes the point that the use of religious ideology allowed for gender ambiguity, where the affectional tradition emphasized the feminine, and in this way could 'allow a woman poet to claim the vatic power that male Romantic poets represented as their birthright, but that female poets were popularly denied'.[69]

Leakey's poetry reflects these shifts, incorporating both an emotional and restrained voice. Much of her poetry is linked to devotional song, and she demonstrates this again in the later poem 'In the Morning' written in Exeter in the 1880s, in which she asks, 'When the cold is keen, and the light is dim, / May be seen the Southernhay bird [...] / He sings till he puts my soul to shame;/ for should not I rise to do the same – / Arise to call on my maker's name / and join the Southernhay bird?' Leakey's rhetorical question is a gender-conscious defence for writing poetry, and she repeats, 'Shall I do *less* than the Southernhay bird? / Shall I be mute when *his* song is heard' (emphasis mine).[70] It functions both to present women's poetry as religious obligation and to position women's poetic voice as both natural and valuable. In poem XIII (Bring flowers for the wearied one) Leakey exemplifies this shift to an emotive poetics of restraint:

> Bring her flowers from the mountains,
> And Wildlings from the hills,
> From the happy sparkling fountains,
> And from the quiet rills.
> And of the sweet 'Forget-me-not',
> Be sure your lap to fill
> 'Twill tell her, though so hard her lot,
> of One that loveth still. (28–29)

The understated expression of emotional pain is here matched to an imagined reception of unfeeling disdain, with the exceptions only of a sympathetic sisterhood and God. That intensity of feeling is instead symbolically held in the flower, recalling a religiosity that is framed as the sympathy missing in society.

This religious framing is significant to the volume's wider reception, in also aligning it with a central aspect of the middle-class domestic ideal. Leakey similarly frames the penal system and transportation symbolically as the incarceration and degradation of women's sexual, financial and intellectual freedoms in relation to the domestic ideal, and attempts to re-accent women's sexuality positively. It is clear that the idea of *Lyra Australis* as 'travel writing' or 'Australian' may have yet overshadowed these political and feminist concerns in the reception of the volume in the nineteenth century and beyond. *Lyra Australis* was received in the context of a more global than previously recognized book trade, with reviews published in London, Ireland and Tasmania. A review in *The Dublin University Magazine* describes *Lyra Australis* in imperialist terms as

> A very laudable thing indeed, especially when that land has yet produced no songsters of its own. Miss Leakey has given us some very sweet verses, composed, we believe, entirely in Australia, and many of them descriptive of the scenery of that country.[71]

A Tasmanian review from *The Courier* alternatively notes that

> The whole have met with favourable review in several of the most select periodicals of the mother-country [...] Yet, as the efforts of 'our poetess' are invested with a local interest which renders them more important in our eye, we should consider ourselves to have failed in our duty by abstaining from a friendly notice.

It goes on to state that

> There are some poems in the collection which, while they cannot be put forward as gems of excellence, or in fact come up to the standard of many which we have seen published in the colony at intervals, and which have not come under the observation of English reviewers, are above the ordinary run of poetic inspiration in the colony.[72]

Unlike the British and Irish reviews, the tone of the Tasmanian review foregrounds how the reception of women's poetry in the Australian colonies was in light of an emergent nationalist canonization process that aimed to promote Australian-born white male poets.

For the poems, *The Courier's* review lists both London and Hobart publishers for the first edition in 1854. These poems were, like Leakey's novel *The Broad Arrow*, a part of a global book trade in the late nineteenth century. Alison Rukavina argues that the publisher of Leakey's novel, Richard Bentley, did not let the fact that a number of the books were not written by Australians stop him from advertising both the authors and the books in the library as Australian. The Australian Library included British author Caroline Leakey's *The Broad Arrow*, which was edited for the series with an Australian readership in mind. The new edition of the novel emphasised the romantic elements in the book and de-emphasised a polemic against the convict system and colonial life. Consequently, the novel, first published by Bentley in 1859 as a religious novel for a British public, became in 1888 a tragic national romance for Australian readers.[73]

While Leakey was a British author, she also lived in Tasmania and produced works based on her experiences and on tropes of fallen womanhood and imprisonment there. These were understood at the time as being simultaneously British and colonial and, later, increasingly through Australian nationalism. Miller and McCartney's *Australian Literature* notes that there was an Australian edition of the novel published in 1860 by J. Walch in Hobart.[74] Rukavina's argument nonetheless reflects the complexities of Leakey's texts placements within competing British imperial, emergent nationalist and global contexts. Leakey's representations of her experience in colonial Tasmania appear to have appealed to both an emergent nationalist Australian context and a global market interested in the colonies. With her work received primarily in these ways, Leakey evidently succeeded in de-emphasizing the unacceptable connections of her sympathetic narrative on the fallen woman to a favoured use of this trope within a broader anglophone women's poetic tradition.

Leakey's novel would come to be seen as a 'companion' to Marcus Clarke's novel and be read in light of an emphasis on a particularly masculine nationalist poetics, if receiving attention at all. More contemporaneously, Leakey was known as a poetess to Tasmanian readers through newspaper publications and individual poems as well as *Lyra Australis*. *Lyra Australis* was reviewed in Tasmanian newspapers from 1854, and six poems from *Lyra Australis* were anthologized in Douglas B. Sladen's *Australian Poets 1788–1888* (1888). Sladen here described Leakey as a 'well-known Tasmanian poetess'.[75] 'Queen Ina' which was included in the anthology, like other poems not included, such as 'The Rock of Martin Vaz', demonstrates the way in which Leakey links the natural environment of the Antipodes with the trope of the fallen woman. The fallen woman is symbolized by the moon in 'The Rock of Martin Vaz', in a scene which describes, what Leakey adds in a footnote, occurred on board the ship, 'on a summer morning in the southern hemisphere, issuing forth from the gloomy twilight of a little cabin [...] the moon, southern cross, Venus, and several larger stars all in the sky with the sun!' (*Lyra*, 77–78). Leakey connects this natural occurrence very deliberately with Romantic tropes of the embowered woman and the woman who waits:

> And the moon's own placid face, through that veil of beauty shown
> She looked, through that morning light, like a bride from her lattice-pane
> [...]
> But her lamp it waxed dim, and her crescent paler grew
> Till with a speechless grace, Heaven's virgin queen withdrew;
> For she knew her lord right well, and her eye it waxed dim,
> For she was aweary quite, with her watching long for him. (78–79)

This poem shows the continued significance of earlier Romantic tropes as a framework for approaching colonial writing, consciously referencing both Tennyson's 'Mariana' and earlier Romantic texts such as Shelley's 'To the Moon', which reads:

> Art thou pale for weariness
> Of climbing heaven and gazing on the earth,
> Wandering companionless
> Among the stars that have a different birth –
> And ever changing like a joyless eye
> That finds no object worth its constancy?[76]

Leakey's usage too emphasizes, perhaps autobiographically, ideas of women's constancy in love. While it has been noted that both Norton and Charlotte Smith came under criticism for being too autobiographical,[77] Leakey's own experience is somewhat obscured in Emily Leakey's hagiographic memoir *Clear Shining Light*. Emily Leakey stresses the virtues of her sister in a way which mirrors the emphasis on humility in Elizabeth Gaskell's *Life of Charlotte Brontë* (1857). Gaskell's *Life* has been noted by Lucasta Miller as functioning to excuse Charlotte Brontë from the supposedly 'unacceptable unfeminine elements of her novels'.[78] Emily Leakey refers to the absences of certain details in her memoir, stating in her dedication to her brother-in-law,

> under whose roof she [Caroline] dwelt so long when in Australia; with the hope that all I have written of her holy and guileless life may meet with their approval, and what I have left unsaid of her [...] eventful life, may be rather considered discreet than blameworthy.[79]

As Mead notes, the only other biographical account of Leakey from her lifetime is in a journal from a fellow passenger on the ship during her voyage to Tasmania, who found Leakey to be 'not pretty, certainly not pretty' and disliked her drinking and flirting:

> Miss L looks a perfect child, but is said to be five and twenty, 'not pretty, certainly not pretty', very much marked with the small pox, little, bad figure, and makes devoted love to Mr. Smith (another passenger) [...] her ankles and feet are if anything a little thicker than Miss Palmer's [...] I forgot to mention one of Donald's (Mr. Cameron) amusements, scolding Miss Leaky [sic] and Miss Palmer...on the heinousness of ladies (particularly young ladies) drinking such a quantity of wine everyday [...] the young ladies turn about reciting their own poetry [...] I think Miss L is rather too unsophisticated.[80]

Leakey's concern with the figure of the fallen woman, with the vulnerabilities of babies, and the fleetingness of life is confirmed in her biography. Emily Leakey also makes reference to a flirtation on board the ship, describing how 'the young officer to whom she administered a playful rebuke when he persisted in calling her a blue stocking, because she was able to give information *when asked*, admired her maidenly propriety and sincere piety'.[81] Emily Leakey adds the impromptu which Caroline returned to Mr. Cameron: 'If I am a blue sock, sir, I was not knit for you; Nor one inch of wool from your thin fleece I drew.'[82] As Shirley Walker suggests, there is a tension between ideas of the religious resignation expected of women and the 'wild and wilful' characteristics in Caroline Leakey's life and writing, including her 'over indulgence in laudanum (opium) and alcohol'.[83]

There is a clear sense in Leakey's short story 'Sentiment from the Shambles' (1959) that geographical spaces are significant for young women's susceptibility to libertine men. Published under the pseudonym of Oliné Keese, the story has hitherto remained absent from discussions of Leakey's works. This short story appeared in the literary magazine *Once a Week* (1859–80) and was published in the same year as *The Broad Arrow*. 'Sentiment from the Shambles' repeats many narrative elements of *The Broad Arrow*, with Bessie Munro seduced and deceived by a digger, Joe Sadlers, who has promised to marry her, but instead robs the Black Bear where Bessie boards. This robbery is a crime for which Bessie is blamed but, unlike Maida, she has an alibi in the form of the gentleman narrator whom her father has met and implored to find her. Set in Hobarton, but never published outside of Britain, this recapitulation of the fallen woman trope focuses particularly on the relationship of

Bessie and the father who has turned her out and seeks to find and forgive her. Unlike Maida, Bessie is 'redeemed' by her return to her father's house and is eventually married.

Popular American examples, such as Fanny Forester's (Emily Chubbuck) short story 'Lucy Dutton' published in *Alderbrook: A Collection of Fanny Forester's Village Sketches, Poems etc* (1847), reflect the widespread popularity of this recurring narrative. 'Lucy Dutton', like Leakey's 'Dora', also makes a wry note of the narrative as one so common as to need little furnishing: 'And so Lucy met the young metropolitan; and Lucy was beautiful, and trusting, and thoughtless, and he was gay, selfish and profligate. Needs the story to be told?'.[84] Where he was metropolitan, she was a country girl in America, so 'her innocence was no match for the sophistry of a gay city youth!'[85] However, the use of Tasmania as a space in which this narrative is played out is particularly important in Leakey's versions of the story.

In 'Sentiment from the Shambles' Leakey seems to suggest, while clearly being aware otherwise, that the betrayal by Joe Sadlers may be a particularly Antipodean situation. As the narrator notes, 'I knew enough of diggers to make me tremble for her; but to shake her faith in her betrothed was impossible.'[86] The emphasis on her trust reiterates the representation of the fallen woman in Leakey's earlier poem 'Dora':

> She, unrequited, loved – she loved too well;
> She too much trusted, and, alas! she fell.
> Her father cursed – and still his ev'ry breath
> Some new curse breathed, to her more dread than death.
> The blow was heavy, and the mother lay
> Long time, twixt life and death – but love bore sway, –
> For her fallen daughter's sake she lived again
> Though what to her life now but one long pain? (205–6)

This European conceptualization of an Antipodean world of strange reversals is arguably drawn on to both emphasize Leakey's sympathetic and even powerful portrayals of the fallen woman figure and to distance these from a tradition of women's writing on this topic, on which she nonetheless clearly models her sympathetic approach.

Leakey's *Lyra Australis* primarily addresses the same 'protesting men's combination of sexual license with their claim to righteous social power' that Nancy F. Cott discusses in relation to American sources from the late eighteenth century.[87] Cott argues that 'The sexual double standard epitomized male usurpation of power, because it allowed men to flaunt the arts of seduction without losing public esteem while it condemned a woman forever if she once succumbed to a deceiver.'[88] This is clearly a point Leakey makes through Maida Gwynnham and Captain Norwell in *The Broad Arrow*. Leakey's 'Dora' and later Maida Gwynnham are strong examples of writing designed to evoke sympathy for the fallen woman. Dora, whose baby did not live, 'Scarce on its head the sacred sign was made / Than on the arms of Jesus it was laid' (206) may also suggest criticism of the failure of the Church to baptize babies born out of wedlock. Describing 'The Cult of True Womanhood' in America, Barbara Welter points out that 'If religion was so vital to women, irreligion was almost too awful to contemplate. Women were warned not to let their literary or intellectual pursuits take them away from God.'[89] It is also clear, however, that within religious and colonial frameworks alike, there was scope for women poets like Leakey to address feminist themes.

In framing these traditions of dissenting literature through a traveller or settler colonial experience, Leakey published political poetry that would not have been considered acceptable in a mid-century British setting. It also appears that the later women poets in this study, such as Leakey and Emily Manning, emphasized religious aspects of their work in response to the increasing constraints on women's sexuality and the woman poet over the nineteenth century. In colonial Australian settler women's poetry this involved exclusions from emergent masculine nationalism and an understanding of feminist dissidence as occurring simultaneously within both transnational and imperial contexts. Accordingly, Eliza Hamilton Dunlop approaches the massacre of Wirrayaraay people within the discourses of broader Irish, British and American women's literary contexts of appropriative writing against slavery. Mary Bailey approaches the penal system, women's poetry and political inclusion in Britain and Tasmania through Grecian antiquity and Romantic Hellenism. Class is also important to a self-identification as exile, and the recurring exilic theme in the work of Dunlop, Bailey and Leakey may be understood as an articulation of a 'fall' in class status as well as a moral conflict with British laws. This identification as a trope in colonial poetry problematically appropriates experiences of imprisonment and obscures agency. For Leakey, a shared tradition of women writing incompatibility with the normative model of British ideal womanhood is articulated as a basis for a sisterhood, and a knowing rejection of the sexism, double standards and classism inherent in British and transnational prejudices associated with the middle-class domestic ideal and purity discourse.

Similarly, *Lyra Australis* when situated in relation to British women's Romantic legacies develops their feminist resistance to increasing conservatism through its close reimagining of earlier key poetic works. Caroline Norton's *The Sorrows of Rosalie* predates Leakey's volume by 26 years and is undoubtedly the source of the narrative of the fallen woman in both Leakey's poems and novel (*Rosalie* itself heavily drawing on the narrative of Bowles' earlier *Ellen Fitzarthur*). Norton had sympathetically portrayed Rosalie as the fallen woman, and she had also critiqued the prison system in *The Undying One* (1830). Like Norton, as well as Dunlop and Bailey, there is a clear engagement with the question of laws as they pertain to rights. These laws are held up against 'natural laws' and experiences such as sexuality, emotional pain, maternal and romantic love, to demonstrate their discrepancies and elite male bias. The moral contestation of such laws in a colonial context did not extend to any understanding of the legal fiction of terra nullius and those laws on Aboriginal land, relating instead to the parallel conceptualizations of progress through imperialism and feminism. Leakey's complicity with the inherent violence of settler colonialism is likewise revealed in the lack of acknowledgement of Aboriginal peoples, laws and rights. Leakey's departures from the earlier Romantic women's tradition and symbolic language reflect the intense reaction away from their highly political poetry, which by the mid-nineteenth century had become unacceptable. Her poetry in this way preserves the political and feminist messages of poets such as Norton, while replacing formal elements and refraining from the more emotive tone and open referencing of women poets seen in earlier Romantic women's poetry. The religious strain is significant to much settler colonial women's poetry. Women's rights activism within these traditions and imperialism also encompassed uncritical presumptions of Christian Western superiority. Religiosity, as a central aspect of the restrictive middle-class domestic ideal, also provided a moral and political space considered acceptable for women and this space is likewise engaged with, in different ways, in the later poetry of Emily Manning. However, Leakey's response to the dominant culture of shaming and controlling women's sexuality is a sustained public reclamation of voice and experience, amplified and shared among a white 'sisterhood' articulated through these earlier women's traditions.

Chapter 4

EMILY MANNING: SPIRITUALISM AND PERIODICAL PRINT CULTURE: 1860–80

The increased religiosity of British women's poetry and spiritualism are both central to Emily Manning's poetry. *The Balance of Pain and Other Poems* (1877) published under the pen name 'Australie' presents a questioning and challenging of gender roles that were part of the spiritualist movement, and spiritualism and theological inquiry operate as intellectual spaces challenging the limitations of separate spheres of ideology. Born to a well-off family, Manning was writing on Warrang lands of the Gadigal people of the Eora nation, called Sydney by settlers. Manning's poetic concerns and approaches to spiritualism, religion and questions of social justice do not encompass any discussion of Indigenous Australians. She was involved with intellectual settler circles, and in 1865 she left for London where she 'had connections which allowed her to move into the literary world, meeting Tennyson, Browning, Huxley and George Eliot' before returning to Australia.[1] Patricia Clarke points out that it was in London that her journalistic career began, with Manning writing for periodicals including Charlotte Yonge's *Monthly Packet of Evening Readings* (1851–99) and *Golden Hours* (1864–84).[2] Her poetry was also originally published in Australian newspapers and periodicals including the *Town and Country Journal* (1870–1919) and the *Sydney Mail* (1860–1938).

Occultism is an important aspect of Manning's title poem 'The Balance of Pain' which was first published in the *Sydney Mail* (1876) over two full pages, and her engagement reflects the vogue of the occult revival. Yet the heightened interest in both spiritualism and religiosity, as well as the connection of these areas to questions and challenges to the domestic ideal, involves three significant aspects. First, Manning's poetry foregrounds the connections between occultism and, more broadly, spiritualism, with nineteenth-century imperial feminism. Second, the occult revival in Manning's poetic practice delineates a continuation of anglophone women's writing traditions. Spiritualism operates as a conceptual theorization in poetry with connections to the legacies of literary Romanticism and political voice. Through the domestic ideal, particularly religious devotion, as well as spiritualist disruptions to the separate spheres ideology, Manning's poetry articulates concerns around social inequality, gender inequality and marriage. Third, the occult revival, like much settler women's poetry, was circulated extensively through periodical print culture.

Manning had published in newspapers and journals in both Australia and England, gaining journalistic knowledge while working on Charlotte Yonge's *Monthly Packet* during her time in London, reflecting the imperial contexts of her writing and its circulation. A reviewer in the *Illustrated Sydney News* of *The Balance of Pain* (1877) reflected on the presence in periodicals of the 'colonial authoress, "Australie"', writing that

> This lady is well known as a contributor of both prose and verse to the public journals, and has by this means already made acquaintance with a large circle of readers, which we doubt not will be considerably extended by the publication of the presentable and handsomely got up volume under notice. 'Australie' is an enthusiastic worker in the somewhat prosaic and certainly unprofitable field of literature (as far as its emoluments in the colonies are concerned), and evidently takes delight in intellectual occupation, as she seldom permits any long interval to elapse without favouring the reading public with an opportune poem or review.[3]

It is important to recognize that Manning was regarded as a poet, or 'poetess', first and foremost. As were many of the poets in this study, she was well-connected socially to literary circles, as well as with intellectually and politically influential people in Sydney and later in London. Her father, Sir William Montagu Manning, was a barrister, politician and university chancellor. Sally O'Neill points out that she was educated at a private school and was encouraged to take an interest in literature by Professor Woolley of the University of Sydney.[4] The significance of women's contributions to periodical and newspaper publications as a part of both transnational and imperial feminist poetics is increasingly apparent. Manning's volume of poetry *The Balance of Pain and Other Poems* was published in London in 1877 and contained many of her poems previously published in Australian newspapers, as well as eight hymns.

The politics of feminized religiosity

The uses of theological argument and occult mesmerism in Manning's title poem 'The Balance of Pain' speak to increasing tensions around gender roles and women's rights, particularly within marriage, and the limitations of the domestic ideal as a means of promoting white women's social and political equality. Manning's *The Balance of Pain* reflects one imperial feminist approach to religious decline, through her departures from the heightened religiosity of poetry such as Caroline Leakey's, discussed in the previous chapter. Egalitarian marriage, like education, was understood within feminist circles as crucial to ideas of individual autonomy and consequently to claims to citizenship and democratic inclusion. As Jane Rendall suggests more broadly of transnational feminist developments in the period, 'by 1860 the ground was clearly laid, and in Britain and America a small but recognisable feminist movement was established'.[5] Manning's presence as a public intellectual and woman writer, generally under the name 'Australie' or anonymously, within various newspapers and journals, was highly regarded.

As well as poetry and correspondence, she published serial fiction in Australian newspapers, including 'Cupid on a Swiss Tour' and 'The Story of a Royal Pendulum', reviews under the title 'Books Worth Reading', and articles and literary criticism. Her reviews reflect her extensive knowledge of British, American and European literary circles and include reviews of works by or about Tennyson, Byron, the Brontës, Browning, Harriet Martineau and the French artist Elisabeth Vigée-Le Brun. Manning's 1879 review article of Elisabeth Vigée-Le Brun provides some further clues to her own views on the institution of marriage. She notes that

> Marriage in France, especially at that time, was merely an alliance for purposes of convenience. If no love followed, each lived and acted without interfering with the other. There were few of the quarrels of an English ill-assorted couple, because by mutual consent they saw as little as possible of each other, but amused themselves after their own fashion.[6]

Manning implies that this French model may have granted a woman a certain amount of personal and sexual freedom as well as artistic autonomy within the legal confines of a loveless marriage.

Although she does not overtly suggest divorce as an option, it is suggested that a de facto divorce would be preferable to such a marriage. This approach to marriage in the period preceding the French Revolution is contrasted favourably in Manning's review with increasingly conservative, later nineteenth-century British views on marriage. In the *Sydney Morning Herald* in April of 1874, Manning had reviewed Rev. Maurice Davies' *Unorthodox London* (1873) which examined various religious and spiritual groups. Her review similarly reveals some sensitivity regarding the plurality of religious varieties:

> There is 'One God, one faith, one baptism', saith Holy Writ: Yet here are more than forty different ways of worshipping that God, forty faiths

and almost as many forms of baptism! Each body has its own prophet, who verily speaks in his own tongue, and, like Greek of old, looks on all other languages as Barbarian, each believes that his one hand alone has grasp of the truth.[7]

This passage suggests that Manning's understandings of religion and spiritualism aspired to plurality and the breaking down of hierarchical thinking.

Manning also reviewed *Harriet Martineau's Autobiography* (1877) in the *Sydney Morning Herald* in 1878. The connections of Manning's writings to Harriet Martineau and to George Eliot demonstrate the imperial feminist contextual basis in her approaches to the religious transitions in women's poetry and public intellectual writings. That lengthy review article discusses Martineau's strong anti-slavery profile, as well as her well-publicized use of mesmerism in recovering from a period of illness, of which Manning notes that 'it seems almost incredible that such bigotry and prejudice should have existed among sensible people, especially the medical profession, as was evinced by their attack upon Miss Martineau for her recourse to this new healing agency'.[8] Well-known British women intellectuals such as Martineau and Eliot were, like Manning, questioning religiosity and embracing periodical literature, and Manning's reviews indicate support of an expansive plurality of spiritual and religious practices, particularly as spaces for women's self-expression.

Manning's awareness of gendered representations of religious devotion and its relationship to 'women's mission' and inequality indicates another conscious level on which she wished to examine gender roles in *The Balance of Pain and Other Poems*, notably in the title poem. While Manning's poetry defends the morality of faith, which was connected to the development of many Western imperialist feminist approaches, Howard Murphy points out that the decline itself was essentially moral, rather than grounded in scientific advances such as Darwin's theory of evolution. Murphy suggests that many in this period felt a 'growing repugnance toward the ethical implications of what they had been taught to accept as essential Christian dogma'.[9] 'The Balance of Pain' addresses questions of faith and rationalism as factors precipitating the decline of religion in the late nineteenth century and is structured as a theatrical dialogue.

Through this dialogue between a husband and wife, Agatha and Theodore, rationalism is presented as functioning within a gendered dichotomy of masculine materialism and feminine spiritualism. 'The Balance of Pain' opens with an oration from Theodore, who decries the suffering of man: 'PAIN and still pain! Pain at each turn of being! / Pain at life's opening and in the last dark hour! / Pain in the flesh and in the soul's vague depths –'.[10] Theodore goes on to assert:

> Yet I could bear it were the throes assign'd
> In equal measure to each human soul.
> But 'tis not thus; on one the woes are heap'd,
> While others pass with strange immunity
> From all save that engrain'd in very living.
> It is a grand injustice of the Lord,
> In whom, alike, all move and have their being. (1)

Theodore's oration implicates material political inequality as the ultimate suffering and as a class-conscious approach speaks to irreconcilability between faith in God and political action.

The poem explicitly states, 'It is a grand injustice of the Lord' (1), for such disparities between affluence, pleasure, poverty and pain to exist. Manning's Theodore represents the position that God is unjust, and that social justice must be the responsibility of the people. Agatha then answers him:

> Nay, speak not thus. The righteous judge is true,
> Creative author of the mortal world.
> Why should he love one creature more or less
> When we are His, the work of His own hands? (2)

In attributing to the wife a defence of religious faith, Manning's poem falls in line with the common practice of representing a split between religious and political (or rationalist) discourses in gendered terms.

However, in approaching poetic voice through dramatic dialogue, Manning's poem encompasses discourses outside the acceptably feminine space of domestic ideology and engages in what Murphy argues was an ethical religious crisis in the nineteenth century. Isobel Armstrong has suggested that the

> Victorian dramatic poem is not the dialogue of the mind with itself so much as the dialogue of the poem with itself, using the dialogue of the mind [...] [i]f the poet knows that the act of representation is fraught with problems [...] then a structure which analyses precisely that uncertainty and which makes that uncertainty belong to struggle and debate [...] is the surest way to establish poetic form. The surest way to answer uncertainty is creative agnosticism.[11]

In the context of increasing secularization, the philosophical nature of debates around alternative ideas such as Gnosticism and atheism was occurring in many cases alongside ongoing essentialist and sexist beliefs that men possessed power to reason where women were more emotional and aligned towards faith.

Concerns with gender and rights were played out in various ways in relation to these developments. Murphy argues, in 'The Ethical Revolt against Christian Orthodoxy in Early Victorian England', that the erosion of religious sentiment was due to 'a sensed incongruity between a vigorous and hopeful meliorism and the doctrinal legacy of the Christian tradition' and lists George Eliot as one public figure in whose work he believes this 'point is strikingly illustrated'.[12] Eliot was openly swayed from her evangelical upbringing by ethical concerns. Murphy bases this assessment of Eliot on her letters, noting that 'Fragmentary as it is [...] the evidence in these letters confirms our thesis that the higher criticism and the idea of evolution were effective solvents of "faith" only in the minds already alienated from Christianity as a system'.[13] Religious decline was important to both Manning and George Eliot.

Manning's 'The Balance of Pain' (1877), like George Eliot's *Agatha* (1869), has a woman protagonist named Agatha, deriving from the Greek agathos, meaning good and associated with Saint Agatha of Sicily. Both Manning's and Eliot's texts are presented as theatrical script. Eliot's *Agatha* (1869) begins by linking imagery of nature with the maternal, 'where the earth spreads soft and rounded breasts / To feed her children', before evoking Mary, after whom the place has been named 'Sancta Maria'.[14] Eliot suggests power through motherhood, stripping away symbols of material riches as she presents Mary: 'What though a Queen? / She puts her crown away, / And with her little boy wears common clothes' (199). Just as the Mother removes her crown,

> the Blessed Virgin's name,
> Sancta Maria, which the peasant's tongue,
> Speaking from out the parent's heart that turns
> All loved things into little things, has made
> Sanct Märgen (199)

Eliot diminishes associations with Mary as a figure of material power and simultaneously venerates spiritual and affectional aspects, such as 'the parent's heart' that binds Mary and the people of Sanct Märgen, in a return to the mode in which the poem begins, where the landscape is maternal. The spirit in the maternal, as distinct from materialism, is presented by Eliot as that which is to be valued. Eliot's *Agatha* is in this way similar to Manning's Agatha in *The Balance of Pain*, and the poems have clear stylistic and thematic resemblances.

Particularly, Manning's use of theatrical dialogue in this poem, in which the husband and wife are engaged in debate around theological discourses, suggests the significance of these themes to gender roles around motherhood and marriage. Although Murphy's arguments on the decline of religion relate to England specifically, we can see how earlier colonialist accounts of Australia 'between 1830 and 1850 [...] [which presented] a new image of Australia as a land of opportunity for all comers, especially the working man', as distinct from the rigid class structure of England, similarly exemplify this ethical bias.[15] Given that from the 1830s to the 1870s England underwent a period of political upheaval as industrialization brought about increasing dissatisfaction with conditions, such representations of Australia should be understood as constructed within a wider imperialist context. The reality was, as Anne Summers has pointed out, that

> Both race and sex ideologies were transported from England with the capitalist system but they have been maintained in Australia with a distinct and explicable fervour. The ideology of racism was used to justify the invasion [...] [and] the ideology of sexism has served several varying purposes in Australia's economic development.[16]

As works that resisted aspects of sexism through a philosophical grounding in many of the underlying assumptions of these ideologies, Manning's poems work to draw closer imperial networks and reproduce empire, as well as sometimes seeking a new emergent nationalist settler aesthetic. Through these positions, her poetry does not acknowledge Indigenous people, constructing the volume as an exclusively white settler 'Australia'.

The absence of any consideration reflects the broader colonial impulse and cultural erasure amid the ongoing dispossession of Indigenous lands. Manning's approach does not acknowledge the connections of Indigenous peoples to the land as sacred, and there is similarly no recognition of how her religiosity was tied up with presumptions of Christian Western superiority and colonization. While spiritualist discourses in America sometimes incorporated discussions of Native American culture, and in New Zealand that of Māori culture, Manning's approach to spiritualism makes no reference to these. John Kucich suggests of the American context, recognized as a source of the Spiritualist vogue, that

> Regular communication with a spirit world features prominently in Native American cultures, and Europeans and Africans brought spiritualism with them to America's shores. As important as it was to each

cultural group, spiritualism also helped shape the terms by which these cultures interacted from the earliest days of contact to the present.[17]

Manning's absence of acknowledgement of Indigenous people, or consideration of questions of human rights and justice in relation to them, reflects literary constructions of a white Australia inherently complicit with imperialist and emergent nationalist agendas. This is despite the fact of First Nations people's survival and strong resistance to colonization, also demonstrated in print culture, through letters written in English by writers including William Barak and Bessie Cameron, as well as petitions.[18]

Manning instead expresses views highly conscious of the falsehood of popular and idealized British, transnational and emergent nationalist representations of Australia as a paradise for the white working-class man, for example, in the poem 'A Plea for the Ragged Schools'. The poem originally appeared in the *Sydney Morning Herald* in 1873 and was later included in *The Balance of Pain and Other Poems*.[19]

> No sign of poverty; all is bright,
> For the capital waxes great;
> No misery here as in older lands;
> No need for our pity, – but wait!
>
> Step back from the broader thoroughfare
> And pass through some narrow lane,
> And find – too many a noisome street,
> With its dwellings of want and pain. (102)

Here Manning's presentation of increasingly closer images of the city is depicted like the device of filmic panning, as she focuses on Sydney as if from a height, which suggests the role of the poet herself as a 'seer' or medium:

> The city of Sydney lies smiling fair
> In the beams of a winter morn
> And the murmuring voices of busy men
> On the southern breeze are borne
>
> The peaceful face of the harbour glows
> With a joy of heavenly blue
> A tender thought and a touch of love
> Shine forth in each changing hue

> The spires point up to the God who paints
> The beauty and joyous life
> For he is worshipp'd sometimes amid
> The hurry of care and strife
>
> The streets are gay and the wharfs are lin'd
> With a fleet of laden ships:
> The buildings are grand and the citizens rich
> "Gold! Gold!" the word on their lips! (102)

In this poem, as in 'The Balance of Pain', Manning displays her concerns with inequality and gendered space.

Particularly, the poem articulates tensions within binary and gendered representations of an ordered separation of public and private spheres. This is evident in lines such as 'the murmuring voices of busy men' with '"Gold! Gold!" the word on their lips!' as masculinity, material wealth and industry are equated with the public life of the city. In the title poem 'The Balance of Pain' the feminine space is associated similarly with the spiritual and the 'God who paints the beauty of joyous life' as something only 'sometimes worshipp'd' by these men. In 'A Plea for the Ragged Schools', a call for political intervention is specifically addressed to maternal sympathy, and it is 'for the babes we plead' (103). This suggests that Manning's view of religion and appeal to maternal sympathy functioned as a means for approaching questions of social reform, seeking to overcome what Murphy described as 'a fundamental conflict between certain cherished orthodox dogmas (of which the infallibility of the word was perhaps the least important) and the meliorist ethical bias of the age'.[20]

Manning's Agatha similarly represents ties between religion and motherhood as tightly woven, so that, as a parent might, Agatha is able to imagine the way in which God might 'weigh and measure out in love / The outward and the inward; balancing / Circumstance 'gainst disposition' (7). Agatha, in line with the domestic ideal, is submissive and pious, but she is able to articulate a moral influence on Theodore through spiritualism. In Sarah Lewis's English translation of Aimé Martin's *Woman's Mission* the idea of moral influence through the domestic ideal is explicit: 'The moral destinies of the world, then, depend not so much upon institutions, or upon education, as upon moral influence. The most powerful of all moral influences is the maternal.'[21] Likewise, in 'A Plea for the Ragged Schools', Manning overtly asserts woman's mission and the idealized 'sweet pure woman' as a feminized solution, when she asks, 'Could no power reach / Those tender young lambs in time?' (103) and answers 'Yes, one power there is' (104). Writing of the American context,

Barbara Welter terms this intense adherence to the domestic ideal 'The Cult of True Womanhood' and points out that 'increasingly, in a political world, women and the church stood out as anti-political forces, as they did in an increasingly materialistic society, dominated by a new species, Economic Man'.[22]

While the occult sciences could seem by their association with the satanic and with witchcraft to undermine Manning's apparently orthodox Christian stance, rather an essentialist discourse of women's power was signified within both the occult and the religious. As Diana Basham argues,

> Victorian literary texts concerned with 'Occult' phenomena, such as those associated with mesmerism, provided an important site for the discussion of gender concepts and gender roles [...] Because occultism works with paradigms that are outside of, or in opposition to, the generally prevailing or generally agreed upon formulas for what constitutes social reality...writers engaged in such potentially threatening fields of exploration frequently deployed strategies of self-protection against the fantasy potential released in their fictions.[23]

Such strategies of self-protection in Manning's poem are particularly expressed through the representation of Agatha in accordance with the values of the domestic ideal. Barbara Welter notes that 'Woman, in The Cult of True Womanhood presented by the women's magazines, gift annuals and religious literature of the nineteenth century, was the hostage in the home.'[24] She points to evidence that 'women's magazines and books of advice also warned against politics as a destroyer of the home', reflecting the immense popularity of these ideas in the print culture of America and Britain in the nineteenth century.[25]

Agatha's power as a medium is that she can present scenes to her husband, which aim to expand his understanding of the nature of suffering as not being purely economically driven or remedied. As Alex Owen suggests, regardless of class, 'the mainstay of spiritualism's democratic impulse was the continued belief that every man, woman and child had the potential for spirit mediumship'.[26] This is a level beyond the straightforward suggestion of gender inequality in the lines 'a woman poor in speech' (3), which have been correctly read for their alignment with the middle-class domestic ideal. Michael Ackland notes that 'although Manning is concerned with the problematical issues raised by social injustice, human restrictions, and the processes of sin and acculturation, she strives throughout to preserve Victorian decorums' adding that Manning 'actualizes in Agatha a current ideal of womanhood'.[27]

The significance to imperial feminist strategies of the affiliation between religion and women within the domestic ideal is a crucial aspect of Manning's adherence to 'Victorian decorums' yet one in which a greater degree of resistance to white women's subjugation than has been generally thought was occurring. As Welter has pointed out of the domestic ideal,

> the very perfection of True Womanhood [...] carried with it the seeds of its own destruction. For if woman was so very little less than the angels, she should surely take a more active part in running the world, especially since men were making such a hash of things.[28]

This sentiment is at the heart of several of Manning's poems, including 'The Balance of Pain' and 'The Angel's Call'.

The linking of woman and angel is explicit in 'The Angel's Call', which depicts a woman on her deathbed, called by angels to 'come home' to heaven:

> On her death-bed lay a woman
> Long with weary suffering worn,
> And her brows throb with the anguish,
> Yet with Christ-like patience borne,
> Lo! A sudden joy breaks o'er her,
> Though her strength is nearly spent
> And her eye in upward rapture
> Is on some bright vision bent.
> Oh! To her the heavens are open'd
> E'en before her soul takes wing!
> Angel choirs to her are calling
> As in joyous tones they sing:
>
> Come home! Come home! We have called you long
> And your place is prepar'd mid the angel throng!
> And the victor's crown shall encircle the brow
> That with earthly wounds is all bleeding now!
> Come home! come home! For the day is done
> The strife is past and the victory won! (94)

The lines 'And her eye in upward rapture / Is on some bright vision bent' suggest again Manning's emphasis on both Christianity and unorthodox spiritualism. In presenting the vision as one which is possible 'e'en before her soul takes wing!' (94), Manning likens the state of trance as an earthly spiritual realm akin to heaven, thereby both emphasizing and challenging hierarchies in connections between poet, woman and angel.

The domestic ideal and the woman question in occultism

Significantly for Manning's interests in occultism and spiritualism, in the 1870s they functioned as active sites for feminist and political discourse. In the colonial context, later women poets such as Louisa Lawson as well as other poets, including Christopher Brennan, John Le Gay Brereton and the 'automatic slate-writer Henry Slade who converted E. Cyril Haviland', were concerned with spiritualism and theosophy.[29] As early as the 1870s, Manning was interested in spiritualism, as were members of her extended social circle. Sydney spiritualists included Margaret Woolley, whom Jill Roe points to as one of the first fellows of the Theosophical Society in 1883, – 'the name of Margaret Woolley suggests that the first responses to theosophy in Sydney came from the liberal intelligentsia of the 1870s'.[30] Spiritualism in the nineteenth century was not necessarily antagonistic to orthodox Christian positions, and Julian Holloway makes the argument that 'spiritualism represented a sort of halfway house between the increasingly separate or separated God (and thus by implication the church) of "hellfire" religious doctrine and the bare materialism of secularism or atheism'.[31] This idea of spiritualism as a middle ground is demonstrated in the narrative of 'The Balance of Pain'. Manning is careful not to posit Agatha as the victor in the debate through the power of mental reasoning, offering up spiritualist alternatives that both fit within and challenge the model of ideal womanhood: Agatha is capable of seeing into the minds of others and describes visions rather than arguing. However, Agatha's success is an imagined victory of a woman's spiritual discourse over a supposedly masculine and materialist one.

It is politically significant that Manning approaches marriage and the ethical questions of the age through spiritualism and mesmerism, especially given that both divorce reform and opposition to women's legal status as femme covert emerged as major feminist concerns in the decades leading up to suffrage. Diana Basham notes that

> Occultism flourishes [...] whenever disruptions of existing hegemonic structures become acute. Thus, witchcraft and witch mania reached its peak in England in the years prior to the civil war, just as mesmerism acquired momentum through its association with pre-revolutionary France.[32]

A reading of 'The Balance of Pain' as a poem primarily concerned with debates around gender, class and religion is supported by its use of occult mesmeric trance:

SCENE II

THEODORE.

WAVE the passes slowly, strongly,
    Eye to eye and breath to breath.
Will that sleep shall hold the body,
    Fast as in the bonds of death.
While the soul, from sin escaping,
    For one Bless'd supernal hour,
Pierces through all earthly barriers
    With ethereal essence power –
And by space nor matter trammell'd,
    Gains awhile a seraph's dower.

Gently now the eyes are closing –
    Respirations long and deep –
One wave more – she lieth dreaming,
    Wrapp'd in strange mesmeric sleep.
Far her soul's eyes now are piercing
    Far beyond the senses' ken;
Still the mortal lips may show us
    Visions real of mortal men.
        Soul of Agatha, where art thou?
        Speak, and tell thy dreaming now. (5)

This 'mesmeric sleep' parallels death in its imagery, 'fast as in the bonds of death'. This allows Agatha's vocalization to emerge as akin to posthumous voice, a tradition in anglophone women's poetry connected with addressing questions of injustice. In this state, Agatha presents arguments against the political morality of rationalism, through the descriptions of her visions.

This conflict signals the increasing problematization of Victorian ideal womanhood, a question Manning pivots around in the poem. Manning questions these values through Agatha who, although considered to be particularly susceptible to religious piety and therefore morally upright, is denied representation and voice in public and political life. Manning points out women's inequality through Agatha, who herself states: 'I dare not argue. I am all too weak. / A woman poor in speech, unlearn'd in art, / Who cannot shape in words the truths she knows' (7). Agatha vocalizes her 'views' in a disembodied and supernatural state, yet significantly these are presented as morally superior and of greater truth than the political views taken by her husband. Agatha in her trance state presents a scene which highlights tensions between spiritualist and materialist discourses as gendered:

AGATHA

How came I 'mid such scenes? 'Tis night.
Within a chamber richly dight
I see a lady, jewell'd, fair,
With costly robes, and stately air.
Nought can she know of struggling life,
Her home with every luxury rife;
Rare pictures hang about each wall,
Sculpture and music, books, and all
That soothe the senses, thrill the mind
With magic touch, are here combined.
But yet her look is sad! She sighs,
And Care's dark circles shade her eyes.
Ne'er heeds she these rich works of art
Which, had we *one* such, to our heart
The thing of beauty we would take,
New joy in our poor home to wake.

She waits alone. The guests long gone,
I hear the great clock chiming one.
She rises, listens, passes now,
A weary look upon her brow,
Through empty halls, into a room
Where one faint night-lamp lights the gloom.
She lays her lace and jewels by;
Rich, yet so lonely, with a sigh
The Countess sits anear the bed
And on the pillow lays her head
Beside a pale boy's sleeping face
Whose features bear a woman's grace –
The prophecy of early death.
Poor mother! Short that heaving breath! (5–6)

In Agatha's vision, Manning presents concerns with material injustice in relation to ideas of maternal suffering, presenting value as characterized by emotion and human love rather than economic possession alone. The mother, who 'lays her lace and jewels by / Rich, yet so lonely, with a sigh' repeats this symbolic action more emphatically, declaring 'While I am envied – I! Who fain / Would give my riches all to gain / Health for my darling'. As Agatha relates the close of the scene, material wealth is again presented as inconsequent to emotional suffering, as 'through silken curtains still she weeps' (7).

Imaginative compassion for others was considered particular to women, as it was understood to be intuitive and emotional rather than reasoned. Manning takes this conceptualization into the realm of the supernatural in her descriptions of Agatha as a seer in 'The Balance of Pain'. A woman medium, as Sarah Willburn points out, can be said to occupy both the public and private spheres simultaneously, and even a third mystical sphere. The use of religious language in 'The Balance of Pain' to describe the mesmeric as free from satanic associations is apparent in images such as 'a Seraph's dower' and 'mortal lips' (5). Just as spiritualism challenged the separate spheres, so too the domestic ideal, itself predicated on the concepts of separate spheres, purity, piety and ideal womanhood, was being increasingly used to 'justify' women's work outside of the home through involvement in charities by arguments of natural compassion and religious duty.

Sarah Lewis's *Woman's Mission* (1839) and John Ruskin's *Sesame and Lilies* (1865) were two widely popular texts dealing with women's roles, marriage and the education of women, to which Manning's strategies in presenting a theological debate between Agatha and Theodore speak directly. Ruskin, for example, wrote of 'wifely subjection' within the domestic ideal, asking 'but how, you will ask, is the idea of this guiding function of the woman reconcilable with a true wifely subjection?'[33] Manning's creative answer to Ruskin's question of how 'a true wifely subjection' is to be reconcilable with a guiding function in the wife is that Agatha is able to intuit and present scenes as a 'seer' in the state of mesmeric trance.

In this way, while conforming to the domestic ideal and its expectations of the wife, Manning simultaneously creates a challenge to the limitations of this model through Agatha. As Sarah Willburn has noted,

> This new theology was not a redundant if strange marker of bourgeois hegemonic respectability, but was, instead, often a new, revolutionary world view that, in turn, changed the boundaries of some women's domestic lives [...] These women used a mystical extra space to expand and redefine the professional and domestic spheres of which they were also a part.[34]

The Balance of Pain in this way both stands against and speaks to popular works, such as *Woman's Mission* and Ruskin's 'Of Queens' Gardens', which Deirdre David describes as 'one of the most conservative and influential treatises on the correct employment of woman's mind'.[35]

Manning's volume appeared the year before women were granted admission to universities in Britain. Her father was chancellor of the Sydney University at this time and delayed the opening of channels for women to pursue university education in New South Wales. The decision allowing colonial women's admissions into universities followed that of the University of London in 1878, as Anne Summers notes, and 'Sydney was the last university to admit women [...] three years after the matter had been first raised in 1878'.[36] Manning was by this time 33 years old and would not benefit from the decision, although, as Patricia Clarke has pointed out, she was regarded as an intellect by her contemporaries.

Manning's Agatha both affirms and attempts to refute patriarchal binary thought on the subject of women's intellect and married role. David notes that a common conflict with the separate spheres is apparent in the work of Eliot, Martineau and Barrett Browning. However, Manning's use of mesmerism as an alternative space along with Agatha's persuasion of Theodore signals increasing tensions around women's limitations within the domestic ideal and Ruskin's well-known ideas. What Ruskin describes as 'one pure kind of kingship [...] which consists in a stronger moral state, and a truer thoughtful state, than that of others; enabling you to guide, therefore, or to raise them'[37] is expressed through Agatha rather than Theodore in Manning's poem. Further, by engaging with the ideas discussed by Ruskin in this way, Manning herself is clearly asserting the right of women's representation in theological, political and intellectual discussion and practice.

Manning's approach, at the same time, is in line with the frequent containment of Victorian anxieties about class within narratives that recuperate 'order' through the domestic marriage. As Patricia Ingham argues of the British context, this social ordering is articulated through the interlocked coding of class and gender, in which the 'Angel in the house' figure increasingly associated middle-class women with purity, while working-class women and women of colour were uniformly coded as impure. Marriage both structurally and legally operated through the concept of coverture. This meant that structurally the process of marriage enabled mercantile men to assume the moral qualities of the idealized middle-class domestic woman, so 'this now morally excellent man thus became well suited to the duty of restraining the irrational and dangerous working classes'.[38] As Lillian Nayder suggests, there is also metaphoric resonance in the process of mesmerism, particularly of a man mesmerizing a woman, with the power structures of marriage and coverture. The recurrent Victorian idea that order was maintained and signified by the middle-class marriage applies to Manning's narrative poetics as well. Nayder points out that mesmerism acts as a re-enactment of the legal status of the married woman, whereby she becomes a 'femme covert', her legal rights subsumed within the legal rights of the husband.[39] The dialogue between Agatha and Theodore also secures their ongoing compatibility through Agatha's reinstatement of the terms of that social order, as defined by her faith and 'moral qualities'.

However, in the use of mesmerism, Manning also does depart from cultural norms. Armstrong points out that as well as being a popular poetic form in the Victorian period, theatrical monologue and dialogue were of particular use to women poets as a means of examining gender from behind the mask of anonymity or multiple voices. She notes too that Romantic women poets, such as Landon and Hemans, were among the first to adopt the technique.[40] She further points out that

> Victorian expressive theory is affective and of the emotions. It is concerned with feeling. It psychologised, subjectivised and often moralised the firm epistemological base of Romantic theory, though its warrant was in Wordsworth's spontaneous *overflow* of feeling. The idea of overflow, of projection and expression, a movement of feeling out of the self, develops metaphorically from a cognitive account of consciousness.[41]

Much of Manning's *The Balance of Pain and Other Poems*, as well as individual poems published in newspapers, suggests the Romantic as well as the dramatic models of poetry as overflow and performance.

This is evident in poems such as the Cantata 'The Emigrants', the hymns and 'The Rising Wind (Written for music)'. This performative model of divine inspiration is also demonstrated in the representation of Agatha's mesmeric vision of a poet in the act of writing in 'The Balance of Pain':

> The pages fill – rich images outflash
> In living words from out the poet's brain
> The hand is weary but the genius' fire
> No sweat can quench nor failing flesh restrain.
> Still glides the pen. The roseate sunlight streams
> Athwart the paper. Starting from reverie
> He rises, watches, till the last red beams
> Have glared to whiteness. Then adown he lies,
> And nature's healing sleep steals o'er the fever'd eyes (13)

Manning's theatrical staging of 'The Balance of Pain', with scenes, visions and speakers, links her poetic voice with the performative and overflow, emphasizing an emotional creativity. Likewise, Agatha's vocalizations in mesmeric trance reflect ideas of poetry as improvised, intuitive and spoken from the spirit.

Occultism and women's political voice

The occult revival of the 1870s built on an earlier fascination with the occult which, in the late eighteenth century, had produced ideas significant for literary Romanticism. Canonical Romantic representations of mesmerism, such as Shelley's 'The Magnetic Lady to her Patient' (1822), demonstrate the significance of magnetism or mesmerism in the production of Romantic poetry and in a questioning of gender roles:

> Sleep, sleep on! forget thy pain:
> My hand is on thy brow,
> My spirit on thy brain;
> My pity on thy heart, poor friend;
> And from my fingers flow
> The powers of life, and like a sign,
> Seal thee from thine hour of woe;
> And brood on thee, but may not blend
> With thine[42]

Nigel Leask argues that Shelley subverts gender roles by having the lady mesmerizing a male patient and furthermore argues that Romantic poetry is intrinsically linked to the mesmeric medium, as with the figure of the 'improvisatrice', in that both involve an improvised spiritual oration that is performed.

The idea of poetry originating organically, representing the close links between the natural environment and the human soul, is encompassed in the metaphor of mesmerism and poetic vision. Leask points out that the competing poetic theories of Shelley and Coleridge suggest these states are even more closely related:

> Coleridge's account of recitation and Shelley's competing theory of improvisation both construct the social vocalisation of Romantic poetry as 'species', albeit distinctive ones, of animal magnetism. The text-centred approach to poetry of modern scholars and silent readers has perhaps blinded the twentieth-century critic to the performative context of much Romantic poetry.[43]

Shelley, in his 'Defence of Poetry', explicitly connects the duality of the spirit and the body with that of the Romantic revaluing of the imagination over reason: 'reason is to the imagination as the instrument to the agent, as the body to the spirit, as the shadow to the substance [...] Poetry, in a general sense, may be defined to be "the expression of the imagination"'.[44]

For Shelley, poetry is linked with the imagination, as the imagination is linked with the spirit. Manning's depiction of mesmeric trance as a practice in which the spirit is freed from the body, 'the soul, from sin escaping / For one bless'd supernal hour / Pierces through all earthly barriers / With ethereal essence power' (5), likewise emphasizes the spirit over the body, and the imagination over reason, with gendered implications given the hierarchical representation of these concepts for women's poetic voice. Manning's use of mesmeric trance in Agatha's dialogue is in line with these Romantic theories of poetry, particularly in her connection of an oration of the spirit in trance with improvisation and divine inspiration in poetry.

In addition to the significance of mesmerism to Romantic theorizations of poetry, the theatricality and political significance of these theories within late nineteenth-century spiritualist approaches to restrictions on women's roles and self-expression are signalled by Manning's poem. These theatrical and occult aspects of 'The Balance of Pain' are particularly significant in relation to gender, as improvised and performative poetry is associated with the Romantic woman poet, as typified by Madame de Staël's *Corinne* (1807). The woman poet as particularly connected with poetic improvisation is also closely related to the oration in a trance state, and, like Corinne's improvisations, Agatha's words suggest divine inspiration:

> How came I 'mid such scenes? 'Tis night
> Within a chamber richly dight
> I see a lady jewell'd, fair,
> With costly robes and stately air. (5)

With Agatha's second vision, Theodore ceases his reflection on the first scene she has presented: 'But Agatha speaks. Mid other scenes she glides; / I see it by her smile. / I listen, wife' (8). Through Theodore's desire to hear Agatha, Manning replicates in some ways Oswald's pleasure in hearing Corinne: 'Oswald was so delighted by these stanzas that he expressed his admiration by the most rapturous applause [...] Indeed, it was to him rather than the Romans that Corinne had addressed her second improvisation.'[45] Manning posits, through Agatha, a nineteenth-century Romantic nostalgia for the expressive and revered woman poet.

Corinne is an important symbol of the woman poet and, as various critics have suggested, also connects to the figure of Sappho. Patrick Vincent has suggested of Landon's 'Sappho' (1822), 'a Sappho leaning on her harp, sublimely centred within a familiar landscape of adoring gazes,' that this 'is the apogee of the Sappho-Corinne myth, the epiphany of full and divine presence'.[46] Angela Esterhammer further connects the development of Romanticism and improvisation in the early nineteenth century, so that

> The poet who performs spontaneous composition now comes to function as a representative or a visualisation of Romantic genius [...] *Corinne*, appearing in French, German and English in 1807, is the foremost example of how the discourse of improvisation makes its way from travel writing into imaginative literature, simultaneously feminising the improviser.[47]

More subtle meditations on the divine inspiration that connects the woman medium and woman poet are consistent throughout *The Balance of Pain*.

The volume, which consists of seemingly disconnected poems, may be seen rather as a group of integrated poems that depict the spiritual and moral journey of the woman poet-as-seer. In presenting scenes outside of the domestic sphere Manning is also presenting, through both the mesmeric and religious, feminist 'resolutions' that framed both ideal womanhood and the expansion of women's moral influence beyond the domestic sphere as allaying contemporary anxieties around religious decline as well as anxieties around social inequality, class, poverty and the effects of industrialization in Britain. These themes are consistent throughout the volume, in poems such as 'A Plea for the Ragged Schools' and 'Blind Little Joe: The Unconscious Missionary' (1877), and indicate further connections to the legacy of women's Romantic poetic traditions. Imperial and transnational women's poetic traditions are important aspects of this, as reflected in Manning's reviews and her dramatizing of these discourses and the figure of Agatha, whose mesmerized oration is linked with ideas of public voice and the roles of the woman and poet.

The depiction of Agatha's mesmerized entry into both theological and political debate in 'The Balance of Pain' raises crucial questions about the boundaries of the domestic ideal, particularly as it related to women's public intellectual expression and political voice. In 'A Plea for the Ragged Schools', it is the 'gentle women with Christ-like wiles' who might be able to bring change through the ragged school:

> There are dens where crime and sorrow reign
> Uncheck'd in their fearful sway –

There are homes that dare not to bare the name —
There are scenes — but we may not say.

Here the drunken father will cruelly beat
A slatternly red-eyed wife,
While hunger is known and squalor is found
And sickness and fever are rife.

'Their own fault? There is work for all, —
Why need they our charity claim?'
Nay not for them, for the babes we plead
In the God of Mercy's name!

The poem reveals a deeply unsympathetic depiction of working-class adults as 'drunken' and 'slatternly' and Manning invites readers instead to 'see that girl, with face so childish fair, / Or the boy with the kindling eye; / What a sweet pure woman she yet might make/ Were she train'd to her mission high!' (103). These lines express the class-condescension of the belief in moral influence through the 'pure woman' and middle-class domestic ideal, presented as a so-called resolution to the poverty and disadvantage depicted. While Manning does not consider racialization, such attitudes of superiority and purity were a basis for immeasurably damaging racist colonialist applications. As Jennifer De Vere Brody points out more broadly of purity discourse and connections between racial and sexual categories in Victorian culture, the idea of 'the pure includes the erasure of the impure other' adding that this means 'purity as a concept-metaphor is not pure. It is defined always through negation [...] Purity and hybridity are therefore mutually constitutive rather than mutually exclusive. Pure purity is an impossibility.'[48] Both 'A Plea for the Ragged Schools' and 'The Balance of Pain' are overtly concerned with juxtaposing wealth and poverty, with a white feminized religiosity and spiritualism presented as providing a resolution.

Periodical culture and spiritualism

Newspapers, like Spiritualism itself, were often understood as having a democratic basis and as extending beyond ideas of national boundaries. Colonial readers' awareness of British, European and American cultural and literary contexts, such as the wider occult revival and 'The Cult of True Womanhood', are evidenced within colonial print culture. Holloway points out that 'Broadly, the spiritualist movement had a loose institutional geography organised around newspapers and journals (such as *Medium* and *Daybreak* and *Two Worlds*), educational lyceums, and, of course, the séance itself.'[49] Bridget Bennett suggests the metaphoric significance of transatlantic spirit travel amid improving technologies for travel and communications, pointing out that

> Nineteenth century spiritualism is routinely conceived of as a phenomenon that originated in the United States and spread across the Atlantic and then eventually worldwide. Given the concurrence of the emergence of spiritualism and the rapid development of faster and cheaper modes of transatlantic travel and communications, it is useful to ask to what extent, and how, the Atlantic affected the development of the aesthetic models spiritualists engaged with [...] Might the Atlantic itself, and the possibility of spirit travels across and beyond it even be invoked as a source of proof of the truth of spiritualisms claims?[50]

Manning's interest in spiritualism, then, is necessarily also linked with the increasing influence of the United States on transnational popular culture, demonstrated by the presence in colonial Australian newspapers of transatlantic articles, stories and poems.

A reviewer in the *Sydney Morning Herald* positioned Manning's use of mesmerism in 'The Balance of Pain' comically in wider literary terms:

> His wife, it seems, possesses the gift of clairvoyance, her husband has corresponding mesmeric power, and by the combination of these rare, and shall we say 'favoured gifts', they manage to see what is going on in the world without leaving their own chamber. That is much better than Jules Verne's 'Round the world in eighty days.'

This reviewer points to the international significance of occultism in this period, satirically adding,

> Nor must Agatha's spirit-trip through space be confounded with Mrs. Guppy's, and the tricks of the London *seances*. The latter had something very uncanny about them, though to what extent the courts of law have been quite unable to decide.[51]

These comparisons with high-profile spiritualist mediums such as Mrs. Guppy, and with the London séances, demonstrate how well known in colonial Australia these popular spiritualist figures of the 1870s were.

The London séances refer to the case in which the spirit known as 'Katie King' was alleged to have materialized at séances, both in London and Philadelphia. This reviewer's mention of the ensuing court case, which had been a major story, suggests that the widespread interest in spiritualism was well known, even to colonial Australian readers who were not involved in spiritualist circles. Alex Owen points out the medium Florence Cook's supposed materializations of 'Katie King', as the 'first full spirit materialisation seen in Britain', that because 'the novelty value of what Florence Cook had achieved was considerable [...] this accounted for much of her fame outside spiritualist circles'.[52] Stories of 'Katie King' had appeared in various international publications as well as colonial Australian newspapers.

Stories such as that of the spirit 'Katie King', as well as more general discussions of spiritualism, were not limited to specialist publications. An article taken from the *New York Times* was republished in the *Portland Guardian and Normanby General Advertiser*, and also appeared in the *Western Australian Times*.[53] The *Sydney Morning Herald* republished another article the same year, entitled 'A Spiritualistic Exposure *(from the Philadelphia Express, December 17)*', referring to both the photographic term (an allusion to photographs allegedly depicting the spirit 'Katie King') and the exposure of fraud.[54] The satirical suggestion that Manning's use of mesmeric mediumship is not to be confused with the 'tricks of the London *séances*' indicates that her literary strategy for inquiry into nineteenth-century theological debates was considered dubious.[55]

Spiritualism in Manning's poetry in the 1870s evokes the significance of ideas of place, emergent nationalist ideologies and distinctions between the so-called old and new worlds. In the *Town and Country Journal's* review of *The Balance of Pain*, the literary connections between settler colonial and British Romantic poets are addressed explicitly, with these earlier women poets such as Hemans and Eliza Cook specifically mentioned:

> Mrs Hemans, Eliza Cook, and other 'Stellae Minorae' of both sexes, sing songs for, and are understood and appreciated for their mere sweetness and homeliness by the great multitude to whom Eschylus, Dante, Milton, Byron and Shelley are 'caviare' [...] We, 'colonials' as we are, have *our* poets, and real ones too; but *place aux dames*, we also have our poetess, and if 'Australie' has not the tireless eagle-wing of the 'deathless few', she has at any rate the pinions of the dove and can bear the olive-leaf.[56]

It is here made strikingly clear that in the minds of colonial readers Manning is undeniably a 'poetess', situated within both emergent nationalist literary constructions and a transnational literary market in which hierarchical representations of gender, class and place were understood as defining factors in reputation. The reviewer concludes with a comment that 'the talented authoress has hardly done herself full justice in the selection of her poems, as we miss some of her best'.[57] Manning's readers were familiar with her poetry. Both publication and gender hierarchies are challenged by Manning's poetic practice, particularly her use of the theme of mesmerism, and in her newspaper and journal publication.

In the case of poetry such as Manning's, which was appearing in journals and newspapers and was later collected and published in a volume, any idea of a conflict between journalistic and literary genres is rather a reflection of the publication hierarchy, as the individual poems themselves remain largely unchanged, but shift from a perceived ephemeral context to a published volume. Ruskin's view on the value of newspaper publications is suggested by his opinion that 'the newspaper may be entirely proper at breakfast time, but assuredly it is not reading for all day'.[58] Comparisons with the lasting importance of published books are typical of the undervaluing of the literary significance of periodical culture. In Manning's poetry there are binary concepts with which she is concerned: domestic and public; religion and free-thinking; and occultism and separate spheres. It is arguably also the case that the print media was considered a more feminized space than printed volumes for settler women, although not an uncontested one.

Connections and contestations around class politics and women in the poetic and print culture communities are demonstrated in colonial newspaper contexts. One example is a letter signed 'Australie' to the editors of the *Sydney Morning Herald* regarding the boycott of two unnamed women's journals in Sydney in 1889. This was the year of the boycott on Louisa Lawson's feminist journal, the *Dawn* (1888–1905). The *Dawn* was boycotted, ostensibly for its use of non-union labour. This arose from the journal's exclusive employment of women who as women were not permitted to join the union. The letter, published the year before Manning's death, suggests the interconnections within Australian literary and feminist circles, and states of the boycott: 'I can understand the Irish tenant farmers boycotting heartless landlords, but not New South Welshmen treating women in this way.'[59] Like Manning, Lawson was interested in the 'ragged schools', as well as spiritualism.

When examined in the transnational context of feminist discourses on 'The Cult of True Womanhood', spiritualism and theology, Manning's volume can be seen to be challenging the boundaries of white women's personal, political and intellectual agency. The connections between religion, spiritualism and periodical publishing in Manning's poetry reflect international feminist trends of the period, exemplifying a degree of challenge to women's subjugation in poetic, intellectual and political discourses. As Sarah Willburn notes, 'some Victorian women theologians used seances and mesmerism to gain insight into how to achieve progress [...] The point here is that Victorian women who engaged in mystical practices do not fit into the identificatory model of separate spheres'.[60] 'The Cult of True Womanhood', which Agatha upholds, as a woman of faith but without intellectual claims, 'a woman poor in speech, unlearn'd in art' (3), is arguably one such protection for the challenges Manning presents to gender roles, particularly as they relate to marriage, as well as women's involvement in issues of social injustice. Despite any protections it may have afforded privileged women, the ideology of ideal womanhood was irrevocably conceptually embedded in various structural attempts to justify and maintain classism and racism.

Print culture and newspapers were essential to the widespread appeal of both the spiritualism and the domestic ideal and what Welter terms 'The Cult of True Womanhood' so crucial to Manning's poetry. It is important to remember that these developing ideas were disseminated broadly through the periodical press and were certainly known to all the women poets of this study, with Mary Bailey referring to the source text of Sarah Lewis' *Woman's Mission* as early as the 1840s. Manning's treatment of religion is particularly bound up with developments of these ideas of gender roles and challenges to them, in what Welter, writing specifically on America, argues was a feminization of religion. Periodical literature, popular literature and overseas travel would have all acquainted Manning with the rigid expectations of the domestic ideal and its relationships to arguments for women's rights. These ideas were prominent in Australian newspapers of the period, one example being an anonymous poem entitled 'Women's Rights'[61] appearing in the ladies column of the *Town and Country Journal*, to which Manning herself was a contributor.[62] This poem is worth quoting as it is a good summary of the connections being made between the values of 'The Cult of True Womanhood' and ideas of an increased feminine influence and power:

> The rights of women? What are they?
> The right to labour, love and pray,
> The right to weep with those that weep,
> The right to wake when others sleep [...]

The penultimate stanza concludes:

> Are these thy rights? Then use them well;
> Their holy influence none can tell:
> If these are thine, why ask for more?
> Thou hast enough to answer for.[63]

While these lines should be regarded as anti-feminist, they also reflect an ongoing concerted push among some Western women of the nineteenth century for greater influence through arguments of moral equality being made through domestic, maternal and religious discourses.

It is also worth noting that when the *Australian Town and Country Journal* published an article on this same poem 17 years later, in 1890, the year of Manning's death, it provoked the following response:

> We find a poem going the rounds of the newspapers [...] we want to know why a woman has any more right than a man 'to labour and to pray?' [...] A woman to our way of thinking has the right to do anything which she can do well.[64]

This exemplifies important shifts in thinking from the 'True Woman' to the 'New Woman'. The conflict these earlier models of True Womanhood and the domestic ideal reveal is the irreconcilability between the demands of overt submissiveness and covert moral influence, through a tension which at once utilizes and attempts to undermine the dominant ideology.

While Manning's volume *The Balance of Pain*, and its title poem in particular, engages with gendered discourses of religious decline and the association of religiosity with the domestic ideal, the roles of women as well as of the woman poet are central concerns. Manning's approach to questions of equality and social justice do not encompass any question of the rights of Indigenous people and her emphasis on class inequality for the white working class in Australia is approached through the middle-class domestic ideal. Yet aspects of that domestic ideal are also challenged. She does not present the occult and mysticism in competition with Christianity, during this period of shifting attitudes to religion. Rather, both the occult and orthodox religious positions signify ideas of women's power through Agatha. Through the use of mesmerism and spiritualist discourses in particular, the dichotomy between the domestic and public as separate spheres is transcended. Manning's engagement with spiritualism, and the representation and oration of spirit travel through Agatha as a woman speaker in mesmeric trance, allows a kind of poetic voice traditionally not accessible to women poets. This poetic voice is related to ideas of the vatic power of the poet and the ongoing legacies of literary Romanticism. Manning's poetry reflects not only the influence of Romantic women poets like Hemans but also the theological transitions of Romantic legacies amid a continuing women's writing tradition. In 'The Balance of Pain' Manning employs rationalist, religious and occult discourses in order to enable a woman's political voice. Through spiritualism and mesmerism, a disembodied supernatural experience situates these articulations of political voice as separate from a woman's body. Her uses of occultism and spiritualism are suggestive of the numerous links between feminism and Victorian poetic re-engagements with Romanticism and performativity as politically engaged spaces. Finally, Manning's embrace of print culture as a public space for women's poetry (as well as journalism and writing more generally) also involves conscious movement across the so-called separate spheres. Like performed improvisation, as distinct from the printed volume of poetry, the periodical press as a space for women's poetry was also seen as ephemeral. The metaphor of the mesmerized woman as poet situates Manning's work within wider contexts of imperial feminist developments and transnational women's writing traditions.

In combining the writing of poetry and literary works with the reviewing of literature in journals, Manning follows examples like Harriet Martineau, as a figure noted for her involvement in periodical literary culture as well as for her contributions to feminist discourses. Martineau, like Manning, was also an acquaintance of Eliot's, and these two major public intellectuals are significant exemplars of the intellectual literary woman. The complex connections of publication mediums and genres in Manning's writing career are also particularly relevant to the question of what Dallas Liddle terms 'discourse genres', the conflict between the journalistic and the literary.[65] As a space transcending the concept of separate spheres, women's writing in periodicals functions similarly to occult practices, in which 'The medium is a part of a new, if ephemeral, political space several decades before suffrage.'[66] Its presence in journals connects to an extended community, in which occultism and mediumship operate as spaces for imperial and transnational feminist communication of poetic and political voice.

Chapter 5

LOUISA LAWSON: FIN DE SIÈCLE TRANSNATIONAL FEMINIST POETICS AND THE *DAWN*: 1880–1910

> The newly combined and (to women) newly available role of author-editor was a position that could influence the way in which fiction was shaped, produced and consumed [...] it gave women writers control over the dissemination of their work; it provided status, contacts, and remuneration.[1]

Louisa Lawson's poetry and her feminist journal the *Dawn* (1888–1905) are closely connected in obvious and more subtle ways. Lawson published her collection of poetry, *The Lonely Crossing*, at the *Dawn* office in 1905. However, much of Lawson's poetry had first appeared in the *Dawn* and other periodicals, including the *Worker* (1892–1913), the *Town and Country Journal* (1870–1919) and the *Bulletin* (1880–2008). As both the first working-class poet and the first poet to take on the roles of both author and editor of this study, the relationship between print politics and poetry is particularly important to understanding Lawson's approach to literary production. The shift that saw women increasingly occupying the dual role of author-editor in late nineteenth-century British periodicals is reflected in Lawson's practice in Australia. While Lawson's poetry and publishing were engaged with nationalism, it is her international context that I want to consider here. This builds on the work of Heather Radi who notes that the *Dawn* 'had an extensive country readership and intercolonial and overseas subscribers. It was in regular communication with English and American feminists.'[2] The international aspects of Lawson's poetry have received little attention in scholarship to date, yet the high level of engagement with transnational poetic and philosophical influences is important for understanding its political significance. The transnational flows of print culture are reflected in Lawson's poetry too, which appeared in Australian periodicals and the *Dawn* and had readers not only in Australia but also in New Zealand, Fiji, England and Scotland, as well as Europe and America. Lawson initially published much of her own poetry in the *Dawn*.

At the same time, Lawson was also publishing a wide range of other periodical poets, that is, poets who were well known primarily through their publications in journals, newspapers and other periodicals, not only from Australia. In American and British literary studies nineteenth-century women's periodical poetry has undergone a re-evaluation in the past 30 years, and this is less the case in Australia. The broader poetic influences on Lawson as a poet have also been little discussed to date. Lawson's literary inheritance was strongly based in British and American poetic traditions and can be most accurately contextualized politically and aesthetically within these women's poetics, as well as those of the aesthetes and the earlier Pre-Raphaelites. Recognizing the importance of international periodical print cultures to the feminist literary contexts of the *Dawn* reveals ongoing relationships with Victorian popular poetry and fiction. These relationships included engagements with earlier women's sensation novels, often vehicles for the 'New Woman' writers of the fin de siècle. Lawson's poetic imagery closely reflects the tropes and symbolism of American and British women's poetry, including that of Christina Rossetti and largely forgotten American women poets such as Kate Tannatt Woods, Lucy Leggett, Sarah Chauncy Woolsey (Susan Coolidge) and Ella Wheeler Wilcox. The success of these women poets at the time Lawson was writing is demonstrated in their publication in Australian periodicals and newspapers, including the *Dawn*.

Like the work of these poets, many of Lawson's poems are concerned with marriage, the sexual double standard, love, its failings and the theme of renunciation. Isobel Armstrong notes of Rossetti's early works as a concern with 'illegitimacy, fallen women, the fierce legal bond of marriage, the sexual fate of the woman who waits, while the male is given social licence to experiment, the experience of exclusion'.[3] Lawson emphasized the British literary context through the *Dawn* and an article encouraging 'The Home Libraries' states that 'The Editress of THE DAWN also agrees to send any one of the books mentioned below as a premium for one new subscriber to THE DAWN'. Authors listed included Dickens, Bulwer Lytton, Sir Walter Scott, Marryat, Alcott, Mrs. Stowe, Thackeray, Carlyle, Ibsen and Charlotte Brontë, as well as 'Longfellow's poems, Shelley's, Wordsworth's, Keats's, Whittier's, Cowper's, Byron's'.[4] Yet unlike many other periodicals at the time, the *Dawn* was predominantly focused on drawing attention to women writers and women's issues across national boundaries.

As Susan Belasco Smith and Kenneth M. Price note in the introduction to *Periodical Literature in Nineteenth-Century America*, 'the periodical – far more than the book – was a social text, involving complex relationships among writers, readers, editors, publishers, printers and distributors'.[5] This social aspect of the publishing context is itself a significant element of Lawson's poetry, which is based on popular and working-class traditions, linked to the idea expressed by Walt Whitman, that a 'bard is to be commensurate with a people'.[6] Both the political and literary contexts of late nineteenth-century philosophical engagement with socialism, women's suffrage, divorce reform and spiritualism are made explicit in the pages of the *Dawn*, perhaps more so than in Lawson's volume containing many of the same poems. These philosophical and political values permeate the poetic and literary contexts of Lawson's poetry, in which Pre-Raphaelitism, American Romanticism, American women's periodical poetry, 'proto-modernism' and erotic poetics are all operating. Her political approaches to sexuality in her poetry utilize popular floral symbolism and spiritualist discourses to challenge double standards. Characteristic of Lawson's poetry is the mixture of popular and elite forms, along with a combination of class-conscious plain language and esoteric symbolism. The incorporation of these forms is a style mirrored more broadly in the *Dawn* itself, much as was occurring in magazines outside of Australia, such as the *Atlantic* and *Harper's Monthly*.

Lawson's poetry relates to British and imperial contexts in its feminist approach, particularly in terms of its engagement with Pre-Raphaelite aesthetics. The frequent symbolism of dreams, flowers, death, birds, cages and the classical allusions in Lawson's *The Lonely Crossing* (1905) all suggest strong links with Pre-Raphaelite poetry. These symbols have further significance in representing femininity as analogous to birds, especially caged birds, which abound in Pre-Raphaelite poetry and art. Likewise, flowers represent women, particularly their sexuality and courtship in a continuation of earlier traditions. Lawson's 'To a bird' was published in the first issue of the *Dawn* (1888) and suggests the so-called gilded cage of women's oppression through the institution of marriage. Lawson's 'city bird', which had 'once in a desperate rage' kicked over its seed, links freedom within nature and death in the wish that

> when they lay me away to my rest
> And bosom and brain are serene
> Some friend would remember to plant over my breast
> A tuft of that city-yard green[7]

This recalls Rossetti's 'Song' (1862):

> When I am dead, my dearest,
> Sing no sad songs for me;
> Plant thou no roses at my head
> Nor shady cyprus tree:
> Be the green grass above me.[8]

Rossetti's poem appeared in the *Dawn* in 1894, and Lawson's lyrics, like those of Rossetti and colonial women poets such as Emily Manning, evoke spiritualism and the posthumous voice, particularly through dreams.[9] These symbolic discourses in Lawson's poetry mark her engagement with radical politics and women's traditions more broadly.

Louisa Lawson's poetry and Pre-Raphaelite aesthetics

In the context of the *Dawn's* poet's pages the transnational poetic culture Lawson's poetry was engaged with becomes evident in ways that are effaced when her poetry is considered only in terms of *The Lonely Crossing and Other Poems*. From the early issues of the *Dawn* the poetry pages included her own poetry, which appeared alongside those of a wide range of other poets such as Christina Rossetti, Bulwer Lytton and Jean Ingelow, as well as numerous American poets. Periodical poets included Charles Follen Adams and American women such as Ella Wheeler Wilcox, Edith M. Thomas, Ellen Palmer Allerton, Sarah Chauncy Woolsey, Julia C. R. Dorr, Ethel Lynn and Kate Tannatt Woods.[10] Paula Bennett has argued for the significance of periodical literature by American women in the late nineteenth century, pointing out that it tends to be characterized by an ironic rather than idealistic voice.[11] Lawson's poetry does present an ironic voice, but arguably not to the exclusion of idealistic qualities.

It is these tensions between the ironic and the sentimental in Lawson's poetry that create a knowing voice, reflecting Lawson's familiarity with women's strategic uses of poetic conventions. Her poetry is thematically preoccupied with the figure of the woman failed by love and marriage and in this regard is closely linked with developments in women's poetry in Britain and America. Poets such as Elizabeth Barrett Browning and Christina Rossetti notably treated love, as a subject bound up with gender and contemporary politics, with irony and scepticism. This treatment of love extends to much earlier traditions of women's poetry, as Andrea Brady and others have shown through their scholarship on seventeenth-century women poets. A cynicism towards love is distinctly in evidence in Lawson's approach, and these later developments in women's poetry were clearly known to Lawson.

The similarity to Rossetti's approach is particularly clear, as poetry that Lawson demonstrably had access to and poetry that perhaps is most characterized by this attitude to romantic love. Rossetti's aesthetics of renunciation are at work in much of Lawson's poetry, particularly the poem entitled 'Renunciation' (1905):

> While love unsatisfied my heart was wringing
> I would not kiss thy close and tempting lips,
> And while my starving soul to thee was clinging
> I would not touch thee even with finger-tips. (40)

Here Lawson's treatment of romantic love consciously blends both the sentimental and ironic poetic voice through a sexual renunciation positioned in terms of both desire and social constraints on female sexuality. Through both floral and spectral symbolism, Lawson turns such restrictive approaches to female sexuality on this love itself, in choosing to 'kill a passion' and 'cast it warm and pulsing in the grave', at the point at which it is still 'in its virgin beauty', in the lines

> I plucked my love while in its virgin beauty
> And memorised it for I was afraid
> That it might warm to lust or chill to duty;
> Or change to hate, or suffer blight and fade.

Much as a woman might be considered 'fallen' by the standards of nineteenth-century morality, Lawson's poem presents the sexual double standard and the concept of love in these same terms, in which a love may remain pure as if in a so-called virginal state. Lawson concludes the poem

> Forget me now, nor seek to reinstate me;
> I have elected hence to walk alone.
> I love a love, not man; oh, do not hate me –
> A love etherealised that's all my own. (40)

This expresses her love for a spiritualized and non-corporeal form of love instead, suggesting spiritual love and *Philautia* as a form of self-love. Lesbian desire was also signified by spectrality, and while it is not known if this was Lawson's meaning, Tatiana Kontou after Terry Castle notes that 'the metaphor of spectrality has been consistently employed to portray female homosexuality in Western culture'.[12] So in de-corporealizing the representation of love itself as a 'love etherealised that's all my own' a preference for queer love as well as spiritual self-love perhaps could be signified to her readers.

Gender and the libertine

Lawson's poetry is in these ways highly self-conscious in its uses of transnational women's poetic traditions to articulate political commentary on sexuality and gendered social institutions. Conley identifies in Rossetti's poetry 'an ironic counter-discourse within Victorian poetry' and this reading also seems appropriate to Lawson's poems, particularly those that employ a male persona, such as 'Song of Bacchus' (1905).[13] This poem has a mocking quality:

> I laugh ha, ha! and I laugh ho, ho!
> For I think it a goodly thing
> To curse the high and to curse the low
> And to rule both Beggar and King. (18)

Writing in the voice of Bacchus, a classical point of access for commenting on contemporary concerns, this carefree tone is at an obvious and calculated remove from Lawson's own feminist position regarding the double standard and negative impact of men's intemperance on women's lives, which she had elaborated on in various articles in the *Dawn*. The line 'I laugh ha ha! And I laugh ho ho!' is from a folk song 'Will-O'-the-Wisp', which relates to jack-o-lanterns and has Hallowe'en and spiritual connotations.

Lawson presents the bacchanalian in accordance with feminist connections with the women's temperance movement and various aspects of men's unrestrained behaviour. This was an international movement in which many of Lawson's correspondents were involved. Amelia Bloomer and Elizabeth Cady Stanton are important American examples of feminists whose writing is linked with women's temperance. Lawson, like other Australian feminist journal editors in the 1890s such as Maybanke Wolstenholme of *Woman's Voice*, also stood firmly against enforced motherhood.[14] 'Song of Bacchus' indicates her critique of the 'nationalist "masculine" culture that privileged male sexual prerogatives'.[15] Lawson's challenge comes through her parodic mimicry of this dominant culture, which Conley describes as operating in poetry 'whereby a woman restages or represents herself in terms of phallocentric discourse but with an excessiveness which marks her failure to be contained by that discourse. Irony, in its doubleness or duplicity, is one such marker.'[16] Such irony is evident in lines such as:

> I fill with lust and I poison trust,
> And I taint the lovers' caress;
> I love to hate, I'm insatiate
> In my hunger for lawlessness. (17)

This dualistic representation of women's virtue and men's lack of virtue was particularly presented in terms of men's lust, and alcohol is also linked to the campaign for suffrage and to women's challenges to the sexual double standard and marriage reform.

Representations that emphasized women's virtue and portrayed men negatively within suffrage movements included cartoons about votes for women that depicted men as so-called lunatics and drunkards who had the vote while women could be doctors and lawyers without it. Lawson's poetry also reflects the relationship of these representations of masculinity as bereft of virtue to the figure of the fallen woman (also exemplified by Caroline Leakey's treatment of the male libertine examined in Chapter 3). Such representations of masculinity could both reinforce and draw critical attention to the double standards around ideas of women's purity and virtue. These were not limited to the *Dawn*, and they abound in transnational feminist periodical culture around the turn of the twentieth century. While the problematic idea of women's purity had been significant for some earlier feminist claims to moral equality and therefore political voice, and played a part in the culture around suffrage, Lawson's writing also reveals a position aligned with shifting attitudes in which women's sexuality was in some cases beginning to be more widely re-accented in positive ways. But as Ellen Carol DuBois notes of the American feminist tradition, 'the only issue within mainstream nineteenth century feminism where "pro-sex" ideas had a significant impact was divorce'.[17]

Lawson's poem 'The Squatter's Wife', published in *The Lonely Crossing* (1905), raises issues about divorce and challenges depictions of women's sexuality as shameful, depicting the husband as an unfaithful drunkard, while his wife, 'Alice Gertler', was 'a beautiful and gifted girl' (31). As Marilyn Lake notes, this poem was based on an account of an actual case. Such biographical poetics continue the strategies of earlier Romantic women poets, such as Hemans, who frequently wrote of real-life events. Lawson's poem presents the case of a woman who is unable to be with the speaker, who is in love with her, due to both the shame placed on women's sexuality and a lack of access to divorce, suggesting that both are unnecessary barriers to their happiness that could and should be changed. However, the inclusion of an Aboriginal woman as the 'mistress' of her husband in this context incorporates colonial racism into Lawson's feminist discourse around masculinity:

> Bound to one who loves thee not,
> Drunken offspring of a sot;
> Riots he in drink and sin,
> Mating with an half-caste gin –
>
> Alice Gertler

> When I think what thou hast borne
> Painfully my breast is torn.
> Meant I but to pity thee
> But love came, unsought, to me,
> And I'm sad with loving thee
>
> Alice Gertler (32)

The depiction of the drunken squatter as promulgating the sexual double standard through already having a 'black mistress and family' (31) in the lines 'Riots he in drink and sin, / Mating with an half-caste gin —' (32) demonstrates how nineteenth-century ideas around white women's so-called purity and racism were deeply connected.

While the exploitation of Indigenous women by settler men as an instance of male corruption is implied, Lawson's representation attempts to dehumanize the unnamed woman based on her Aboriginality and conceptually links whiteness with moral purity, rather than standing in solidarity. Liz Conor describes how settler colonial constructions had from the 1790s typecast Aboriginal women, replacing individual identity with anonymized terms like 'gin' to discriminate through sexual and racial difference.[18] Lawson's usage of these racist ideas is positioned in terms of her attempt to increase sympathy for Alice Gertler and opposition to men's unrestrained behaviour. Sara Cousins notes that the focus on the changing nature of femininity in historians' approach to the *Dawn* has tended to ignore its representations of masculinity, which she argues 'presented a distinct view of "manhood" to their readers in an attempt to gain positions of power for women' (85). However, where such depictions of masculinity and the sexual double standard involved racism, as Lawson's poem does, they did not mean to empower all women. In the kind of exclusive feminism advocated by settler women, such challenges to inequality were for white women. The ideas of 'purity' central to their arguments for equality were already based in oppressive hierarchical thought, reproducing presumptions of superiority and ignorance of the extreme injustices of colonization.

Lawson's representations of masculinity more broadly reflect those in international journals, as is demonstrated by the cartoon of the American suffragist Victoria Woodhull by Thomas Nast, entitled 'Get Thee Behind Me (Mrs.) Satan', published in *Harper's Weekly* in 1872, in which Woodhull is demonized for her advocacy of 'free love' (Figure 5.1). This demonization of women who did break the bonds of their marriage is feared by Alice Gertler in 'The Squatter's Wife' where Alice would 'talk of sin and shame' (32). The discourse around women's morality is represented in the depiction of a suffering wife as virtuous in the cartoon by Nast.

Figure 5.1 Nast, Thomas, *Get Thee Behind Me (Mrs.) Satan!*, 1872.

The wife who must carry her drunk husband and their children along the path of life symbolically depicts the difficulties and responsibility heaped on a woman in her married life. The caption shows the wife telling Woodhull, who is visually represented as Mrs. Satan with horns and wings, 'I'd rather travel the hardest path of matrimony than follow in your footsteps.'[19] In representing Alice Gertler as a sympathetic figure and portraying the faults of her husband, Lawson's feminist approach differs from Nast's representation in positioning the focus on women's unhappiness in marriage alongside the legal and societal barriers to divorce as well as presenting men's intemperance as unjust.

As Audrey Oldfield has noted, 'In the early 1880s the Women's Christian Temperance Union spread from America to Sydney and other capitals [...] Lawson was never a member of the WCTU but she vehemently condemned the use of alcohol [...].'[20] Intemperance was also conceptually linked with libertinism as examples of uncontrolled behaviour that could include a disregard for its harmful consequences to others. However, there are complex and subversive ways in which Lawson's poetry is positioned against the idea of what Nancy F. Cott later termed 'passionlessness' in women.[21] In Lawson's poem 'Renunciation' and others, women's repression of sexual desire is represented as a conscious choice and a struggle, not a natural state. The ideology of passionlessness is questioned and challenged in Lawson's verse and this critique constitutes a rebellion against expected modes of nineteenth-century femininity.

Divorce and the fate of women

Lawson subverts the perceived immorality of free love and divorce in 'The Squatter's Wife' by presenting Alice Gertler as a tragic figure, trapped in her marriage with a 'fiend', simply because she had not met her true love in time. In the poem, the speaker is Alice Gertler's would-be lover. The speaker tells us that she would not break the bonds of her marriage, however unloved and ill-treated she is within it:

> Still I may not tell thee so.
> Thou would'st scorn me well, I know
> With thy fair cheek all aflame
> Thou would'st talk of sin and shame,
> And with me dishonour blame –
>
> Alice Gertler (32)

Lawson's 'The Squatter's Wife' resembles American poet Kate Tannatt Woods' 'Dan's Wife' (1890) not only in its thematic concerns of unhappiness within marriage but also in its feminist challenges to cultural representations that denied many women's emotional suffering within the institution of marriage. The poems are also similar in their poetic structure, using rhyming couplets with a repeated refrain at the end of each stanza:

> [...] Closed piano, unused books,
> Done the walks to cosy nooks:

Brightness faded out of life –
Saddened woman

Dan's wife[22]

Lawson had published 'Dan's Wife' in January of 1890 in the *Dawn*, 15 years before 'The Squatters Wife' appeared in *The Lonely Crossing*. Woods' poem was widely circulated in American and Australian periodicals. Lawson's representation of marriage in 'The Squatter's Wife' foregrounds the issues of divorce reform and free love, reflecting her stand on divorce reform in the *Dawn*.

Lawson's views closely mirror those of the American suffragist Elizabeth Cady Stanton. Stanton, along with Susan B. Anthony and others, published *The Revolution* (1868–72), a weekly women's rights and suffrage newspaper, in America. In *Voices of Revolution: The Dissident Press in America*, Rodger Streitmatter notes that, 'Elizabeth Cady Stanton and other feminists who raised their voices in *The Revolution* had, in the late 1860s, begun to question the sanctity of the vows that permanently bound a wife to her husband […] Stanton went so far as to advocate that in cases of domestic violence, the only viable solution was divorce.'[23] The exact language used by Stanton is used and expanded to include drunken or criminal husbands in Lawson's 'The Squatter's Wife', and Lawson's 1890 article in the *Dawn*, 'The Divorce Extension Bill; Or, the Drunkard's Wife', puts the question: 'with all due reverence for the sanctity of marriage, can there be anything sacred in the bond which binds a good woman to a sot, felon or brute?'[24] Alice Gertler's love urges her to

> Go to those good men again,
> They who bound with ring and pen,
> Say he's ta'en thy peace away,
> Wronged and used thee cruelly.
> Will they touch thy burden? Nay

Alice Gertler (32)

In addition to the representation of the squatter as lacking virtue, the poem questions the virtue of 'those good men' who represent the legal institutions and uphold double standards in laws of marriage.

However, Lawson does not acknowledge the far greater extent of legal double standards in relation to Indigenous people. Lawson's lack of consideration of Aboriginal people's rights similarly does not recognize that this was also the case in relation to suffrage, in which different sets of laws were enforced. As Judith Smart notes,

The very legislation that granted women the Commonwealth franchise also denied it to Aborigines[sic] except where they retained rights under colonial suffrage provisions. Apart from South Australia, this provision was effective in New South Wales and Victoria, but did not, of course, extend to Aboriginal women in these two states.[25]

Susan Magarey also points out that 'those legislators, who had just passed an Act installing the infamous White Australia policy, explicitly disenfranchised those Aboriginal women admitted to the vote in South Australia and Western Australia and those Aboriginal men who had [...] been enfranchised since the achievement of manhood suffrage decades earlier'.[26] It was not until the 1962 Commonwealth Electoral Act that all First Nations peoples could vote in federal elections.[27]

Lawson instead contextualizes challenges to legal double standards in terms of white men's behaviour and white women's 'purity' and presents their emotional pain within marriage as having a wider international and imperial relevance. Writing of European examples, Linda L. Clark points out that under Napoleonic law in France, the 'husband could seek divorce if his wife was unfaithful, but she could do so only if his adultery reached the extreme of bringing another woman into their home [...] an adulterous woman might be jailed for up to two years, but a man who kept a mistress in the family home faced only a fine'.[28] The law in New South Wales was based on English Common Law, under which, as Joan Perkin states, in addition to the significantly greater requirements for women than for men seeking divorce, 'far fewer divorces were granted to women [...] [I]f a husband ill treated his wife or was unfaithful to her there seemed little likelihood of her getting a full divorce (even if she could afford the action)'.[29] Lawson's own relationship with her estranged husband Niels (Peter) Larsen was financially strained. Brian Matthews notes that Lawson received irregular support and took in sewing and boarders to support herself and their children, adding that 'Louisa learned, when Peter died, just how difficult it was for a woman to inherit from her husband'.[30]

While Lawson's activism around legislature and laws as they pertained to marriage and divorce reform is a strong theme in the *Dawn*, her poetry also advocates for these reforms through the politics of love and marriage. While 'Alice Gertler' presents a deliberately Australian context, Lawson explicitly parallels the lovers in Alice Gertler with the John Everett Millais painting 'A Huguenot on St. Bartholomew's Day refusing to shield himself from danger by wearing a Roman Catholic Badge' (Figure 5.2) painted in 1851–52, in England:

Figure 5.2 Millais, John Everett, *A Huguenot on St. Bartholomew's Day*, 1852.

Millais makes a face like thine
On the Huguenot to shine
What would I not give to be
Like him, forced all else to flee,
But beloved by one like thee,

                 Alice Gertler

This comparison links Alice Gertler's denied ability to love freely with a failure to act politically for fear of persecution. The suggestion is that it would be a political act to reject the social attitudes towards women's sexuality and divorce that prevent their union, while the repression of the desires of Alice Gertler and the poem's speaker, as an act of cowardice, is equated with the wearing of a Roman Catholic badge for protection as in the painting of the Huguenot lovers. Lawson's use of the work of Millais, an important member of the Pre-Raphaelites, is one of the few overt references to this group in her volume. Other references to Pre-Raphaelite themes are less overt, such as the classical allusions to Cupid and Psyche, in Lawson's manuscript poem 'The Flower and the Book', reflecting their significance in Pre-Raphaelite art, particularly the work of John William Waterhouse.

In poetry, Lawson's use of Psyche reflects developments from earlier preoccupations, such as Keats' 'Ode to Psyche' and Mary Tighe's 'Psyche'. Harriet Kramer Linkin notes 'the importance of Tighe's poem as a literary source for much of Keats' writing'.[31] Lawson's usage of Psyche also suggests Lady Psyche in Tennyson's *The Princess*. She may be referring to Tennyson's Lady Psyche's vow never to wed when she refers to 'faint ambush o'er loves quest' (161) in 'The Flower and the Book' (first published in *Louisa Lawson Collected Poems* in 1996 from an undated manuscript poem). The fallen woman is symbolized by flowers in many of Lawson's poems, including 'The Common Lot' and 'The Flower and the Book':

> I bought once in an idle hour
> From off a city stall
> A book, and from its leaves a flower
> I carelessly let fall.
>
> I found a page all deeply stained
> With its dark blood so blue,
> And then I read with senses strained
> This short sad story through.
>
> 'I kept the tryst where Psyche throws
> Faint ambush o'er love's quest,
> And you will find my blood red rose
> Upon her marble breast.' (161)

The 'blood red rose' laid on the 'marble breast' of Psyche suggests a desire for passionate love. This repeats the imagery of the 'dark blood so blue' staining the white page, which suggests the blue blood and the fate of the fallen woman, the financial dependency even of aristocratic women on men and their capacity to 'fall' through sexual desire. The speaker of the poem recalls 'a flower / I carelessly let fall' (161) – a fallen woman whose story mirrors that told by the book, of a woman who 'kept the tryst where Psyche throws / faint ambush o'er love's quest' (161). In Greek mythology, particularly Apuleius's *Metamorphoses*, or *The Golden Ass*, Psyche (who represents the soul) would not marry a mortal but would instead marry Cupid (who represents Eros).[32] Marriage, the soul and Eros are all central to Lawson's late Victorian poetic concerns with white women's political autonomy and equality.

Shifting arguments for women's claims to citizenship from questions of the soul, religiosity and morality into later feminist challenges to the institution of marriage, repression of sexual desire and temperance are evident in Lawson's use of Psyche and Cupid. Rather than idealizing heterosexual love, the poem presents a cynicism towards the 'fruitless tryst' (161). The poem explores the speaker's discovery of another woman's emotional pain through 'a page all deeply stained' in the book, which reads:

'And now I go to hide my pain
Where death's dark shadows creep,
I go but ne'er will come again
A fruitless tryst to keep.'

And as I read the plaint of years,
The word, 'God make us kind',
I found all stained by woman's tears,
Upon the margin lined. (161)

Lawson's cynical approach to romantic love, expressed through the mythology of Cupid, is similar to that in much earlier women's poetry, such as Lady Mary Wroth's 'Late in the Forest I did Cupid see', written in the seventeenth century:

Late in the forest I did Cupid see
Colde, wett, and crying hee had lost his way,
And beeing blind was farder like to stray
Which sight a kind compassion bred in mee,
[...]
Carrying him safe unto a Mirtle bowre
Butt in the way hee made me feele his powre,
Burning my hart who him had kindly warmd.[33]

Lawson's usage likewise, and in accordance with Pre-Raphaelite representations, reiterates the classical in terms of the significance of Psyche to contemporary preoccupations with inequalities in marriage and gender. There is a redemptive quality to the ending of 'The Flower and the Book' in the lines 'Then as I felt the bitter power / Of those sad lovers' pain, / I stooped and raised the withered flower / And placed it back again' (161). In addition to Grecian antiquity as a sexualized discourse, she employs a range of other common tropes that were significant to women's writing traditions, including flowers, and often brings these together.

The contrast between red and white floral imagery reiterates the virgin and whore dichotomy. The 'blood red rose' is commonly understood to be symbolic of sexual desire and passion in women, and the floral imagery and 'dark blood' is juxtaposed with images of 'whiteness' in both the pages of the book and the marble breast, symbolizing sexual purity. The repeated juxtaposing of these images in terms of 'blood' and the 'page all deeply stained' represents women's social punishment in the context of cultural valuation of purity. In Lawson's poetry white is repeatedly linked to death, femininity, purity and the lily. In her 'In Memoriam' (the second poem with this title in *The Lonely Crossing*),

> White and waxen a fair maiden lay,
> White as the snowdrift her beautiful clay.
> White raiment clothed her, and over her bier
> White lilies faded, sweet emblems they were.
> White was her record, and where she is gone
> White is the stone that her new name is on. (58)

The poem's anaphora strongly emphasizes the colour white and takes the traditional English form of heroic couplets.

Lawson's poetry is typically formal verse, employing traditional rhyme schemes and popular and folk forms from working-class literary culture such as the ballad, as forms suited to periodical print culture, rather than a formally innovative poetics. As scholars such as Florence Boos have pointed out, many working-class poets in the nineteenth century utilized traditional forms, particularly those suited to song and oral traditions. While little has been written about working-class poetics in colonial Australian women's poetry, the connections with traditions outside of Australia including Britain suggest 'preferences for ballads and songs over more "formal" genres such as blank verse and the dramatic monologue'.[34] The ballad form, like newspaper publication, was also often understood as having democratic potential. In Lawson's 'In Memoriam' the accessibility, repetition and simplicity of the poetic form are similarly expressed by the repeated emphasis on the colour white.

The repeated use of white in much of Victorian women's writing could be a signifier of the feminine, purity, virginity, the wedding gown, as well as death and the ghostly. Sandra Gilbert and Susan Gubar expand upon the treatment of the colour white in nineteenth-century women's poetry, and particularly in that of Emily Dickinson.[35] They suggest that it functions symbolically as 'a two-edged blade of light associated with both flame and snow, both triumph and martyrdom [...] it paradoxically represents both a divine intensity and a divine absence, both the innocence of dawn and the iciness of death, the passion of the bride and the snow of the virgin'.[36] Yet as Jennifer DeVere Brody also points out, 'the production of purity (for example wholesomeness) depends on the erasure of hybridity',[37] adding that

> So too, the colour white was related to the 'material' in an equation that reads as follows: White = pure = solid = cold = complete = perfect. These concept-metaphors were equated and understood as being not only analogous but synonymous. In Victorian discourse, almost invariably, one term connotes and signifies the others. Thus when most Victorians [...] spoke about the beauty of sculpture, of its pure white forms, smooth unblemished surfaces, and unchanging solid structure, they spoke simultaneously of an idealized form of white beauty that complimented their racialized nationalistic ethos.[38]

DeVere Brody's point demonstrates the ways in which Victorian approaches to the concept of purity as linked to the colour white often connected and intertwined racist and sexist ideas, particularly around sexuality, and Lawson's uses of such imagery demonstrate their connections to the colonial racism of the period. In 'The Flower and the Book' there is a juxtaposing of the white marble breast of Psyche with the 'blood red rose' in the final lines 'And you will find my blood red rose / Upon her marble breast' (161). Although immersed in these ideas of 'purity', Lawson in this way also challenges the ideology of 'passionlessness' in suggesting eroticism, through the placement of the blood red rose, representing passion, on the marble breast, associated with purity, the classical and historical, as an act suggesting both memory and change taking place in the late nineteenth century.

Paula Bennett points out that, for early twentieth-century critics, 'Victorian women's poetical effusions were, as everyone knew, "flowery" (i.e. Sentimental), not erotic' and argues that it is now clear that such poetry reflects 'the evolution of a nineteenth century female erotic discourse *within* the sentimental'.[39] The symbolism of flowers is recurrent in *The Lonely Crossing*. The lily is a repeated motif in Rossetti's poetry as well:

> White and golden Lizzie stood,
> Like a lily in a flood, –
> Like a rock of blue-veined stone
> Lashed by tides obstreperously,
> Like a beacon left alone
> In a hoary roaring sea,
> Sending up a golden fire, –
> Like a fruit-crowned orange-tree
> White with blossoms honey-sweet
> Sore beset by wasp and bee, –
> Like a royal virgin town
> Topped with gilded dome and spire
> Close beleaguered by a fleet
> Mad to tug her standard down[40]

Her poem 'Consider the Lilies of the Field' likewise points to floral symbolism in feminized religion. Lawson's floral imagery and use of classical mythology in *The Lonely Crossing* as well as in her manuscript poetry reiterate constructions of masculinity and femininity that emphasize 'purity' as well as sexual passion and the sexual double standard, through Bacchus as masculine and Psyche as feminine. Idealized classical mythology is used to comment on contemporary social issues, such as references in the *Dawn* to rational dress as encompassing the natural beauty of Grecian antiquity. Robert Dixon notes that neoclassical culture in New South Wales from 1788 and into the nineteenth century formed part of an imperialist approach that was another mode of emergent nationalism and signified connections to Empire through 'the movement of civilization from ancient Greece to Augustan Rome to Georgian England' as well as ideas of 'progress' and colonization in the southern hemisphere.[41] Lawson's usage of the classical to comment on contemporary gender inequality follows that of earlier women poets like Mary Bailey in Tasmania. Lawson's later uses also echo Pre-Raphaelite tropes including an ironic or cynical stance on romantic love. This cynicism is depicted visually in English Pre-Raphaelite artist Evelyn De Morgan's painting, 'Love the Misleader' (Figure 5.3), also featuring Psyche and Cupid (1889).

Along with her ironic voice, an erotic quality is notable in Lawson's poetic approach to romantic love. As Michael Ackland has pointed out, Lawson, like the later poet Mary Gilmore, treats her own experience of marriage as a personal subject rather than a poetic one. Gilmore would state that 'wifehood is a little world apart where none may come in – and so I only write of outside things'.[42] Taboos around women's honest accounts of marriage as a poetic subject are nonetheless broken down by Lawson, and

Figure 5.3 De Morgan, Evelyn, *Love the Misleader*, 1889.

although avoiding direct references to her own experience of marriage, Louisa's treatment of 'the outside things' suggests a profound disenchantment with stock romantic notions. Unless dealing expressly with 'Woman's Love', attraction between the sexes is invariably depicted as ending in the horrors of betrayal and the hardships epitomised by bush unions, or in permanent emotional scarring.[43]

This treatment of love in Lawson's poetry is not only an isolated response to the hardships of bush union, as Ackland has suggested in line with the dominant nationalist reading, but a marker of her positioning within imperial and transnational women's poetry of the late nineteenth century. Such irony is flagged in Susan Conley's critical appraisal of Christina Rossetti too, for example. Likewise, Claire Raymond in *The Posthumous Voice in Women's Writing from Mary Shelley to Sylvia Plath* notes that the poem 'After Death', in which 'a suitor visits the fresh corpse of a woman just deceased and longs for her whom in life he ignored [...] is exemplary of Rossetti's deployment of a lush cynicism'.[44] Rossetti's popularity in America as well as Britain and Australia was significant for developments in the use of ironic voice in women's poetry.

In addition, Lawson engages with challenges to gender inequality through her uses of floral symbolism, as poets like Caroline Leakey had done in the mid-century to question the legal circumscribing of women's sexuality and fallen womanhood. Sam George illuminates the tradition of feminist resistance to the sexual double standard through botanical language, particularly in relation to earlier examples such as Mary Wollstonecraft's *A Vindication of the Rights of Woman* (1792). George points out that Wollstonecraft 'defended botany against prudery [...] attacking those who would limit women's access to Linnaean knowledge. She approved of botany as a female pursuit but she deplored sentimental analogies between women and flowers.'[45] Leakey's usage conversely emphasized these analogies in arguments connecting natural laws and sympathy, while Lawson's use of this language in the late nineteenth century draws on these as established tropes that both reinforce and critique the binary representation of women as virgin or whore. She seems to suggest an active desire present in both the lilies and the roses in the lines in 'A Grave' (1904) 'where lilies grow tall and white / And vie with the moist red roses' (51). Significantly, the churchyard, in which this scene is set, reflects the legality of marriage as an institutional context for the sexual dichotomy.

Lawson's use of this symbolism is highly conscious of Pre-Raphaelite aesthetics and politics. Indeed, the Virgin Mary is said to have been represented by both the lily and the rose, and Debra N. Mancoff states that 'the white lily or *Lilium candidum* was first associated with a fifth century legend of Mary's assumption'.[46] Mancoff's study examines the significance of this floral symbolism, including that of the lily and the rose, to Pre-Raphaelite art and poetry, such as Dante Gabriel Rossetti's 'The Blessed Damozel', in which both roses and lilies appear as emblems. Mancoff points out that 'years later, Rossetti's sister Christina would observe that "Love wears the lily's whiteness, and love glows in the deep-hearted Rose," and by pairing these flowers as the Damozel's emblems, Rossetti declares that love merges the passions of the sacred and the profane'.[47] The churchyard, like the lilies, in Lawson's 'A Grave', suggests both the bridal and the funereal. While the lily is associated with sexual purity, it is also an emblem of death. 'A Grave' demonstrates these preoccupations with connections between floral symbolism, women's sexuality and how fallen womanhood could result in these women's deaths. The 'undecayed' and unmarked grave of the 'Hermit, unknown and found dead on / Rocks at the foot of the cliff' (52) evokes both an alternate solitary experience outside of romantic love and death.

The significance of this Pre-Raphaelite symbolic language can be seen not only in the poetry of colonial Australian women such as Louisa Lawson but also in anglophone women's poetry in India, reflecting the wider imperial contexts informing the reiterations of Pre-Raphaelite poetry in colonial and imperial examples. Toru Dutt's 'The Lotus', published posthumously in *Ancient Ballads and Legends of Hindustan* (1882), demonstrates the ways in which floral symbolism was adapted and reiterated within specific colonial and cultural contexts as part of differentiation from Britain:

> Love came to Flora asking for a flower
> That would of flowers be undisputed queen,
> The Lily and the Rose long, long had been
> Rivals for that high honour. Bards of power
> Had sung their claims. 'The rose can never tower,
> Like the pale lily with her Juno mein' –
> 'But is the Lily lovelier?' Thus between
> Flower factions grew the strife in Psyche's bower.[48]

As K. T. Sunitha argues, in this poem Dutt 'deconstructs the myth of the supremacy of the English flower to valorise the sanctity of a beautiful Indian flower like Lotus. She deconstructs to create anew and refigures postcolonial displacement by synthesising the two flowers – the rose and the lily.'[49] This synthesis of floral characteristics also has important implications for the symbolic separation of 'purity' and sexual passion signified by the lily and the rose, with the lotus representing both at once.

Lil, an abbreviation of Lilly, is the name Lawson gives to the woman in 'The Digger's Daughter' (1905) which begins 'The waratah has stained her cheek / Her lips are even brighter' (*Collected*, 16). In this poem, as in 'A Libertine' (1905), Lawson reworks gender construction, sex and the use of floral allusion. The waratah, a settler-appropriated name for a red native Australian flower, is employed by Lawson very deliberately, incorporating symbolically a flower specific to the region in which she is writing into the transnational significance of floral symbolism. In Dutt's 'Lotus' the speaker similarly links broader floral symbolism with a local flower:

> 'Give me a flower delicious as the rose
> And stately as the lily in her pride' –
> 'But of what colour?' – 'Rose-red,' Love first chose
> Then prayed – 'No, lily white, – or both provide';
> And Flora gave the Lotus, 'Rose-red' dyed
> And 'lily-white' – the queenliest flower that blows.[50]

The meanings associated with this floral symbolism, as Lawson and Dutt's poems both suggest, are also closely linked with colour, creating shorthand ways of representing thought around women's sexuality.

The closely interconnected relationships between women's writing and publication, transnationally advanced by both a feminist poetics and print culture, can be seen in the resonances between the language used across Lawson's writing and that of the American women's press. Earlier American women-run publications such as Amelia Bloomer's *The Lily* were concerned not only with causes that also mattered to Lawson's feminism in the *Dawn*, such as the temperance movement, but also with women's involvement in print culture and the poetic symbolism of the language used. Bloomer wrote, in the first editorial for *The Lily*:

> It is woman that speaks through the *Lily*. It is upon an important subject, too, that she comes before the public to be heard. Intemperance is the great foe to her peace and happiness. Surely she has the right to wield the pen for its suppression [...] Like the beautiful flower from which it derives its name, we shall strive to make the *Lily* the emblem of 'sweetness and purity'.[51]

The symbolic use of the lily reiterates imperial ideas of 'purity' related to the domestic ideal, of women having a powerful moral influence, as well as linking the suffering of Christ with the suffering of women, as Lawson's lines in 'The Petunia' suggest:

> Looked I then up to the river-blue sky,
> 'God of the lily stars, if Thou be nigh
> Show me a sign.' Then my pleading eyes fell
> On a petunia's tender white bell.
>
> Looking straight up to the same God as I,
> Trustingly seeking no sign from the sky. (45)

Lawson's use of the lily also reflects her connection to earlier Romantic women's traditions, particularly Hemans's later poems such as 'Flowers and Music in a Room of Sickness'. of which Julie Melnyk discerns, 'Herbert identifies Edith with the lily, and Lilian's very name evokes "the saviour's flower"'.[52] Religious significance in a flower is also found in 'The Petunia', although Lawson's approach to faith is not consistent, and she articulates a struggle to reconcile white women's suffering with religious faith in several poems, including 'The Petunia' and 'A Mother's Answer' (1905). In 'A Mother's Answer' the speaker questions faith, in her grief for her dead child:

> I doubt for the time where her spirit has flown
> If the love e'en of angels can fully atone

For the loss of a mother's, mysterious and deep.
I own that thought sinful, yet owning it – weep. (59)

In 'The Petunia', in contrast to the woman, there is a religious purity in the white bell of the petunia, 'Looking straight up to the same God as I, / Trustingly; seeking no sign from the sky. / Wafting upon the oblivious air / Exquisite odour – the incense of prayer' (45). Lawson presents the woman speaker without religious faith, walking at night, 'Weeping because I was left by my own / Crushed by misfortune, to suffer alone!' (45).

Dreams and spiritualism

The repeated motif of walking at night or dreaming recalls Millais' image of 'The Somnambulist' (Figure 5.4); it is important to note that this state was perceived by Victorians to have a sexually suggestive quality. Many of Lawson's poems are suggestive of sleeping as a state that may represent a border between life and death, with sleepwalking also being perceived as occult in the nineteenth century, a heightened state of spiritual receptivity akin to mesmeric trance. These themes are also connected with questions of gender, sexuality and morality in the living world, particularly through the tropes of the fallen woman and the angelic woman.

As Leonie Rutherford notes, the poem 'A Life's Dream' first appeared in the pages of the *Dawn* in 1904 as 'Lawson's tribute to the suffragist struggle, "Two Dreams – Twenty years Apart"'.[53] In this poem, the speaker narrates a dream in which 'a woman's form' appears 'to tell thee, sister, we are free':

Then as I rose and dried my tears
It surely did meseem
That they had helped me with their prayers –
The women of my dream. (37)

These lines suggest a spiritual visitation and a sisterhood of spirits supporting women's suffrage. Several of Lawson's poems, particularly 'A Dream', also originally published in the *Dawn* under the pseudonym of Dora Falconer, reflect themes of death, dreaming and walking at night ('Last night as I lay on my bed / I dreamed a sad strange dream' in 'A Dream' (*Collected*, 41) and in 'The Petunia' where, 'Wrung by heart-hunger and pledges unkept / Sleepless I walked while a silent world slept' (45). The poem 'After Many Days', uses the repeated imagery of white in the form of a bird or 'lily stars' or flowers. These are frequently seen against a landscape 'bathed in golden light' contrasted with a 'dark blue sky' or 'river-blue sky' (45)). 'A Dream', originally published

Figure 5.4 Millais, John Everett, *The Somnambulist*, 1871.

in the *Dawn*,[54] narrates a meeting, seemingly on a spiritual plane, with the lover who has betrayed:

> His outstretched hand he offered me,
> And said, 'Shall we be friends?
> And, oh, believe, the change in thee
> My heart with sorrow rends'
>
> 'The rose has fled that once bright cheek,
> The fire has left thine eye.
> Why silent stand? Wilt thou not speak?
> Oh make me some reply!'
>
> I answered 'why dost thou desire
> To open wounds half healed,
> Or, fan to flame a dying fire,
> Deep in my sad heart sealed?'
>
> 'Sad heart', I said, 'no longer sad,
> For I have found a balm
> For every sorrow that I had
> For every storm a calm.
>
> I gave thee honour due by right
> unto a jealous God
> And in thy sudden, causeless flight
> I kissed his chastening rod.'
>
> [...]
>
> I turned to gaze upon the stream
>   Where it had rippled by
>   'Twas gone. Ah me! Deluding dream
>   Nor friend of old was nigh.
>
> Then o'er me did rebellion steal;
> The fight was lost, not won.
> Nor could I say, with righteous zeal,
> 'My God, Thy Will be done'. (18)

The penultimate stanza recalls Tennyson's fifth stanza in 'Mariana in the South': 'Dreaming, she knew it was a dream / She felt he was and was not there / She woke: the babble of the stream' (75). The original version is longer, and the additional stanza between the lines 'My heart with sorrow rends' and

'I answered "Why dost thou desire' reads: 'The rose has fled that once bright cheek / The fire has left thine eye / Why silent stand? Wilt thou not speak? / Oh make me some reply!' This suggests again Lawson's use of the red rose as a sexual symbol, and the imagery is repeated in the later lines 'Hadst thou not blasted on my way / each bud with deadly blight'.[55] These lines remain in both versions.

The explicit suggestion of rebellion and the popular appeal of the poetry of the American Ella Wheeler Wilcox (1850–1919) which also appeared in the *Dawn* are notably apparent in Lawson's own style. Wilcox, like Lawson, had her poetry published in radical papers including the *Worker* in Australia. 'Communism' from her collection *Poems of Passion* (1883) is an overt political gesture; in the preface to *Poems of Passion*, she writes:

> In 'Communism' I endeavoured to use a new simile in illustrating that somewhat hackneyed theme of the supremacy of Love over Reason; and simply to carry out my idea, I represented the Communist emotions against King Reason.[56]

The context of ironic and renunciatory poetry on love provides some ambiguity for the radicalism that is arguably advocated by the 'supremacy of Love over Reason' in both Wilcox's and Lawson's poems. This struggle would seem to refer to the fight between desire and renunciation, and 'The Squatter's Wife' sequentially follows the poem 'Renunciation' in *The Lonely Crossing* and precedes several poems that deal with desire through a spiritual framing. In 'Buried Love' (1905) Lawson depicts a woman speaker haunted by desire for lost love, who asserts:

> But the love we buried deep out of sight
> On the day that we said 'good-bye'
> Must go back in the grave whence it came tonight
> And its ghost in the grave must lie. (47)

Wilcox, like many women involved in literary and suffrage circles, including Victoria Woodhull, Harriet Martineau, Emily Manning and Louisa Lawson, was also involved in spiritualism. The immense popularity of Wilcox suggests that she was a significant influence on Lawson, who published her in the *Dawn's* poet's pages.[57] Wilcox was also widely published in various Australian newspapers and poems by her frequently appeared in the *Worker*, including 'The Rising of Labour', a poem celebrating the uprising of the working class in the tradition of mid-century British Chartist poetry,[58] suggesting the significance of her poetry for radical working-class political circles.[59]

She was extremely popular as a 'people's poet', noted for her plain and colloquial language. In Wilcox's 'From the Grave' we find the same preoccupations with spiritualism and romantic love as in Lawson's work:

> And deep – ah! deep was the grave I made
> But now I know that there is no killing
> A thing like Love, for it laughs at Death.[60]

Lawson's similar use of death's metaphoric relationship to love in 'Buried Love' is linked in her poetry with the idea of dreams and communication with the dead, particularly in several poems grouped together in *The Lonely Crossing* between 'A Life's Dream' and 'In Memoriam'.

Hades is evoked from the beginning of Lawson's volume, in the title poem, 'The Lonely Crossing':

> In it sat one of the fairest ladies
> That mind could mould, in a crown of white
> But close behind a fiend from Hades
> In a chariot black as the heart of night. (9)

Hades is noted by Conley as significant to the poetry of Christina Rossetti, and similarities to Rossetti's treatment of death, and particularly the use of the posthumous voice, are also evident in Lawson's poetry. Claire Raymond contends that 'because they are nearly contemporaneous, Dickinson's troped posthumous poems ask to be read in conversation with Christina Rossetti's death lyrics'.[61] Following Angela Leighton, Conley points out that it is from beyond the grave that Rossetti's women voice a challenge to religious faith, and that the voice of 'the living dead, one who speaks from the grave, is as paradoxical a being as the woman poet; both speak from the traditional position of silence and radical otherness'.[62] Lawson's 'A Dream' (the second poem in *The Lonely Crossing* with this title) uses posthumous voice.

The final stanza of Lawson's 'Buried Love' seems also to suggest spiritualism in the lines:

> For you love to look on a lotus feast
> And drift in a westering way
> But I've set my face to the pregnant east
> Where I watch for a broad new day. (47)

Lawson's poems that involve a sense of communication beyond the grave, such as 'To My Sister' and 'To a Libertine', in which the speaker addresses us from 'hell's awful gate' (17) are suggestive of a poetic mediumship or spirituality and theology that are common to the work of women poets such as Christina Rossetti (exemplified by poems such as 'After Death') and Emily Dickinson.

In Lawson's second poem entitled 'A Dream', the posthumous voice is presented through a dream:

> Just as the grey dawning 'gan faintly to beam
> One still summer's morning I dreamt a fair dream.
> I thought that my body was tenantless clay
> And friends were preparing to lay it away
> They stood at my bedside, one weeping aloud
> While two with deft fingers placed on me a shroud.
> And one who had loved me and knew all my care
> Placed flowers about me and braided my hair. (49)

Catherine Bernard points out that 'in the Victorian age, dreams belonged as much to the supernatural world as to science [...] spiritualists argued that dreams were miraculous events that permitted communication with the supernatural world'.[63] The ghostly use of white in poems such as 'Memoriam' and others likewise links spiritualism with both ideas of sexual purity and challenges to them.

Spiritualism and erotic poetic discourse

Constructions of masculinity, femininity and sexuality are major preoccupations in Lawson's poetry, particularly in poems like 'The Flower and the Book' (which reflects the trope of the fallen woman), 'Song of Bacchus' and 'To a Libertine' (which present the male philanderer):

> I wooed her in delicate fashion
> Then sullied her soul with my lust;
> I poisoned her life with my passion
> And murdered her beautiful trust.
>
> And now her sweet spirit is flitting
> To where other sweet spirits wait
> While I with soul-lepers am sitting
> In torment at hell's awful gate. (17)

The narrative poem is spoken in the posthumous voice of the male libertine. He reflects on the damage done to the woman in life after hearing her speaking the words: 'My life I no longer can bear, / For death I am constantly praying, / Oh, when will God answer my prayer?' (17). 'To a Libertine' draws on the figure of Don Juan, reflecting Washington Irving's ghost story 'Don Juan: A Spectral Research' (1841) which had appeared in *The Chronicles of Wolfert's Roost* (1854). Irving's story is of Don Manuel, who repents after death. He is contrasted with 'the object of his pursuit', a beautiful village girl, who he sees being taken into a convent:

> The ceremony proceeded; the crown of flowers was taken from her head; she was shorn of her silken tresses, received the black veil, and went passively through the remainder of the ceremony. Don Manuel de Manara, on the contrary, was roused to fury at the sight of this sacrifice [...] never had the object of his pursuit appeared so lovely and desirable as when she was within the grate of the convent and he swore to have her, in defiance of heaven and earth.[64]

There is an explicit connection to the libertinism of Don Juan in Irving's story: 'you will find that Don Juan is not the only libertine that has been the object of supernatural castigation in Seville'.[65] As the author of *Don Juan* (1819) and a figure symbolizing the libertine, Byron himself was the topic of an article in the *Dawn*, in which he is described by the anonymous author as being 'in his relations with women [...] singularly cruel and heartless'.[66] Lawson's libertine reflects that he had 'spoiled her sweet spiritual beauty / Then turned her away from the right' (17). This line in the original publication of 'A Libertine' in the *Dawn* suggested violence rather than influence: 'Then spoiled her sweet spiritual beauty / And dragged it down into the night.'[67] These lines also suggest that in Lawson's poetic challenges to the sexual double standard, via the corporeal body and the spiritual, the spirit is given priority.

Spiritualism as a philosophical position emphasized the spirit over the material with important implications for class and gender. Jill Roe gives further insight into the spiritualist leanings of Lawson in *Beyond Belief: Theosophy in Australia 1879–1939*, stating that a 'spiritually distressed Louisa Lawson learned "Zooistic Science, Free Thought, Spiritualism and Harmonial Philosophy" all together from a spiritualist organisation in Sydney during the "Freethought craze" of the 1880s'.[68] This was the decade in which her poems were first published in the *Dawn*. Brian Matthews writes of Lawson's home life that

> Their various dwellings were meeting places for all kinds of people, many of whom were already eminent: Thomas Walker – spiritualist and political radical; Gerald Massy – public lecturer; Justice William Windeyer;

the Hon. Bruce Smith; Chief Justice Sir William Cullen. Louisa's close association with the Progressive Spiritualistic Lyceum at Leigh House brought her into contact not only with spiritualists but also with socialists and republican radicals, as well as many of the women who were to become activists in the Womanhood Suffrage Movement.[69]

As Roe points out, Sir William Windeyer was involved in the theosophical movement in Sydney together with Mrs Woolley (widow of Sydney University professor John Woolley). Lady Windeyer, who was Lawson's friend and a suffragist, chaired the meeting at an afternoon soirée of theosophist Mrs Cooper-Oakley, who had been invited to speak by Rose Scott. Roe notes that some members were concerned about the Women's Suffrage League of New South Wales being associated with theosophy.[70] This concern was a result of the conflation of spiritualist thought with both radical politics and sexuality.

Not only were spiritualist ideas linked closely with marriage reform and free love, spiritualism was also strongly associated with socialist politics, as Perkin notes.[71] The term 'free love' in this context did not mean libertinism within the sexual double standard, which Lawson deplored, but matches made out of spiritual and economic freedom, according to the laws of desire, rather than man-made laws. These ideas had implications too for non-heterosexual relationships. Free love was an idea espoused by Fourier and also by Andrew Jackson Davies, with whose work on harmonial philosophy Lawson was familiar. Earlier in the nineteenth century harmonial philosophy, spiritualism, Fourierism and free love were interconnected, particularly through challenges to the institution of marriage, and 'the Pre-Raphaelite movement revived in the 1850s and 1860s the criticism of coercive sanctions on sexual unions that had been voiced earlier in the century'.[72] This places Lawson's Pre-Raphaelite aesthetic in the 1880s and 1890s into an international context of the poetics and politics of marriage reform and feminist challenging of the sexual double standard and man-made laws. In this context, Lawson's poetry was comparatively radical by the standards of many other late nineteenth-century suffragists.

Through both spiritualism and popular literary culture, Lawson's construction of the *Dawn* signifies connections similarly voicing demand for political representation around class and gender. Ann Vickery has already noted the influence of Tennyson on Lawson, and that the epigraph 'The Shadow passeth when the tree shall fall' from Tennyson's 'Love and Death' also begins Caroline Leakey's *Lyra Australis, or Attempts to Sing in a Strange Land*.[73] This is a reflection of the link between Tennyson and women's rights. Thirty-four years after Leakey published *Lyra Australis*, Louisa Lawson in her introductory article for the *Dawn* had as its first words:

> 'Woman is not uncompleted man, but diverse', says Tennyson, and being diverse why should she not have her journal in which her divergent hopes, aims and opinions may have representation.[74]

Lawson's quotation is from Tennyson's *The Princess*, from which some poems were individually published in Australia, with the volume advertised for sale in various Australian newspapers from as early as the year of Lawson's birth, 1848.[75] As Howard W. Fulweiler points out, 'John Killham has shown that Tennyson was regarded favourably by early Victorian feminists and that *The Princess* had a clear relationship to the feminism of the Saint Simonians, the Fourierists and the Owenite Socialists.'[76]

Lawson's referencing of Tennyson was likely designed to contextualize the journal within the wider feminist and utopian socialist discourses signified to readers in the late nineteenth century. As Leslie F. Goldstein argues, 'Saint-Simonians specifically criticized the modern marriage institution not only on its double standard of sexual morality and its abominably inequitable property relations but also for its rule that the wife be obedient and do the housework.'[77] Tennyson was influential on this emerging aesthetic, which saw depictions of women's emotional and mental states, as in his lyric poem 'Mariana' (1851), in which Mariana waits for her fiancé in vain after her dowry was lost in a shipwreck. Vickery notes that Tennyson's 'Mariana' is echoed in Lawson's 'Lines Written during a Night in a Bush Inn'.[78] The Pre-Raphaelite painting 'Mariana', by John Everett Millais, takes its epigraph from Tennyson. Andrew Leng also points out that Millais' 'A Huguenot' was 'originally planned as an illustration of the line "two lovers whispering by a wall" from Tennyson's short poem "Circumstance"'.[79]

The literary *Dawn*, print culture and socialist politics

Lawson's *Dawn* was highly literary from its first issue. As the publishing context for many of her poems it should be viewed as a vehicle for her own literary aspirations and a political context for her poetry. It is through periodical culture in particular that Lawson would have been familiar with a wide range of women poets, although there has been a tendency in discussion of Lawson's international context to focus much more on the feminist and suffrage circles than on the literary. Through Pre-Raphaelite poetics, Lawson engages with women's rights, class politics and marriage reform in her poetry. The political and intellectual theories of Fourier, Marx and spiritualists in the nineteenth century about gender, romantic love and marriage are also significant for her poetry.

Lawson's all-women operation of the *Dawn* and her use of her own press to print *The Lonely Crossing and Other Poems* reflect her awareness of class as connected with gender politically. While Lawson's was a highly significant all-women-run journal in Australia, such connections are also strong in international examples. The mid-nineteenth-century French utopian socialist feminist paper, *La Voix des Femmes*, founded by Eugenie Niboyet, has been claimed as the first to be all-women produced. *La Voix des Femmes* was also available in Britain in the late 1840s. Claire Goldberg Moses states that the situation in France involved attacks upon women from both the left and the right of politics:

> In 1848–49, the French feminist movement was the most advanced and the most experienced of all Western feminist movements. Yet for the next twenty years, feminists would be unable to move forward. They would have to contend with attacks from the Left as well as the Right. And the only weapons that they would be able to employ would be their pens.[80]

Other journals such as the British *Eliza Cook's Journal*, a weekly magazine for women that began in 1849, also aligned working-class and women's issues. Eliza Cook is best known as a poet and her journal similarly included her own poetry as well as articles and household advice. Cook's poetry was popular in America and was also often reprinted in Australian newspapers.[81] Closer to Lawson's period, women-run journals included that of the suffragist Victoria Woodhull, who ran *Woodhull & Claflin's Weekly*, along with her sister, and was the first in America to reprint Marx's *Communist Manifesto* in 1871.[82]

While the feminist nature of its articles, particularly on women entering the workforce, is overt in the *Dawn*, Lawson's poetry has been seen to be less politically engaged. However, the intellectual engagement with radical philosophical movements in the late nineteenth century evident in the *Dawn* is intrinsic to Lawson's poetry. Likewise, the literary nature of the *Dawn* has been overshadowed by the intensity of its political activism. In the *Dawn*'s first issue Lawson included as an epigraph to the list of contents, 'a day, an hour, in virtuous liberty, is worth a whole eternity in bondage' from Addison's *Cato*. Addison's play has been suggested as a significant text for the American Revolution, given its themes of liberty and resistance to tyranny.[83] *Cato*'s inclusion as a literary text referenced in the *Dawn* demonstrates Lawson's linking of such values with feminism and further suggests the role of international dialogues in this process. As both a revolutionary ideal and a significant element of much Romantic poetry, liberty is a central concept of Lawson's political and poetic practice.

Lawson's engagement with themes of marriage and divorce, for instance, encompasses an ideal of liberty that is consciously opposed to the law as an instrument of oppression, particularly regarding gender, and the way in which gender relates to the erotic. The pseudonym Dora Falconer, which Lawson used both as the editor as well as for some of her own poetry, is another literary allusion – the name of a character in the novel *Only Herself* by (Mrs. Pender Cudlip) Annie Thomas, published in London in 1869. The fictional character of Dora Falconer plays out the fallen woman trope; she ends up alone, having had a flirtation with another man during her engagement to Mr. Falconer. Since Lawson was writing articles under various pseudonyms, it is telling that her poetry in the first issue of the *Dawn* appeared under her own name, as this suggests that she hoped to be known primarily as a poet. On page seven were 'notes by L.A.L.' (Louisa Albury Lawson), a different sign-off that seems to deliberately evoke Letitia Elizabeth Landon's preferred signature of L.E.L.

Yet the poignant reference to Dora Falconer points to the fact that Lawson had produced the *Dawn* herself, as well as to her status as a mother separated from her husband, and highlights the significance of the married state to Lawson's concerns. Largely forgotten today, Thomas's *Only Herself* appears to have been a fairly popular novel, as Lillian Nayder notes in *The Other Dickens: A Life of Catherine Hogarth*:

> Catherine Dickens realized that men often placed heavy restrictions on the property they left to their wives. In the year preceding her husband's death she read Annie Thomas's *Only Herself* (1869), in which these very restrictions provide the central theme. The novel hinges on the status of a widow, Mrs. Bruton, whose husband 'left everything to his wife, subject to [...] one condition': 'If she married a second time she was to forfeit every shilling of the wealth he had endowed her.'[84]

Beth Palmer has pointed out the importance of women sensation writers to the changing roles of women's involvement with print culture, stating that writers like 'Braddon, Wood, and Marryat [...] tread a path on which fewer women had ventured – that of editorship'.[85] Palmer suggests the ongoing significance of these writers to the newer generation of women writers of which Lawson was a part.

Lawson's transnationalism may also be tracked beyond such intertextual referencing. American women poets featured in the poet's page of the *Dawn* included Lucy Leggett who, like Lawson herself, was at the vanguard of women's increasing role in the production of periodical culture. As Willah Weddon has outlined, Martha Rayne had opened a School of Journalism in Detroit in 1886 with the help of several women 'including her good friend Mrs. Lucy Leggett' dedicated to 'helping women enter the field of journalism (at a time when fewer than 3 percent of full time journalists were women)'.[86] Marion Marzolf states that Leggett was the honorary president of the Detroit Women's Press Club.[87] Leggett's poem 'Tired' appeared in the *Dawn* on 1 March 1896 and included an epigraph, 'So tired, so tired, my heart and I', taken from Elizabeth Barrett Browning's 'My Heart and I'. Pauline Simonsen points out that

> In Elizabeth Barrett Browning's poem 'My Heart and I', a woman mourns her dead lover, and reveals her consequent sense of redundancy [...] Redundant women had, by the year of EBB's death in 1861, become an issue of concern [...] Given the Victorian middle-class ideology that a woman's career was marriage and a family [...] the debate about 'excess' women featured in the periodical press from 1860 to 1880. The debate became a starting point for many of the feminist movements of the late nineteenth century.[88]

Leggett's reference to Browning's poem with its links to debates on women's employment is a clear indication of the significance of earlier writers to ongoing debates.

Like Lawson, Leggett was familiar with both periodical debates and poetry. In light of these issues, Leggett's poem is a call to arms: 'What though we're tired my heart and I / It matters not there's more to come / We must live on, we cannot die / Must rise and gird our armour on' (24). One of Lawson's own poems 'All's Well', published in the *Dawn* in 1896 (the poem, although first published there, bears the date 1888 beneath the title), appears on the same page as Leggett's and explores maternal grief. Lawson had also addressed this topic in earlier poems, including 'My Nettie' (published in 1878 in the *Mudgee Independent*), a poem about the loss of her own daughter. 'All's Well' is similar to Leggett's poem in broadly suggesting women's strength in the face of adversity.

The issue of women's employment was of enormous significance to Leggett, as well as Lawson. Both were late nineteenth-century women poets who were actively involved in increasing employment opportunities for women as writers and within the print media. Simonsen also notes the importance of class in these debates, adding that the 'majority of "surplus" women were working class'.[89] Lawson, however, as a working-class woman poet, editor and writer, was entering an especially male-dominated field.

Women aesthetes and 'New Woman' writers: Late Victorian literary contexts and the *Dawn*

Louisa Lawson's poetry was also closely engaged with other related late nineteenth-century literary cultures, including the aesthetes and 'New Woman' writers, as is evident when attention is turned to the literary contexts of the *Dawn*. In *Worldwide Pre-Raphaelitism*, Juliette Peers notes the 'denunciation' of Pre-Raphaelitism by the conservative Australian critic James Smith in the *Argus* in 1870.[90] Peers views this as an embodiment of 'the separateness of Australian critical thought: although Pre-Raphaelitism encountered hostility in England in the 1850s, by the 1870s the movement was largely accepted in Europe and America'.[91] Peers suggests that such opposition to the Pre-Raphaelites was 'rooted in the idea of naturalist *plein air* landscapes as the "proper" expression of white Australian identity' also noting the popular appeal of Pre-Raphaelite art in colonial Australia, and the 'fervour surrounding the Australian tour of William Holman Hunt's *Light of the World* in 1906'.[92] Peers's account of colonial responses to Pre-Raphaelitism, in light of Lawson's engagement, suggests gendered popular and high culture binaries and a perceived hierarchy in cultural value, in which the local or emergent national culture was often presented as oppositional to and devalued in comparison with the continued preference among many colonial Australians for international and imperial culture, like *Light of the World*, even post-federation. Lawson's complication of these binaries can be seen as a significant aspect of late nineteenth-century feminist and working-class approaches. The conservatism of critics like Smith, as a factor informing colonial resistance to Pre-Raphaelite aesthetics, was evidently being challenged by popular engagement such as Lawson's.

Louisa Lawson's poetry was extensively connected with Pre-Raphaelite aesthetics, as suggested already, particularly through the recurrent symbolism of the lily. Peers suggests a lag, or absence even, in the Australian reception of Pre-Raphaelitism in the visual arts, connected with emergent nationalist ideas. Moreover, rather than simply reflecting delayed colonial acceptance, the popular and literary significance of Pre-Raphaelite aesthetics in Lawson's poetry in the *Dawn* in the 1890s reflects an up-to-date connection with the women writers of the fin de siècle. Studies such as Susan Sheridan's *Along the Faultlines* have discussed the ways in which canonical colonial writers, including Joseph Furphy in *Such Is Life*, satirized writers like Ouida.[93] However, the fin de siècle 'New Woman' has a particularly clear relationship to the Pre-Raphaelite woman, and these connections are discussed by Talia Schaffer who also points to the popularity of major women aesthetes such as Ouida with Ruskin. As Schaffer contends, this paradox is what structured the experience of being a female aesthete. The female aesthetes were constantly trying to reconcile competing notions of identity – being female yet being aesthetic; living like New Women while admiring Pre-Raphaelite maidens; trying to be *mondaines* (Ouida's term for cosmopolitan female dandies) but also emulating Angels in the House.[94]

Edited by Oscar Wilde between 1887 and 1888, the aesthetic magazine the *Woman's World* provided a much more feminized and popular culture alternative to the high culture of the *Yellow Book*.[95] Schaffer also notes lilies as an important aesthetic symbol and, likewise, wit as an important aspect of aestheticism. Perhaps following this, the *Dawn* included a 'Wit and Wisdom' section.

Such connections with late-Victorian British literary culture are pervasive in the *Dawn*, with noted women aesthetes and particularly feminized areas of this discourse taking precedence. For instance, the *Dawn* appears to make no mention at all of Oscar Wilde but does make reference to 'Mrs. Oscar Wilde' (Constance Lloyd) in relation to work she was involved in with the free dress movement.[96] Other major aesthetic writers, such as George Moore, are mentioned in the *Dawn* primarily in relation to female writers, such as 'Martin J. Pritchard' (the pseudonym of Mrs. Augustus Moore), noted in the *Dawn* as George Moore's sister-in-law in the section on 'Books – new and old by "Elaine"',[97] an ongoing segment in the *Dawn*.

Literary women associated with the aesthetes, including Ouida (the pseudonym of Marie Louise de la Ramée), appear in the *Dawn*:

> Those who have created an ideal 'Ouida' in their own minds will be shocked to hear that she has a 'ghastly look' with large bold features, haughty and unpleasant though large eyes.[98]

The critical tone of this description is likely a response to Ouida's reputation as an anti-feminist writer. On the poet's page for November 1890 are two poems, possibly by Lawson herself. The first is under the name A. S. Falconer (Dora Falconer being a known pseudonym) and is entitled 'The Dead Baby'. The second, '"Novel" Nursery Rhyme' includes a stanza on Ouida:

> Ouida, Ouida oh indeed-a
> How does *your* novel grow
> With a princess shady, a lord and a lady
> And guardsmen all in a row.[99]

Other writers included in this parody of 'Mary Mary Quite Contrary' were Marie Corelli (another anti-feminist writer), along with 'Mistress Ward' and Edna Lyall. The poem concludes:

> Oh all ye writers of penny soul-smiters
> How does your novels grow?
> With endless chatter of amorous matter
> And wedding rings all in a row.[100]

The poem suggests not only close knowledge of these popular contemporary writers but a tension in the relationship of the woman poet to themes of romantic love in the work of popular and anti-feminist women novelists. As is sometimes the case with Lawson's own poetry, the poem is another example of the working-class tradition noted by Florence Boos, of reworking a well-known rhyme to provide a dissenting truth. In this case, the poem critiques the proliferation of cheap literature aimed at women that limited representation of women's experiences to the sphere of happy romances and marriages, and instead expresses the tensions between cynical and sentimental approaches to romantic love. The uncritical assumptions of these texts that the subject of marriage is always both happy and the only suitable narrative option to be presented to women is, by its placement in the children's rhyme 'Mary Mary, Quite Contrary', likened to over-simplification and fantasy more suited to children's literature than to the literary tastes of a knowledgeable woman.

Such feminist engagements with children's literature and voice in Lawson's writing could explore tensions between innocence and cynicism around gender roles. Ouida, like Lawson herself and many other women poets included in the *Dawn*, was also a writer of children's literature. The title of Lawson's children's book *Dert and Do* (1890–99) is a childlike mispronunciation of the names 'Gert and Joe'. A child's voice is employed by Lawson in her 'Dolley Dear' series, which are addresses from a child to her doll and very consciously written as popular, humorous and light-hearted poetry. In 'Dolley Dear No.14' the child's voice asks:

> I wondered if I prayed would Dard
> Send someping down to me
> And Dranma said 'in torse he would'
> But, dest you wait and see.
>
> I prayed that Dard would send me down
> A nice long drey moustartche, (114)

revealing adult cynicism through a child's vocalization of confusion around questions of gender and ideas of faith in God. These poems are notably absent from Lawson's volume but were published separately.

Louisa Lawson's editorship of the *Dawn* and particularly its literary content may reflect not only the increasingly feminist space of print culture but also feminist reactions away from its perceived limitations. Beth Palmer, in her recent study *Women's Authorship and Editorship in Victorian Culture: Sensational Strategies*, notes that

> The generic characteristics of the periodical form (its capacity for direct address from the editor and response from the reader, its chronological continuity, and its polyvocality) have special significance for women readers at this time, when the woman's magazine as we know it and the women's movement were both taking shape.[101]

Palmer adds that 'Despite the fact that the press was fundamentally enabling for "new woman" writers, there was a widespread perception that fiction published in newspapers or magazines was not culturally valuable and that serial publication was old-fashioned and restrictive.'[102] This was almost certainly even more pronounced in the case of poetry, and this sense is conveyed in the notice of Lawson's own forthcoming book publications that appeared in the *Dawn* in 'Answers to Correspondents':

> As our readers will see the little story '"Dert" and "Do"' written originally for 'Dawn' readers, has been issued in book shape, and by those not bound by prejudice or self-interest has been well and flatteringly reviewed [...] Perhaps it may not be out of place to here further inform our readers that we expect a more pretentious volume from the same pen and office to appear early in March, to wit, 'Poems by Louisa Lawson' to be followed by 'Bush boys' etc, etc.[103]

The passage highlights a number of issues of genre, and particularly hierarchies, in relation to medium, print and gender.

Poetry, here described as 'a more pretentious volume from the same pen', is noted to occupy a higher place within this hierarchy of genre than 'the little story "Dert' and 'Do"', which is both a short story and children's literature, so ranking lowest within these hierarchies. The above passage similarly alludes to the hierarchy of value assigned when any genre of literature is seen as having only been published in the popular and ephemeral space of periodicals, rather than having the prestige of a book. Given that women's writing was often relegated to these more 'ephemeral' and 'maternal' literary spaces, there is an implication that women's writing is less valuable, an idea which is undermined and strongly critiqued here by the assertion that 'those not bound by prejudice or self-interest' had 'flatteringly reviewed' 'Dert' and 'Do'.[104] This feminist assertion about the value of women's writing within these spaces is included in the announcement of Lawson's forthcoming volume of poetry, which represents a departure from these more feminized and devalued spaces.

Lawson's poetic engagement with mid-nineteenth-century Pre-Raphaelites in 1880s and 1890s Australia is highly relevant to the feminism of the 1890s, through both its radicalism and its thematics of death, love, gender and isolation. Lawson's use of restrained lyricism is also marked by a deliberate departure from the stylistics of a high literary elitism, in preference for a simplified, working-class vernacular. This strategic move by Lawson marks an important shift in the development of poetics in Australia. Geographically distant from the poetic contexts of Pre-Raphaelitism, popular American poetry and late nineteenth-century metropolitan literary culture, particularly of women poets working in these modes, Lawson's poetry has not been recognized for its literary or politically radical qualities. Likewise, the perception that poems such as 'To a Libertine' are morally opposed to sex in general rather than having a complex relationship to the sexual double standard is too simplistic.

Rather, Lawson's poetry shows her support for the frankness of the 'New Woman' towards sex and her vision of the liberation of 'the coming woman'. She had represented the future generation of Australian girls in the article 'The Australian Bush Woman' as a source of strength and hope for the women's movement. Through her immersion in periodical print culture, Lawson was in discourse with various women's publications internationally and this article is one example, having been first published in the *Woman's Journal* in Boston, then reprinted in *The Englishwoman's Review of Social and Industrial Questions* in 1889.[105] Lawson's poetry likewise reflects how transnational discourses on woman's love, and its relationships to class and gender, were articulated through strategies such as ironic voice and the use of floral symbolism. Moreover, these were also adapted to Australian flowers and contexts, often simultaneously supporting a feminized emergent nationalism as linked to ideas of 'progress' and white women's rights. While Mary Arseneau points out in her introduction to *The Culture of Christina Rossetti* that recent scholarship 'debunks the obsolete portrait of Rossetti as an unlearned and reclusive spinster, remote from current ideological debate' the misconception that Lawson's poetry is not connected closely with international contexts of suffrage, divorce reform and feminist activism is yet to be adequately addressed.[106]

By recontextualizing Lawson's poetry in terms of the legacy of Romantic traditions and Pre-Raphaelite aesthetics, its philosophical grounding and limitations are better understood. As well as thematic similarities, Lawson's poetry utilizes restrained, ironic and posthumous voice in its challenges to inequalities. Lawson's approaches as a poet can be best understood by resituating these works within a wider imperialist context of late-Victorian feminist literature and earlier Pre-Raphaelite and Romantic women's poetry and writing in the nineteenth century. The restrained lyricism of apparent straightforward simplicity reflects strategic relationships to women's sentimental poetic traditions. Dolores Rosenblum has shown that this restrained poetics is part of a nineteenth-century women's writing tradition and can be traced also to some of the much earlier sentimental women poets, notably Carolina Nairn and Caroline Southey.[107] The development of both a restrained and sentimental poetics relates as well to working-class women's traditions and song forms, in their memorability, accessibility and dissenting voice. Florence Boos points out that much working-class women's poetry refers to well-known poetry or song, but with a desire to reinterpret it with what she terms a 'corrective truth – a dissenting "memorie"'.[108] Lawson's poetry operates in connection to working-class traditions and reinterprets popular women poets such as Ella Wheeler Wilcox and Kate Tannatt Woods. Her poetry was also highly conscious of the role of popular poetry of America and Britain in political causes such as woman suffrage and socialist organization, though anti-racism is crucial to any poetics genuinely aimed at liberation. Lawson's poetry is often poised between the sentimental and ironic in its activism, as much as it also incorporates a popular class-conscious voice with symbolic, mythological, spiritualist and theological poetic discourses. Lawson's poetry, particularly when viewed as part of imperial feminist literary traditions, reveals shifting approaches to women's rights and sexuality. Lawson's use of plain language and her approach to themes of love, class and sexuality mark her influence in Australian poetry.

CONCLUSION: BEYOND THE *DAWN*

The consideration of some of the ways political voice operated in settler women's poetry, especially that published in newspapers and journals, has implications for how colonial poetry and its relationships to poetry in the twentieth century and beyond are read. In concluding this book with a chapter on the poetry of Louisa Lawson, I mean to situate the links her poetry has to the ongoing legacies of earlier Romantic and Victorian women's traditions as well as to poets who would follow. This book considers a sample of nineteenth-century white settler women poets in Australia and ways their poetry, far from being isolated and apolitical, demonstrates close relationships to rights movements outside of Australia and the connections between imperial feminism and colonialism. Their close continuations and engagements with British and European poetic traditions and discourses differ greatly in that these women were published in the contexts of colonialism, horrific genocidal intent, massacre, enslavement, human rights abuses and dispossession of Indigenous peoples. Settler women's poetic expressions of political voice must be understood in connection to the extreme injustices of invasion and colonialism.

The examination of political voice in these women's poetry makes clear that the relationships of rigid colonialist ideas of binary gender to the developments of colonial poetry and emergent nationalism, and to how these have subsequently been represented and understood, is more significant than has been recognized. The themes of the women poets discussed reflect political concerns and positions in relation to gender, including engagements with classical mythology, religious and theological debates, floral symbolism and spiritualism. These themes situate these five poets within the imperial feminist and transnational contexts of anglophone women's poetry in the nineteenth century. As Aileen Moreton-Robinson notes, these contexts were influenced by Mary Wollstonecraft, who 'showed that the Enlightenment's ideal of a universal human nature meant in practice two codes: one code constituted the feminine and the other the masculine'. Yet, such analyses 'by making invisible race and class in their representation of gender oppression, were by omission centring the life experiences of middle-class white women [...] The articulation of gender as the primary form of identity and oppression became the basis of white feminist epistemology and political action.'[1]

The engagements of these poets with white feminist, canonical and popular British, European and North American literary and philosophical texts are particularly focused on the implications for them in terms of gender. Their reworking of aspects of now canonical British texts, such as Byron's *The Giaour* (1813) in Dunlop's 'Morning on Rostrevor Mountains' or 'Hints from Horace' in Bailey's Hellenism and *Don Juan* (1819) in Leakey's and Lawson's fallen woman trope, similarly renegotiate these texts only with awareness of gender inequality and building arguments for white women's claims to citizenship. Isobel Armstrong has suggested of the British context that 'the politics of women's poetry in this century cannot necessarily be associated with the uncovering of particular political positions but rather with a set of strategies or negotiations with conventions and constraints'.[2] Such negotiations and strategies necessarily relate to limited degrees of resistance that could operate through binary approaches based in Western conceptualizations of women's 'deficient' intellectual, moral, sexual and political value and the domestic ideal. While negotiations are often an aspect of nineteenth-century settler women's poetry in colonial Australia, these poets also built on and looked back to earlier British Romantic women's traditions.

These Romantic women's writing traditions and legacies are particularly significant in terms of the question of political voice, and as a part of resistance to the increasing constraints these women faced. This feminist resistance, in association with imperialism, was subsumed into capitalist imperialist Western expansion rather than liberation. As Anne Mellor has pointed out on British women's Romanticism, this movement, like that of 'masculine' Romanticism, can be understood broadly as 'a reformist bourgeois movement, one that served the interests of upper- and middle-class women at the expense of working class women' and, as such, was one that 'too easily fell prey to a conservative Victorian backlash that reasserted a bourgeois patriarchal authority over both the public and private sphere'.[3] Yet Anne Janowitz has demonstrated that the legacy of Romanticism also had a clear ongoing significance to political movements during the nineteenth century, in situating 'the power of romantic lyric discourse, not as an ideology of seamlessness, but as a matrix within which debate about past and present was invented and persists'.[4] In drawing on earlier British and transnational women's traditions in accessing themes of abolition, 'fallen' womanhood, sexuality and spiritualism, common across British and settler women's poetries, including North American examples, these connections aimed to challenge aspects of white women's inequality amid concerns with increasing constraints and their continued exclusion from citizenship and suffrage.

CONCLUSION

These settler women's publishing, openly as women, in newspapers and journals and particularly in ballad form, was often understood as active participation in a more democratic and accessible space than published books, but also as one connected with imperialist reproduction. As a continuation of the periodical literary culture that had been the underworld of British Romantic literary culture, these women's poetry in colonial newspapers could be circulated widely and could be readily understood in terms of its relationships to popular culture, song and working-class forms. While these poets often consider class, especially its relationships to transportation, sexuality and gender, their poetic expressions of political voice were most often without any questioning at all of racism and imperialism. These women's imperial feminist approaches and limited considerations of questions of rights operated through presumptions of Western superiority and the linking of ideas of feminist 'progress' with imperialism. Their complicity with imperialism and the inherent violence of settler colonialism, as well as frequent lack of any acknowledgement of Indigenous peoples and attitudes of superiority, were deeply harmful and racist. The women poets of this study demonstrate a consistent engagement across the nineteenth century with white women's rights movements and understandings of gender, as well as various aspects of developing imperial and emergent nationalist feminist discourses.

It is important to recognize that these settler women's political voices in a developing feminist poetics were characteristically connected with imperial world views and discourses, reproducing empire and centring white women's experiences in approaching questions of rights. These could operate through imperialist ideas of settler women's independence being linked to the colonies as well as through arguments for reforms to existing legislation that maintained inequality there. This most often included participation in the arguments that were developing across the nineteenth century through imperial and transnational movements in the lead-up to white women's suffrage, within the structures of an imposed representative democracy. As such, their writing participated in rather than directly challenged broader structural oppression, most obviously the invasion, genocidal intent, human rights abuses and enforcement of British colonial law on Aboriginal land through the legal fiction of terra nullius.

In recognizing an imperial feminist poetic movement within colonial poetry, and the imperialism in which that writing participates, it is also useful to situate these writing traditions within the plurality of feminisms. Within imperial feminism, arguments were being made through developing discourses around ideas of a gender binary that emphasized white women's sympathy, motherhood and 'purity' in relation to 'morality' over the course of the nineteenth century. The description of the figure of the 'sympathetic' white woman in colonial literature as 'unsettling' is euphemistic. Rather it reveals a deeply damaging structural position serving the interests of both an exclusive feminism and those of imperialism. Just as the middle-class domestic marriage can be understood as signifying a particular social 'order' based in separate spheres ideology and the interlocked coding of class and gender in nineteenth-century British literature, we might similarly understand the functioning of feminine 'sympathy' and 'morality' as being coded within the imperial concept of 'civilizing' in white settler women's poetry.

These popular imperial feminist discourses often presupposed gender to be middle class, white and essentially binary and hierarchical. Consequently, they reproduced hierarchical thinking in taking ideas of women's supposed essential differences as a moral starting place to counter arguments of women's 'inferiority', rather than acknowledging the inherent equality of all people as a starting point. In falsely positioning white women's rights as attainable only through demonstrations of 'moral superiority' and 'purity' as values that would deem them worthy, the imperialist discourse simultaneously positioned those very same values as central to the expectation that white women fulfil a so-called civilizing role. As such these arguments for rights were deeply entrenched in racist ideology. These women's poetics demonstrate networked engagements with such approaches, remaining in dialogue with imperial and transnational feminist developments in anglophone women's poetry across the nineteenth century.

These developments linked discourses and communities of writers through print culture and particularly newspapers, and through women's Romantic traditions, legacies of literary Romanticism and Victorian poetics. These connections are important to recognize in breaking down the myth of settler women poets in colonial Australia as either absent or isolated, marginal and apolitical. Rather, these women's poetic relationships to British and transnational Romantic and Victorian women's traditions, as well as the connections they involved between imperial and feminist discourses, have been effaced through white masculine nationalist constructions of literary history. In the subsequent reading and categorization of these settler women's poetry, where it has been considered, the political implications of their work have often been lost through nationalist prioritization and the legacies of bush nationalism. The subsequent absence or misunderstandings of these women's political poetic voices from constructions of colonial poetry in literary histories has facilitated readings that present colonial poetry as failed sporadic attempts at establishing an emergent nationalist literature and an 'absence' of Romanticism.

This supposed absence has allowed for a later nineteenth-century white masculine nationalist 'Australian' literature characterized by the idea of the supposedly anti-authoritarian, communal and egalitarian ballad, to be positioned as a 'national' literature disconnected from Britain and British imperialism. The poetry of women like Eliza Hamilton Dunlop, Mary Bailey, Caroline Leakey, Emily Manning and Louisa Lawson, on the contrary, demonstrates a lineage of closely connected poetics highly engaged with imperial feminist discourses and Romantic poetic traditions and legacies, that was consistently politically engaged in the deployment of these 'negotiations' in colonial contexts. In considering how relationships between binary constructions of gender and settler poetry functioned within nineteenth-century imperialism, British Romantic traditions and the emergence and development of Australian nationalist literature must be recognized as connected. Foremost, these connections must be viewed in relation to justice and rights of First Nations peoples and traditions as the oldest living cultures in the world.

APPENDIX: SELECTED POEMS

As the newspaper poetry discussed in Chapters 1 and 2 may not be available, the following poems are included for reference.

Eliza Hamilton Dunlop

THE ABORIGINAL MOTHER

Oh! Hush thee – hush my baby,
    I may not tend thee yet.
Our forest-home is distant far,
    And midnight's star is set.
Now hush thee – or the pale-faced men
    Will hear thy piercing wail,
And what then would thy mother's tears
    Or feeble strength avail!

Oh, couldst thy little bosom,
    That mother's torture feel,
Or could'st thy know thy father lies
    Struck down by English steel;
Thy tender form would wither,
    Like the *kniven* in the sand,
And the spirit of my perished tribe
    Would vanish from our land.

For thy young life my precious,
    I fly the field of blood,
Else had I, for my chieftain's sake,
    Defied them where they stood;
But basely bound my woman's arm,
    No weapon might it wield:
I could but cling round him I loved,
    To make my heart a shield.

I saw my firstborn treasure
      Lie headless at my feet,
The goro on this hapless breast,
      In his life-stream is wet!
And thou! I snatched thee from thy sword,
      It harmless passed by thee!
But clave the binding chords – and gave,
      Haply, the power to flee.

To flee! My babe – but wither?
      Without my friend – my guide?
The blood that was our strength is shed!
      He is not by my side!
Thy sire! Oh! Never, never
      Shall Toon Bakra hear our cry:
My bold and stately mountain-bird!
      I thought not he could die.

Now who will teach thee, dearest,
      To poise the shield and spear,
To wield the *koopin*, or to throw
      The *boommering*, void of fear;
To breast the river in its might;
      The mountain tracks to tread?
The echoes of my homeless heart
      Reply – the dead, the dead!

And ever must the murmur
      Like an ocean torrent flow:
The parted voice comes never back,
      To cheer our lonely woe:
Even in the region of our tribe,
      Beside our summer streams,
'Tis but a hollow symphony –
      In the shadow-land of dreams.

Oh hush thee, dear – for weary
      And faint I bear thee on –
His name is on thy gentle lips,
      My child, my child, *he's gone!*
Gone o'er the golden fields that lie
      Beyond the rolling clouds,
To bring thy people's murder cry
      Before the Christian's God.

Yes! o'er the stars that guide us,
  He brings my slaughter'd boy:
To shew their God how treacherously
  The stranger men destroy;
To tell how hands in friendship pledged
  Piled high the fatal pire;
To tell, to tell of the gloomy ridge!
  and the *stockmen's human fire.*
              (*The Australian* (1838): 13 December, 4)

INSCRIBED TO THE MEMORY OF E. B. KENNEDY,

Who lost his life on an exploring expedition in tropical Australia.

'O'er that forsaken sepulchre banner and plume might wave' – L.E.L

Bewail him not! – Oh, bewail him not! –
  Though sunk to his rest in his spring-tide of fame;
For oh, there are hundreds who, mourning his lot,
  Yet sigh for the triumph that circles his name!

Bewail him! – no! – 'twas a glorious quest
  His spirit sustained in that far-off wild;
Upborne by a gift, ever blessing and blest,
  The resolve of a martyr, the trust of a child!

Bewail him not! – Oh, bewail him not! –
  Even there, where the spear of the savage was hurled,
No holy affection, no duty forgot,
  He passed to his Saviour, unscathed by the world!

Bewail him not! – Oh, bewail not the dead! –
  No malice can taint him, no envy pursue! –
Wild palms and glycenes shall shadow his bed!
  Mementos of Kennedy – 'tender and true!'
      (*The Maitland Mercury & Hunter River General Advertiser* (1849): 8
                                                            August, 4)

MORNING ON ROSTREVOR MOUNTAIN,
IN ULSTER IRELAND

'Tis morning! from their heather bed
  The curling mists arise;
And circling dark slieve-dhonard's head

　　　　Ascend the drowsy skies.
'Tis morning! And beside 'CHLOCH-MHOR'
　　　　In solitude I stand,
A stranger on my natal shore,
　　　　And this my Fatherland!

ROSTREVOR! Each illumined line
　　　　Of early life's romance,
Within this beauteous page of thine
　　　　Lies mirror'd to my glance:
Clonullen's spire, *Rosetta's* shades,
　　　　From classic *Arno's* vale,
To *Ballyedmond's* groves and glades –
　　　　Land of my homage, hail!

Morning! The beautiful, the bold,
　　　　Hath left his ocean bride.
And from her couch of wavy gold
　　　　Comes forth, in regal pride.
Ah me! I've seen that crown of rays
　　　　As gallantly put on,
And watched thy robe of crimson haze
　　　　O'er other waters thrown.

Rocked on the billowy bed that heaves
　　　　Beneath the burning *Line*,
I've marked where the horizon weaves
　　　　Its purple threads with thine
And hailed in all their pride of birth,
　　　　Thy purest lustres given,
To gladden scenes more fair than earth –
　　　　The sea! The sea, and heaven!

Where the wild emu leads her brood
　　　　Across the trackless plains,
And lord of nature's solitude –
　　　　The stately cedar reigns;
Even there, through exile's cheerless hours,
　　　　Lighted by Austral skies,
I've linger'd amid orange flowers
　　　　To catch thy scented sighs.

Yes, and where GUNGA'S mighty streams
    Their sacred waters spread,
I've seen, beneath thy worshipped beams,
    Ten thousands bow the head:
And by the *Brahmin's* funeral pile,
    In that far hemisphere,
Young MORN! Have I not met thy smile,
    Mocking the burning bier?

In SAUGUR'S sickly jungle met?
    And on the arid sand,
Where the dark domes of JUGHERNAUGHT'S
    Profane PAGODAS stand?
Aye, met, ev'n 'mid the grave-yard gloom,
    Piercing the tainted air,
Thy sick'ning rays – a marble tomb –
    Engulphs my memory there.

Once, high o'er Afric's southern seas
    In solitary mood,
Within the 'vale of SILVER TREES',
    On Table hill, I stood –
The fresh free breeze, the morning beam –
    The vapour-crested brow,
Of CAFFRE-HOLLAND, as a dream,
    All come before me now!

Again adown *that* deep ravine
    I gaze on fruit and flower –
A labyrinth maze of silky green,
    A many-tinted bower.
Tall *Aloes* crown the rocky steep.
    Pomegranate blossoms spread,
And the umkoba's branches sweep
    Across the torreut's bed.

Blushes yon crassula, as when
    Its scarlet blossoms lay
In the wild fig or *sumach glen*,
    That looks on Table Bay;
And, bearing up by ROBEN ISLE,

From farthest India's shore,
That ship – false dreams! Ye but beguile –
I stand beside *Chloch-mhor*!

(*The Atlas* (1845): 25 April, 257)

Mary Bailey

A VOICE, FROM ASS-MANIA!!
OR
NEDDY'S BRAY

Suggested by a perusal of a poem entitled 'A Voice from Tasmania' by Edward Kemp, Esq.

Ass intones to Ass,
Harmonic twang.
POPE; Dunciad, Book II

By good master Aesop we're told of an Ass,
Who in impudence did all his fellows surpass; –
He'd fain be a *Lion*, but how this could be
The aspiring young Jackass was unable to see;
So he shook his long ears, and, in sorrowing mood,
Traversed slowly and sadly the skirts of the wood.
Not '*the Sun up above nor the fresh flowers below*'
Afforded him the least solace for woe –
So sad was his heart, while he lifted his eyes
Which '*searched*' long '*in vain for their own bright skies!!!*'
It chanced that he found the old skin of a Lion
Which the asinine beast thought at once he would try on.
The beasts of the forest, in terrible fright,
When they saw this strange monster, at once took to flight:
Till a cunning old Fox chanced to pass by that way,
As this *Lion-that-wou'd-be*, 'gan loudly to bray;
Says the Fox – 'a Lion you wish to appear,
But I know what you are now your braying I hear;
Could you keep your own counsel, conceited young Ass,
For a Lion, with some, *perhaps* you might pass:
But that voice so *disgusting*, so *brazen*, so *loud*
Would dub you an Ass – if you're ever so proud!'

M. B. Sandy Bay, 5 July 1847 (*Hobarton Guardian* (1847):
10 July, 4)

THE EXILE'S WIFE TO HER HUSBAND
(Written for the *Guardian*)

'Urge me no more: I could not bear
Thee to go forth alone.
Thou wert indeed an exile then
A hopeless friendless one.

I *will* go with thee, I have weighed
The dangers that betide;
And I am sure the safest place
Is by my husband's side.

Oh! There are other skies as bright,
And other lands as fair;
Where yet thou mayest dwell in peace,
Although an exile there.

Exile! I had not thought to hear,
That coupled with thy name;
Yet, Dearest, it can never be,
To thee the brand of shame.

There is no crime upon thy head –
No guilt upon thy brow:
I still may honour, while I love –
Then, could I leave thee now.

My kindred – friends – when thou wert gone
What would they be to me?
I quit my native land – but, Oh!
My home is still with THEE.'

    Mary, Hobarton, 29 June 1847
  (From the *Guardian, or True Friend of Tasmania* (1847):
          3 July, 4)

THE DEATH OF POMPEY

Upon occasion of a friend's dog, called POMPEY, being accidentally strangled to death by the chain of another canine playmate, called SAPPHO.

'All fall alike – the fearful and the brave'
     POPE: Homer

Shall I in Sapphic verse, relate
Poor curly POMPEY'S wretched fate?

Or shall my plainer verses tell
The awful chance which him befell?

Fair was the day! The sky was bright.
And POMPEY frisk'd with great delight:
By SAPPHO'S kennel he would play
Upon that jocund holiday!

Alas! Old POMPEY, for the hour,
Which brought him near dark SAPPHO'S bower;
Her ponderous chain she o'er him cast,
And iron links secured him fast!

Round went the chain – his throat around
And raised poor POMPEY from the ground;
While SAPPHO marvelled much to see
Her favourite thus in jeopardy!

He struggled – but, t'was all in vain –
Death soon released him from his pain:
While even SAPPHO almost cried,
When thus her aged playmate died.

SAPPHO and POMPEY – mighty names!
They each have set the world in flames!
POMPEY THE GREAT by wars and arms
But SAPPHO – by poetic charms!!

M. B. Sandy Bay, 15 September 1848
        (From the *Colonial Times* (1848): 19 September, 4)

NOTES

Introduction: Rereading Colonial poetry

1 Alexis Easley, *First-Person Anonymous: Women Writers and Victorian Print Media 1830–1870* (Burlington: Ashgate, 2004), 2.
2 Anita Heiss and Peter Minter, eds, 'Aboriginal Literature', *Macquarie Pen Anthology of Aboriginal Literature* (Crows Nest: Allen and Unwin, 2008), 1–9 (2).
3 Ibid.
4 Ann Vickery, 'A "Lonely Crossing": Approaching Nineteenth-Century Australian Women's Poetry', *Victorian Poetry* 40.1 (2002): 33–54 (34).
5 David Damrosch, *What Is World Literature?* (Princeton: Princeton University Press, 2003), 4.
6 Lynda Ng, 'Inheriting the World: German Exiles, Napoleon's Campaign in Egypt, and Australian Multicultural National Identity', in *Scenes of Reading: Is Australian Literature a World Literature*, ed. Robert Dixon and Brigid Rooney (North Melbourne: Australian Scholarly, 2013), 156–67 (158).
7 Clare Midgley, *Feminism and Empire: Women Activists in Imperial Britain, 1790–1865* (Oxon: Routledge, 2007), n.p.
8 Isobel Armstrong, Joseph Bristow and Cath Sharrock, *Nineteenth Century Women Poets: An Oxford Anthology* (New York: Clarendon Press, 1996), 254.
9 Elizabeth Webby, 'Australian Literature and the Nation', Rev. of *The Oxford Literary History of Australia*, by Bruce Bennett, Jennifer Strauss and Chris Wallace-Crabbe, *Southerly* 59.1 (1999): 167.
10 Philip Butterss and Elizabeth Webby, 'Introduction', in *The Penguin Book of Australian Ballads* (Ringwood: Penguin, 1993), xvii.
11 Michael Ackland, *That Shining Band: A Study of Australian Colonial Verse Tradition* (St Lucia: University of Queensland Press, 1994), xi.
12 Susan Pfisterer-Smith, 'The Louisa Factor: The Historical Treatment of Louisa Lawson', in *Louisa Lawson: Collected Poems with Selected Critical Commentaries*, ed. Leonie Rutherford and Megan Roughley with Nigel Spence (Armidale: University of New England, 1996), 275–83 (275).
13 Rosalind Smith, 'Australie (Emily Manning)', in *Australian Dictionary of Biography: Australian Literature 1788–1914*, ed. Selina Samuels (Detroit: Gale Group, 2001), 20.
14 Ackland, *That Shining Band*, xi.
15 Elizabeth Webby, 'Born to Blush Unseen: Some Nineteenth Century Women Poets', in *A Bright and Fiery Troop: Australian Women Writers of the Nineteenth Century*, ed. Debra Adelaide (Ringwood: Penguin, 1988), 41–52.
16 Ann Vickery, *Stressing the Modern* (Cambridge: Salt, 2007), 1.

17 Sharyn Pearce, 'From Bush Battler to City Editor: Louisa Lawson and the *Dawn*', *Journal of Australian Studies* 21 (1997): 12–21 (12).
18 Susan Lever, 'The Social Tradition in Australian Women's Poetry', *Women's Writing* 5.2 (1998): 230.
19 Hans Robert Jauss, *Toward an Aesthetic of Reception*, trans. Timothy Bahti (Sussex: Harvester Press, 1982), 19.
20 Elizabeth Schüssler Fiorenza, *Congress of Wo/men: Religion, Gender, and Kyriarchal Power* (Cambridge: Feminist Studies in Religion Books, 2016), 50–51.
21 Vickery, *Stressing the Modern*, 7.
22 Jill Roe, 'Cambridge, Ada (1844–1926)', Australian Dictionary of Biography, National Centre of Biography, Australian National University, published first in hardcopy 1969, accessed 30 August 2019.
23 Elizabeth Webby, *Early Australian Poetry: An Annotated Bibliography* (Sydney: Hale and Iremonger, 1982), ix.
24 Midgley, *Feminism and Empire*, 66.
25 Meghan Roughley, 'Introduction', in *Louisa Lawson: Collected Poems with Selected Critical Commentaries*, ed. Leonie Rutherford and Megan Roughley with Nigel Spence (Armidale: University of New England, 1996), v–xi (v).
26 Morris Miller and Frederick McCartney, *Australian Literature A Bibliography to 1938* (Sydney: Angus and Robertson, 1956), 283.
27 Katherine Bode and Carol Hetherington, eds, *'To Be Continued …'*: The Australian Newspaper Fiction Database, http://cdhrdatasys.anu.edu.au/tobecontinued/, accessed 9 July 2020.
28 Ken Gelder and Rachel Weaver. *The Colonial Journals: And the Emergence of Australian Literary Culture* (Crawley: UWA, 2014).
29 Anne K. Mellor, *Romanticism and Gender* (New York: Routledge, 1993), 11.
30 Anne Janowitz, *Lyric and Labour in the Romantic Tradition* (Cambridge: Cambridge University Press, 1998), 13.
31 Ibid., 25.
32 See Larisssa Behrendt, *Slave or Servant*, Documentary film (Director: Steven McGregor), 2015. https://www.screenaustralia.gov.au/the-screen-guide/t/servant-or-slave-2015/33088/.
33 Emma Lazarus, 'The New Colossus', in *The Norton Anthology of Poetry*, 4th edn, ed. Margaret Ferguson, Mary Jo Salter and Jon Stallworthy (New York: W. W. Norton, 1996), 1068.
34 Stephen Behrendt, 'Foreword', in *Romantic Periodicals and Print Culture*, ed. Kim Wheatley (London: Frank Cass, 2003), vii–ix (viii).
35 J. V. Byrnes, 'Howe, George (1769–1821)', in *Australian Dictionary of Biography*, vol. 1 (Melbourne: Melbourne University Press, 1966), 557–59 (557).
36 Robert Dixon, 'Hostilities between *The Month* and the *Empire*, 1857–8', *Southerly* 39.4 (1979): 394–416 (415).
37 Margaret De Salis, *Two Early Colonials* (Sydney: Author, 1967), 27.

Chapter 1 Eliza Hamilton Dunlop: Anti-Slavery, Imperial Feminism and Romanticism: 1820–40

1 Jennifer DeVere Brody, *Impossible Purities: Blackness, Femininity, and Victorian Culture* (Durham: Duke University Press, 1998), 26.

2   Clare Midgley, 'British Women, Women's Rights and Empire 1790–1850', in *Women's Rights and Human Rights*, ed. Marilyn Lake, Katie Holmes and Patricia Grimshaw (New York: Palgrave Macmillan, 2001), 3–15 (4). Subsequent references are to this edition and appear in parentheses in the text.
3   Margaret De Salis, *Two Early Colonials* (Sydney: Author, 1967), 27.
4   Ibid. Subsequent references are to this edition and appear in parentheses in the text.
5   Eliza Hamilton Dunlop, 'The Aboriginal Mother', *The Australian* (13 December 1838): 4.
6   Lyndall Ryan, *Tasmanian Aborigines: A History since 1803* (Sydney: Allen & Unwin, 2012), 237.
7   John O'Leary, 'Giving the Indigenous a Voice – Further Thoughts on the Poetry of Eliza Hamilton Dunlop'. *Journal of Australian Studies* 82 (2004): 85–93 (86).
8   Ibid.
9   Mary Loeffelholz, 'Poetry, Slavery, Personification: Maria Lowell's "Africa"', *Studies in Romanticism* 38.2 (1999): 171–202 (198).
10 Eliza Hamilton Dunlop, Letter, 'The Aboriginal Mother', *The Sydney Herald*, (1841): 29 Nov, 2.
11 Ibid.
12 William Lloyd Garrison, 'The Negro Mother's Appeal, by Anon'. *The Abolitionist* 1.1 (1833): 160. Subsequent references are to this edition and appear in parentheses in the text.
13 Alan Richardson, '"The Sorrows of Yamba" by Eaglesfield Smith and Hannah More: Authorship, Ideology and the Fractures of Antislavery Discourse', *Romanticism on the Net* 28 (2002): n.p.
14 Hannah More (attributed), *The Sorrows of Yamba or The Negro Woman's Lamentation* (London: J. Marshall, 1795), The Electronic Text Centre, ed. David Seaman, 1995, University of Virginia Library, 9 March 2010. http://etext.virginia.edu/toc/modeng/public/AnoSorr.html.
15 Jane Rendall, *The Origins of Modern Feminism: Women in Britain, France and the United States 1780–1860* (Hampshire: Macmillan, 1985), 3.
16 Ibid.
17 Midgley, 'British Women, Women's Rights and Empire 1790–1850', 3–15 (4). Subsequent references are to this edition and appear in parentheses in the text.
18 Tanya Dalziell, *Settler Romances and the Australian Girl* (Fremantle: University of Western Australia Press, 2004), 74.
19 Peter Minter, 'Settlement Defiled: Ventriloquy, Pollution and Nature in Eliza Hamilton Dunlop's "The Aboriginal Mother"', 142.
20 Roxanne Eberle, '"Tales of Truth?": Amelia Opie's Antislavery Poetics', in *Romanticism and Women Poets: Opening the Doors of Reception*, ed. Harriet Kramer Linkin and Stephen C. Behrendt (Kentucky: University Press of Kentucky, 1999), 71–98 (77).
21 Isobel Armstrong, Joseph Bristow and Cath Sharrock, *Nineteenth Century Women Poets: An Oxford Anthology* (New York: Clarendon Press, 1996), 167.
22 Felicia Hemans, *The Poetical Works of Mrs. Felicia Hemans: Complete in One Volume* (Philadelphia: Thomas T. Ash, 1836), 170.
23 Ibid., 179. Subsequent references are to this edition and appear in parentheses in the text.
24 O'Leary, 'Giving the Indigenous a Voice'. *Taylor and Francis*. Web. 3 February 2009, 88.
25 Margaret Ferguson, Mary Jo Salter and Jon Stallworthy, *The Norton Anthology of Poetry*, 4th edn (New York: W. W. Norton, 1996), 828.

26 Tim Fulford, 'The Mission to Civilize and the Colonial Romance', in *Romantic Indians: Native Americans, British Literature and Transatlantic Culture 1756–1830* (New York: Oxford University Press, 2006), 194–210 (201).
27 Anna Laetitia Barbauld, 'Epistle to William Wilberforce Esq. on the Rejection of the Bill for Abolishing the Slave Trade, 1791', in *Nineteenth Century Women Poets: An Oxford Anthology*, ed. Isobel Armstrong, Joseph Bristow and Cath Sharrock (New York: Clarendon Press, 1996), 2–4 (2).
28 William McCarthy, *Anna Letitia Barbauld: Voice of the Enlightenment* (Baltimore: Johns Hopkins University Press, 2008), 294.
29 Stephen C. Behrendt, *British Women Poets and the Romantic Writing Community* (Baltimore: Johns Hopkins University Press, 2009), 9. Subsequent references are to this edition and appear in parentheses in the text.
30 Eliza Hamilton Dunlop, Letter. 'The Aboriginal Mother', *Sydney Herald* (2 November 1841): 2.
31 Mary Birkett, *A Poem on the African Slave Trade: Addressed to Her Own Sex. Part 1* (Dublin: J. Jones, 1792); *Brycchan Carey e-text*. Web, 22 August 2012. Subsequent references are to this edition and appear in parentheses in the text.
32 Caroline Leakey, *Lyra Australis or Attempts to Sing in a Strange Land* (London: Bickers and Bush, 1854), v.
33 John O'Leary, '"Unlocking the Fountains of the Heart" – Settler verse and the Politics of Sympathy', *Postcolonial Studies* 12.1 (2010): 55–70 (55).
34 A. W. Martin, 'Parkes, Sir Henry (1815–1896)', in *Australian Dictionary of Biography*, vol. 5, ed. Douglas Pike (Melbourne: Melbourne University Press, 1974); Australian Dictionary of Biography, National Centre of Biography, Australian National University, http://adb.anu.edu.au/biography/parkes-sir-henry4366/text7099, accessed 20 August 2019.
35 Henry Stooks Smith, *The Register of Contested Parliamentary Elections*, 2nd edn (London: Marshall, 1842), 220.
36 Tim Fulford and Peter J. Kitson, 'Romanticism and Colonialism: Texts, Contexts, Issues', in *Romanticism and Colonialism: Writing and Empire, 1780–1830*, ed. Tim Fulford and Peter J. Kitson (New York: Cambridge University Press, 1998), 1–12 (1).
37 Paul Kane, *Australian Poetry: Romanticism and Negativity* (Melbourne: Cambridge University Press, 1996), 9.
38 Charles Harpur, 'An Aboriginal Mother's Lament', in *The Bushrangers: A Play in Five Acts and Other Poems* (Sydney: W. R. Piddington, 1853), 56. Subsequent references are to this edition and appear in parentheses in the text.
39 Kane, *Australian Poetry*, 11.
40 O'Leary, 'Giving the Indigenous a Voice', 85–93 (88–89).
41 Anne K. Mellor, *Romanticism and Gender* (New York: Routledge, 1993), 103. Subsequent references are to this edition and appear in parentheses in the text.
42 Isobel Armstrong, *Victorian Poetry: Poetry, Poetics and Politics* (London: Routledge, 1993), 325.
43 Midgley, 'British Women, Women's Rights and Empire 1790–1850', 5.
44 Claire Connolly, 'Irish Romanticism, 1800–1830', in *Cambridge History of Irish Literature*, vol. 1, ed. Margaret Kelleher and Philip O'Leary (Cambridge: Cambridge University Press, 2006), 407–8 (407).
45 Nini Rodgers, *Ireland, Slavery and Anti-Slavery: 1612–1865* (New York: Palgrave Macmillan, 2009), 259.

46 Neil Gunson, 'Dunlop, Eliza Hamilton (1796–1880)', in *Australian Dictionary of Biography*, vol. 1, ed. Douglas Pike (Melbourne: Melbourne University Press, 1966), 337–38.
47 Eliza Hamilton Dunlop, 'The Irish Mother', *The Australian* (30 November 1838): 4.
48 H. Halliday Sparling, *A Facsimile Reproduction of Irish Minstrelsy Being a Selection of Irish Songs, Lyrics and Ballads* (London: Walter Scott, 1887), 270.
49 Eliza Hamilton Dunlop, 'Songs of an Exile (No.2)', *The Australian* (22 November 1838): 3.
50 Anne Janowitz, *Lyric and Labour in the Romantic Tradition* (Cambridge: Cambridge University Press, 1998), 33.
51 Florence Boos, 'Class and Victorian Poetics', *Literature Compass* 115.2 (2005): 1–20 (2).
52 'I Stood Among the Glittering Throng', in *The Irish Melodist: A Collection of the Newest and Most Admired Songs* (Dublin: Printed for the Booksellers, 1843), 141–2 (141).
53 Armstrong, *Victorian Poetry*, 324.
54 Eliza Hamilton Dunlop, 'Morning on Rostrevor Mountains', *Dublin Penny Journal* 4 (1835): 42. Subsequent references are to this edition and appear in parentheses in the text.
55 Lata Mani, *Contentious Traditions: The Debate of Sati in Colonial India* (Berkeley: University of California Press, 1998), 1.
56 Isobel Armstrong, Joseph Bristow and Cath Sharrock, *Nineteenth Century Women Poets: An Oxford Anthology* (New York: Clarendon Press, 1996), 218.
57 Clare Midgley, *Feminism and Empire: Women Activists in Imperial Britain, 1790–1865* (Oxon: Routledge, 2007), 66–7.
58 Dale Spender, 'A Difference of View', in *Writing a New World: Two Centuries of Australian Women Writers* (London: Pandora Press, 1988), 60–65 (61).
59 Eliza Hamilton Dunlop, 'Morning on Rostrevor Mountains', *The Atlas* (25 April 1845): 257.
60 Eliza Hamilton Dunlop, Letter, 'The Star of the South', *Sydney Morning Herald*, (30 August 1842): 3.
61 Elizabeth Webby, 'Born to Blush Unseen: Some Nineteenth Century Women Poets', in *A Bright and Fiery Troop: Australian Women Writers of the Nineteenth Century*, ed. Debra Adelaide (Ringwood: Penguin, 1988), 45.
62 Webby, 'Born to Blush Unseen', 47.
63 Robert Dixon, 'Hostilities between the *Month* and the *Empire*, 1857–8', *Southerly* 39.4 (1979): 394–416 (415).
64 Susan Sheridan, *Along the Faultlines: Sex, Race and Nation in Australian Women's Writing* (New South Wales: Allen & Unwin, 1995), xiii.
65 Dixon, 'Hostilities between the *Month* and the *Empire*, 1857–8', 415.
66 Anna Johnston, 'Mrs Milson's Wordlist: Eliza Hamilton Dunlop and the Intimacy of Linguistic Work', in *Intimacies of Violence in the Settler Colony*, ed. Penelope Edmonds and Amanda Nettelbeck (Cham: Palgrave Macmillan, 2018), 225–47 (236–37).
67 Susan Sheridan, *Along the Faultlines: Sex, Race and Nation in Australian Women's Writing* (New South Wales: Allen & Unwin, 1995), 31.
68 Eliza Hamilton Dunlop, 'The Aboriginal Mother', *Sydney Herald* (29 November 1841): 2.
69 Henry Halloran, 'The Late Mr Kennedy', *Sydney Morning Herald* (31 July 1849): 2.
70 O'Leary, '"Unlocking the Fountains of the Heart"', 55–70.

71 Eliza Hamilton Dunlop, *The Vase, Comprising Songs for Music and Poems*, n.d. MS. Mitchell Library, Sydney.
72 Brandy Ryan, '"Echo and Reply": The Elegies of Felicia Hemans, Letitia Landon and Elizabeth Barrett'. *Victorian Poetry* 46.3 (2008): 249–77 (256).
73 Ibid., 249–77 (249).
74 Ibid., 264.
75 Eliza Hamilton Dunlop, 'To the Memory of E.B. Kennedy', *Maitland Mercury and Hunter River General Advertiser* (8 August 1849): 4.
76 Hemans, *The Poetical Works of Mrs. Felicia Hemans*, 133.
77 O'Leary, 'Giving the Indigenous a Voice', 85–93 (85).

Chapter 2 Mary Bailey: Hellenism, Bluestockings and the *Colonial Times*: 1840–50

1 Mary Bailey, *Palmyra*, 2nd edn (London: C. G. and F. Rivington, 1833). No copy or record of the date of the first edition could be located.
2 T. B. McCall, 'Bailey, William (1806–1879)', *Australian Dictionary of Biography*, vol. 1. ed. Douglas Pike (Melbourne: Melbourne University Press, 1966), n. p., *Australian Dictionary of Biography*, Web, 16 May 2012.
3 Virginia Blain, Patricia Clements and Isobel Grundy, eds, *The Feminist Companion to Literature in English: Women Writers from the Middle Ages to the Present* (London: B.T. Batsford, 1990), 49–50.
4 Mary Bailey, Letter, 'Contamination! And Pollution! Or England and Tasmania Compared', *Colonial Times* (7 May 1847): 4.
5 Shanyn Fiske, *Heretical Hellenism: Women Writers, Ancient Greece and the Victorian Popular Imagination* (Athens: Ohio University Press, 2008), 5.
6 Bailey, Letter 'Contamination! And Pollution! Or England and Tasmania Compared', 4.
7 Elizabeth Schüssler Fiorenza, *Congress of Wo/men: Religion, Gender, and Kyriarchal Power* (Cambridge: Feminist Studies in Religion Books, 2016), 50.
8 Shayne Breen, 'Extermination, Extinction, Genocide: British Colonialism and Tasmanian Aborigines', in *Forgotten Genocides: Oblivion, Denial and Memory*, ed. René Lemarchand (Philadelphia: University of Pennsylvania Press, 2011), 71–90 (73).
9 Lyndall Ryan, *Tasmanian Aborigines: A History since 1803* (Sydney: Allen and Unwin, 2012), xvii.
10 Ibid. All subsequent references are to this edition and appear in parentheses in the text.
11 James Boyce, *Van Diemen's Land* (Melbourne: Black, 2008), 284.
12 Ibid., 295.
13 'Insolvency Court – Wednesday', *Hobart Town Daily Mercury* (11 March 1858): 2.
14 Mary Bailey, 'Imprisonment for Debt', *Colonial Times* (29 August 1848): 4.
15 Deirdre Coleman, *Maiden Voyages and Infant Colonies: Two Women's Travel Narratives of the 1790s* (London: Leicester University Press, 1999), 7–8.
16 Angela Y. Davis, *Are Prisons Obsolete?* (New York: Seven Stories Press, 2003), 1.
17 'The Colonial Times', Advertisement, *Colonial Times* (9 February 1847): 2.
18 E. Flinn, 'Macdougall, John Campbell (1805–1848)', *Australian Dictionary of Biography*, vol. 2, ed. Douglas Pike (Melbourne: Melbourne University Press, 1967), n.p., *Australian Dictionary of Biography*, Web, 16 May 2012.

19 Stephen C. Behrendt, 'Foreword', *Romantic Periodicals and Print Culture*, ed. Kim Wheatley (London: Frank Cass, 2003), vii–ix (ii).
20 Kim Wheatley, ed., *Romantic Periodicals and Print Culture* (London: Frank Cass, 2003), 1.
21 Mary Bailey, 'Woman's Love', *Colonial Times* (21 August 1846): 3.
22 Blain, Clements and Grundy, eds, *The Feminist Companion to Literature in English*, 49.
23 Timothy Webb, 'Romantic Hellenism', in *The Cambridge Companion to British Romanticism*, ed. Stuart Curran (Cambridge: Cambridge University Press, 1993), 150.
24 Susan Brown, 'The Victorian Poetess', in *The Cambridge Companion to Victorian Poetry*, ed. Joseph Bristow (Cambridge: Cambridge University Press, 2000), 180–202 (183–4).
25 Edward Kemp, *A Voice from Tasmania* (Hobart: John Moore, 1846), iii. All subsequent references are to this edition and appear in parentheses in the text.
26 Michael Roe, 'Eardley Wilmot, Sir John Eardley (1783–1847)', in *Australian Dictionary of Biography*, vol. 1, ed. Douglas Pike (Melbourne: Melbourne University Press, 1966), n.p., *Australian Dictionary of Biography*, Web, 16 May 2012.
27 Roe, 'Eardley Wilmot, Sir John Eardley (1783–1847)'.
28 Morris Miller, 'Chapter XV: Notes to Chapter VII (Eardley Wilmot)', in *Pressmen and Governors: Australian Editors and Writers in Early Tasmania* (Sydney: Sydney University Press, 1973), 281.
29 Mary Bailey, 'A Voice from Ass-Mania or Neddy's Bray', *Guardian, or True Friend of Tasmania* (10 July 1847): 4. All subsequent references are to this edition and appear in parentheses in the text.
30 The 'Monody on Sir John Eardley Wilmot' by Mary Bailey is missing from digitized records of the *Colonial Times*.
31 Roe, 'Eardley Wilmot, Sir John Eardley (1783–1847)'.
32 Ibid.
33 E. D. Daw, 'William Bailey and the Free Church of England in New South Wales', *Journal of the Royal Australian Historical Society* 58.4 (1972): 249.
34 Mary Bailey, 'The Exile's Wife to Her Husband', *Hobarton Guardian, or, True Friend of Tasmania* (3 July 1847): 4.
35 Mary Bailey, 'Woman's Love', *Colonial Times* (1846): 21 Aug, 3.
36 Bailey, *Palmyra*, 10. Unica Project Rare Book and Manuscript Library University of Illinois at Urbana-Champaign Digitization Project, *2011*, Web, 18 October 2011. http://hdl.handle.net/10111/UIUCUNICA:palmyr0001bailma. All subsequent references are to this edition and appear in parentheses in the text.
37 Bailey, 'Odes of Anacreon', 4.
38 Ibid.
39 Letitia Landon, *The Improvisatrice and Other Poems* (Boston: Munroe and Francis, 1825), 11.
40 Webb, 'Romantic Hellenism', 160.
41 Thomas Moore, *The Poetical Works of Thomas Moore* (Paris: A. and W. Galignoni, 1829), 205.
42 Voltaire, *A Philosophical Dictionary from the French of M De Voltaire*, 2nd vol. (London: Dugdale, 1843), 186.
43 Mary Bailey, 'The Death of Pompey', *Colonial Times*, (1848): 19 Sep, 4.
44 Ibid.
45 Susan C. Jarratt, 'Sappho's Memory', *Rhetoric Society Quarterly* 32.1 (2002): 11–43 (25).
46 Claire Goldberg Moses, *French Feminism in the Nineteenth Century* (Albany: State University of New York Press, 1984), *ACLS Humanities e-book*, 243–44.

47 Goldberg Moses, *French Feminism in the Nineteenth Century*, 41–42.
48 Sarah Lewis, *Woman's Mission*, 2nd edn (New York: Wiley and Putnam, 1840), 65.
49 Ibid., vi.
50 Baron George Gordon Byron, *Lord Byron: The Complete Poetical Works*, vol. 2, ed. Jerome J. McGann (Oxford: Oxford University Press, 1980), 56.
51 Felicia Hemans, *The Poetical Works of Mrs. Felicia Hemans: Complete in One Volume* (Philadelphia: Thomas T. Ash, 1836), 333.
52 Andrew Stauffer, *Anger, Revolution, and Romanticism* (Cambridge: Cambridge University Press, 2005), 6.
53 Geneviève Fraisse, *Reason's Muse: Sexual Difference and the Birth of Democracy*, trans. Jane Marie Todd (Chicago: University of Chicago Press, 1994), 177.
54 Ibid., 171.
55 'Palmyra, by Mrs Bailey', Rev. of *Palmyra*, by Mary Bailey, *The Gentlemen's Magazine* 156 (1834): 202–4 (203).
56 Charlotte Brontë, 'Part II: Marian v. Zenobia', *The Juvenilia of Jane Austen and Charlotte Brontë*, ed. Francis Beer (London: Penguin, 1986), 195–222.
57 M.C. Howatson, ed., 'Zenobia', in *The Oxford Companion to Classical Literature*, (Oxford: Oxford University Press), n.p.
58 Bailey, *Palmyra*, 9.
59 Bailey, 'Odes of Anacreon', 4.
60 Mary Bailey, 'Ariphron's Hymn to Health. By Mrs. Wm Bailey, Over-Hall, Essex', *Blackwood's Edinburgh Magazine* 4 (September 1833): 424.
61 Mary Bailey, Letter 'The Greek Anthology'. *Blackwood's Edinburgh Magazine* 4 (September 1833): 423–24.
62 Jane Rendall, 'Bluestockings and Reviewers: Gender, Power, and Culture in Britain, c 1800–1830', *Nineteenth-Century Contexts* 26.4 (2004): 355–74 (356).
63 Mary Bailey, Letter 'The Greek Anthology', *Blackwood's Edinburgh Magazine* 4 (September 1833): 423–24 (423).
64 John Wilson, 'An Hour's Tete-a-Tete with the Public', *Blackwood's Edinburgh Magazine* 8 (1820): 78–105 (99).
65 Rendall, 'Bluestockings and Reviewers', 359.
66 Noah Comet, 'Letitia Landon and Romantic Hellenism', *Wordsworth Circle* 37.2 (2006): 76–80 (79).
67 Mary Bailey, Letter, 'Keep Down the Poets', *Colonial Times* (2 March 1847): 4. Subsequent references are in parentheses in the text.
68 Elizabeth Webby, *Early Australian Poetry: An Annotated Bibliography* (Sydney: Hale and Iremonger, 1982), ix.
69 Miller, 'Chapter XV: Notes to Chapter VII (Eardley Wilmot)', 282.
70 'C.D.' Letter, 'To the Editor of the Colonial Times and Tasmanian', *Colonial Times* (5 March 1847): 3.
71 Elizabeth Webby, 'Writers, Printers, Readers: The Production of Australian Literature before 1855', *Australian Literary Studies* 13.4 (1988): 113–25 (113–14).
72 'Cosmopolite', Letter 'M.B. and Sacred Poetry', *Colonial Times* (1 January 1847): 4.
73 Ibid.
74 'A Catholic, But Not Bigotted', Letter, 'M.B., Rev. Mr. Gell, and the New College', *Colonial Times* (27 October 1846): 4.
75 'Philalethes', Letter, 'M.B. and Colonial Poet-Haters', *Colonial Times* (9 March 1847): 3.
76 Miller, 'Chapter XV: Notes to Chapter VII (Eardley Wilmot)', 284.

77 Stephen C. Behrendt, *British Women Poets and the Romantic Writing Community* (Baltimore: Johns Hopkins University Press, 2009), 41.
78 'Literary Women', *Sydney Gazette* (9 April 1827): 4; 'The Letters of Mrs Elizabeth Montagu. Part the Second, Published by Matthew Montagu Esq. Volumes III and IV', *Quarterly Review* 10.19 (October 1813–January 1814): 32; 'The Letters of Mrs Elizabeth Montagu. Part the Second, Published by Matthew Montagu Esq. Volumes III and IV [from the Quarterly Review]', *Analectic Magazine* 3 (1814): 215.
79 'The Letters of Mrs Elizabeth Montagu. Part the Second, Published by Matthew Montagu Esq. Volumes III and IV'. Rev. of *The Letters of Mrs Elizabeth Montagu*, by Elizabeth Montagu in *Quarterly Review* 10.19 (1814): 32.
80 Caroline May, *The American Female Poets: With Biographical and Critical Notices* (Philadelphia: Lindsay and Blakiston, 1848), 5.
81 Bailey, 'Odes of Anacreon', 4.
82 Ruth Hoberman, 'Women in the British Museum Reading Room during the Late Nineteenth and Early Twentieth Centuries: From Quasi – to Counterpublic', *Feminist Studies* 28.3 (2002): 489–511 (494).
83 Sharon M. Setzer, ed., *A Letter to the Women of England and the Natural Daughter, by Mary Robinson* (Ontario: Broadview Press, 2003), 21.
84 Adriana Craciun, 'Mary Robinson, the *Monthly Magazine*, and the Free Press', in *Romantic Periodicals and Print Culture*, ed. Kim Wheatley (London: Frank Cass, 2003), 19–40 (30).
85 Bailey, 'Odes of Anacreon', 4.
86 Ibid.
87 Timothy Webb, 'Romantic Hellenism', in *The Cambridge Companion to British Romanticism*, ed. Stuart Curran (Cambridge: Cambridge University Press, 1993), 148–77 (169).
88 Moses, *French Feminism in the Nineteenth Century*, 264.
89 Mary Bailey, 'Private Tuition for Young Ladies', *The Courier* (18 April 1846): 1.
90 Craciun, 'Mary Robinson, the *Monthly Magazine*, and the Free Press', 20.
91 Ibid., 28.
92 Qtd in Amanda Gilroy, 'Women Poets 1780–1830', in *Romantic Writings*, ed. Stephen Bygrave (London: Routledge, 1996), 183–204 (189).
93 Ibid., 189.
94 Stephen C. Behrendt, 'The Gap That Is Not a Gap: British Poetry by Women 1802–1812', in *Romanticism and Women Poets: Opening the Doors of Reception*, ed. Harriet Kramer Linkin and Stephen C. Behrendt (Kentucky: University Press of Kentucky, 1999), 25–45 (25).
95 Morris Miller and Frederick McCartney, *Australian Literature: A Bibliography to 1938* (Sydney: Angus and Robertson, 1956), 263.

Chapter 3 Caroline Leakey: The Embowered Woman and Tasmania: 1850–60

1 Caroline Leakey, *Lyra Australis or Attempts to Sing in a Strange Land* (London: Bickers and Bush, 1854), 271.
2 Shirley Walker, '"Wild and Wilful" Women: Caroline Leakey and The Broad Arrow', in *A Bright and Fiery Troop: Australian Women Writers of the Nineteenth Century*, ed. Debra Adelaide (Victoria: Penguin, 1988), 86.

3 Emily Leakey, *Clear Shining Light; a Memoir of C.W. Leakey* (London: John F. Shaw, 1882), 1.
4 Ibid., 37–38.
5 Susan Brown, Patricia Clements and Isobel Grundy, eds. **CAROLINE LEAKEY** entry: Writing screen within *Orlando: Women's Writing in the British Isles from the Beginnings to the Present* (Cambridge: Cambridge University Press, 2006).
6 Leakey, *Lyra Australis or Attempts to Sing in a Strange Land*, 272. Subsequent references are to this edition and appear in parentheses in the text.
7 Sam George, *Botany, Sexuality and Women's Writing 1760–1830* (New York: Manchester University Press, 2007), 2.
8 Jenna Mead, 'Caroline Woolmer Leakey (1827–1881)', in *Dictionary of Literary Biography*, vol. 230, ed. Selina Samuels (Detroit: Gale Group, 2001), 249.
9 Although 'best known today as a political reformer, who played a crucial role in the passage through Parliament of the Infants Custody Bill (1839) and the Marriage and Divorce act (1857), Caroline Norton was also recognized in her own time as a poet'. See Paula R. Feldman and Daniel Robinson, eds, *A Century of Sonnets: The Romantic-Era Revival* (Oxford: Oxford University Press, 1999), 204.
10 Richard Davis, 'Exile', in *The Companion to Tasmanian History*, ed. Alison Alexander (Hobart: University of Tasmania, 2005), 442.
11 Isobel Armstrong, *Victorian Poetry: Poetry, Poetics and Politics* (London: Routledge, 1993), xxvi.
12 Mead, 'Caroline Woolmer Leakey (1827–1881)', 86–87.
13 Ibid.
14 Caroline Norton, *The Sorrows of Rosalie: A Tale with Other Poems* (London: John Ebers and Co., 1829), 69.
15 Ibid. 70.
16 Ibid., 3. Subsequent references are from this edition and appear in parentheses in the text.
17 William Shakespeare, *The Dramatic Works of William Shakespeare: With the Corrections and Illustrations of Dr. Johnson, G. Steevens and Others*, ed. Isaac Reed (New York: H. Durell, 1817), 201.
18 Gail Marshall, 'Women Re-Read Shakespeare Country', in *Literary Tourism and Nineteenth-Century Culture*, ed. Nicola J. Watson (New York: Palgrave Macmillan, 2009), 95–105 (95).
19 Feldman and Robinson, eds, *A Century of Sonnets*, 204.
20 Letitia Landon, 'To the Author of the Sorrows of Rosalie', in *The Lyre Fugitive Poetry of the Nineteenth-Century* (London: Tilt and Bogue, 1840), 73–76 (75).
21 Ibid., 73.
22 Rufus Wilmot Griswold, *The Poets and Poetry of England, in the Nineteenth Century* (Philadelphia: Carey and Hart, 1846), 360.
23 Geraldine Macpherson, *Memoirs of the Life of Anna Jameson* (Boston: Roberts Brothers, 1878), 190.
24 Edward Morris, *A Dictionary of Austral English* (Cambridge: Cambridge University Press, [1898] 2011), 140.
25 Ken Buckley and Ted Wheelwright, *No Paradise for Workers: Capitalism and the Common People in Australia 1788–1914* (Melbourne: Oxford University Press, [1988] 1992), 53.
26 Ibid., 50.

27 Patricia Ingham, *The Language of Gender and Class: Transformation in the Victorian Novel* (London: Routledge, 1996), 23.
28 Ibid., 20.
29 Tim Bonyhady and Greg Lehman, 'Exile – Wybalenna', in *The National Picture: The Art of Tasmania's black War*, ed. Tim Bonyhady and Greg Lehman (Canberra: National Gallery of Australia, 2018), 214–15 (215).
30 James Boyce, *Van Diemen's Land* (Melbourne: Black, 2008), 307.
31 Ibid., 315.
32 Henry Reynolds, *Fate of a Free People* (Victoria: Penguin, [1995] 2004), 15.
33 Lyndall Ryan, *Tasmanian Aborigines: A History since 1803* (Sydney: Allen and Unwin, 2012), 250.
34 Jennifer DeVere Brody, *Impossible Purities: Blackness, Femininity, and Victorian Culture* (Durham: Duke University Press, 1998), 11.
35 Ryan, *Tasmanian Aborigines*, 44.
36 'Lyra Australis: Or, Attempts to Sing in A Strange Land, By Caroline W Leakey', Rev. of *Lyra Australis or Attempts to Sing in A Strange Land*, by Caroline Leakey, in *The Gentlemen's Magazine* 196 (1854): 399.
37 Mead 'Caroline Woolmer Leakey (1827–1881)', 250.
38 Ibid.
39 Armstrong, *Victorian Poetry*, 323.
40 Leakey, *Clear Shining Light*, 6.
41 Caroline Leakey, *The Broad Arrow, Being Passages From the Life of Maida Gwynnham, A Lifer* (London: Richard Bentley, 1859), 49. Subsequent references are to this edition and appear in parentheses in the text.
42 Felicia Hemans, *The Poetical Works of Mrs. Felicia Hemans: Complete in one Volume* (Philadelphia: Thomas T. Ash, 1836), 168.
43 Ibid., 169.
44 Letitia Landon, *The Improvisatrice and Other Poems* (Boston: Munroe and Francis, 1825), 188.
45 Ann Vickery, 'Feminine Transports and Transformations: Textual Performances of Women Convicts and Emigrants to Australia from 1788–1850', *JASAL* 7.3 (2007): 71–83 (78).
46 Leakey, *Clear Shining Light*, 6.
47 Vickery, 'Feminine Transports and Transformations', 79.
48 Armstrong, *Victorian Poetry*, 325.
49 Nina Auerbach, *Woman and the Demon: The Life of a Victorian Myth* (Cambridge: Harvard University Press, 1982), 2.
50 Shakespeare, *The Dramatic Works of William Shakespeare*, 27.
51 Ibid.
52 Caroline Leakey, Letters to Octavian Blewitt, 24 February 1871. MS. (MSS/loan/96 RLF/1844/6) Archives of the Royal Literary Fund. British Lib., London.
53 Ibid.
54 Tim Fulford, 'Cobbett, Coleridge, and the Queen Caroline Affair', *Studies in Romanticism* 37.4 (1998): 523–43 (523).
55 Felicia Hemans, *The Works of Mrs. Hemans, with a Memoir of Her Life*, vol. 3 (Edinburgh: William Blackwood and Sons and Thomas Cadell, 1839), 153.
56 Auerbach, *Woman and the Demon*, 8–9.

57 Glennis Stephenson, 'Letitia Landon and the Victorian Improvisatrice: The Construction of L.E.L', *Victorian Poetry* 30.1 (1992): 1–17 (4).
58 Nina Auerbach and U.C. Knoepflmacher, eds, *Forbidden Journeys: Fairy Tales and Fantasies by Victorian Women Writers* (Chicago: University of Chicago Press, 1992) 7.
59 Leakey, *Clear Shining Light*, 23.
60 Caroline Leakey, 'The Rock of Martin Vaz', *Sunday Magazine* (1882): 160; Caroline Leakey, 'The Muezzin's Cry', *Anglo-American Magazine* 6 (1855): 219 respectively.
61 Caroline Leakey, 'God's Tenth', *Sunday School World* 39.12 (1899): 459.
62 Richard Davis and Stephan Petrow, eds, *Varieties of Vice-Regal Life (Van Diemen's Land Section) By Sir William and Lady Denison* (Hobart: Tasmanian Historical Research Association, 2004), 86–87.
63 Caroline Leakey, Letters to Octavian Blewitt, Feb 24 1871. MS. (MSS/loan/96 RLF/1844/6) Archives of the Royal Literary Fund. British Lib., London.
64 Ibid.
65 Mead, 'Caroline Woolmer Leakey (1827–1881)', 50.
66 Leakey, *Clear Shining Light*, 50.
67 Julie Melnyk, 'Hemans's Later Poetry: Religion and the Vatic Poet', *Felicia Hemans: Reimagining Poetry in the Nineteenth Century*, eds. Nanora Sweet and Julie Melnyk (New York: Palgrave, 2001), 74–94 (82).
68 Emma Mason, " 'Her Silence Speaks': Keble's Female Heirs", *John Keble in Context*, ed. Kirstie Blair (London: Anthem Press, 2004), 125–42 (125).
69 Melnyk, 'Hemans's Later Poetry', 74–94 (74–76).
70 Leakey, *Clear Shining Light*, 48–49.
71 'Attempts to Sing in a Strange Land', Rev of. *Lyra Australis or Attempts to Sing in a Strange Land*, by Caroline Leakey, *Dublin University Magazine* 43 (1854): 741–43 (743).
72 'Lyra Australis or Attempts to Sing in a Strange Land', Rev. of. *Lyra Australis or Attempts to Sing in a Strange Land* by Caroline Leakey, *The Courier* (8 September 1854): 2–3.
73 Alison Rukavina, *The Development of the International Book Trade 1870–1895: Tangled Networks* (New York: Palgrave Macmillan, 2010), 31.
74 Morris Miller and Frederick McCartney, *Australian Literature: A Bibliography to 1938* (Sydney: Angus and Robertson, 1956), 284.
75 Douglas B. W. Sladen, ed., *Australian Poets 1788–1888* (London: Griffith, Farran, Okeden and Welsh, 1888), 319.
76 Percy Bysshe Shelley, *The Poetical Works of Percy Bysshe Shelley*, ed. Mrs Shelley (London: Edward Moxon, 1839), 45.
77 Charlotte Smith, *Emmeline the Orphan of the Castle* (London: Oxford University Press, 1971), viii.
78 Lucasta Miller, *The Brontë Myth* (London: Jonathan Cape, 2001), 34.
79 Leakey, *Clear Shining Light*, 1–2.
80 Mead, 'Caroline Woolmer Leakey (1827–1881)', 247.
81 Leakey, *Clear Shining Light*, 10.
82 Ibid.
83 Shirley Walker, ' "Wild and Wilful" Women', 88.
84 Emily Chubbuck Judson, 'Lucy Dutton', in *Alderbrook: A Collection of Fanny Forester's Village Sketches, Poems etc.* (Boston: William D Ticknor, 1847), 121–27 (123).
85 Ibid., 123.
86 Caroline Leakey, 'Sentiment from the Shambles', *Once a Week* 1 (1859): 505–9 (508).

87 Nancy F. Cott, 'Passionlessness: An Interpretation of Victorian Sexual Ideology 1790–1850', *Signs* 4.2 (1978): 219–36 (230).
88 Ibid., 227.
89 Barbara Welter, 'The Cult of True Womanhood', *American Quarterly* 18.1 (1966): 151–74 (154).

Chapter 4 Emily Manning: Spiritualism and Periodical Print Culture: 1860–80

1 Patricia Clarke, *Pen Portraits: Women Writers and Journalists in Nineteenth Century Australia* (Sydney: Allen and Unwin, 1988), 113.
2 Ibid.
3 'The Balance of Pain and Other Poems, by Australie', Rev. of *The Balance of Pain and Other Poems*, by Emily Manning, *Illustrated Sydney News* (18 August 1877): 18.
4 Sally O'Neill, 'Manning, Emily Matilda (1845–1890)', in *Australian Dictionary of Biography*, vol. 5, ed. Douglas Pike (Melbourne: Melbourne University Press, 1974), n.p.
5 Jane Rendall, *The Origins of Modern Feminism: Women in Britain, France and the United States 1780–1860* (Hampshire: Macmillan, 1985), 276.
6 Emily Manning, 'Review. Souvenirs of Madame Vigée Le Brun', Rev. of *Souvenirs of Madame Vigée Le Brun*, by Louise Elisabeth Vigée Le Brun, *Sydney Morning Herald* (17 July 1879): 15.
7 Emily Manning, 'Unorthodox London', Rev. of *Unorthodox London*, by Maurice Davies, *Sydney Morning Herald* (30 April 1874): 6.
8 Emily Manning, 'Harriet Martineau', *Sydney Morning Herald* (16 February 1878): 3.
9 Howard R. Murphy, 'The Ethical Revolt against Christian Orthodoxy in Early Victorian England', *American Historical Review* 60.4 (1955): 800–17 (801).
10 Emily Manning, *The Balance of Pain and Other Poems* (London: George Bell, 1877), 1. Subsequent references are to this edition and appear in parentheses in the text.
11 Isobel Armstrong, *Victorian Poetry: Poetry, Poetics and Politics* (London: Routledge, 1993), 14.
12 Murphy, 'The Ethical Revolt against Christian Orthodoxy in Early Victorian England', 801.
13 Ibid., 811.
14 George Eliot, 'Agatha', *Atlantic Monthly* 24 (1869): 199–207 (199). Subsequent references are to this edition and appear in parentheses in the text.
15 Richard White, *Inventing Australia: Images and Identity 1688–1980* (Sydney: George Allen and Unwin, 1981), 29.
16 Anne Summers, *Damned Whores and God's Police: The Colonization of Women in Australia* (Ringwood, Victoria: Penguin, 1975), 230.
17 John J. Kucich, *Ghostly Communion; Cross-Cultural Spiritualism in Nineteenth Century American Literature* (Hanover: University Press of New England, 2004), xi.
18 See Anita Heiss and Peter Minter, eds, 'Aboriginal Literature', in *Macquarie Pen Anthology of Aboriginal Literature* (Crows Nest: Allen and Unwin, 2008), 1–8.
19 Emily Manning, 'A Plea for the Ragged Schools', *Sydney Morning Herald* (11 August 1873): 2.
20 Murphy, 'The Ethical Revolt against Christian Orthodoxy in Early Victorian England', 800–1.

21 Sarah Lewis, *Woman's Mission*, 2nd edn (New York: Wiley and Putnam, 1840), 22.
22 Barbara Welter, 'The Cult of True Womanhood', *American Quarterly* 18.1 (1966): 151–74 (139).
23 Diana Basham, *The Trial of Woman: Feminism and the Occult Sciences in Victorian Literature and Society* (New York: New York University Press, 1992), 74.
24 Barbara Welter, 'The Feminization of American Religion 1800–1860', in *Clio's Consciousness Raised*, ed. Mary S. Hartman and Lois W. Banner (New York: Octagon Books, 1974), 137–57 (151).
25 Ibid., 138.
26 Alex Owen, 'Power and Gender: The Spiritualist Context', in *The Darkened Room: Women, Power, and Spiritualism in Late Victorian* England (Chicago: University of Chicago Press, 1989), 1–17 (5).
27 Michael Ackland, *That Shining Band: A Study of Australian Colonial Verse Tradition* (St Lucia: University of Queensland Press, 1994), 84–85.
28 Welter, 'The Cult of True Womanhood', 174.
29 Jill Roe, *Beyond Belief: Theosophy in Australia 1879–1939* (Kensington: New South Wales University Press, 1986), 39.
30 Ibid., 14.
31 Julian Holloway, 'Enchanted Spaces: The Séance, Affect and Geographies of Religion', *Annals of the Association of American Geographers* 96.1 (2006): 182–87 (183).
32 Basham, *The Trial of Woman*, 90.
33 John Ruskin, 'Of Kings Treasuries', in *Sesame and Lilies: Two Lectures* (New York: John Wiley, 1865), 89.
34 Sarah Willburn, 'Victorian Women Theologians of the Mystical Fringe: Translation and Domesticity', in *Women's Theology in Nineteenth Century Britain: Transfiguring the Faith of their Fathers*, ed. Julie Melnyk (New York: Garland, 1998), 188–207 (190).
35 Deirdre David, *Intellectual Women and Victorian Patriarchy* (New York: Cornell University Press, 1987), 14.
36 Summers, *Damned Whores and God's Police*, 324–25.
37 Ruskin, 'Of Kings Treasuries', 75.
38 Patricia Ingham, *The Language of Gender and Class: Transformation in the Victorian Novel* (London: Routledge, 1996), 22.
39 Lillian Nayder, *The Other Dickens: A Life of Catherine Hogarth* (New York: Cornell University Press, 2011), 90.
40 Armstrong, *Victorian Poetry*, 318.
41 Ibid., 340.
42 Percy Bysshe Shelley, *The Poetical Works of Percy Bysshe Shelley*, ed. Mrs Shelley (London: Edward Moxon, 1839), 161.
43 Nigel Leask, 'Shelley's "Magnetic Ladies": Romantic Mesmerism and the Politics of the Body', in *Beyond Romanticism: New Approaches to Texts and Contexts, 1780–1832*, ed. Stephen Copley and John Whale (London: Routledge, 1992), 53–78 (62).
44 Percy Bysshe Shelley, 'A Defence of Poetry', in *A Defence of Poetry and Other Essays by Percy Bysshe Shelley, Project Gutenberg*. Web, 29–48 (29).
45 Germaine de Staël, *Corinne, or Italy*, trans. and ed. Sylvia Raphael (Oxford: Oxford University Press, 1998), 33.
46 Patrick Vincent, 'First Last Songs: The Public Voice of Sentiment', in *The Romantic Poetess: European Culture, Politics and Gender 1820–1840* (Durham: University of New Hampshire Press, 2004), 52–71 (54).

47 Angela Esterhammer, 'The Spectacle of the Romantic Improviser: Corilla, *Corinne*, and British Women Poets of the 1820s', in *Romanticism and Improvisation, 1750–1850* (Cambridge: Cambridge University Press, 2008), 78–103 (78).
48 Jennifer DeVere Brody, *Impossible Purities: Blackness, Femininity, and Victorian Culture* (Durham: Duke University Press, 1998), 66–67.
49 Holloway, 'Enchanted Spaces', 183.
50 Bridget Bennett, 'Crossing Over: The Spiritualist Atlantic', in *Transatlantic Spiritualism and Nineteenth-Century American Literature* (Gordonsville: Palgrave Macmillan, 2007), 27–53 (27).
51 'The Balance of Pain and Other Poems by Australie', Rev. of *The Balance of Pain and Other Poems*, by Emily Manning, *Sydney Morning Herald* (23 July 1877): 5.
52 Alex Owen, 'Star Mediumship: Light and Shadows', in *The Darkened Room: Women, Power, and Spiritualism in Late Victorian England* (Chicago: University of Chicago Press, 1989), 41–74 (48).
53 'America. The Katie King Fraud and The Deceptions of Spiritualism (New York Times)', in *Portland Guardian and Normanby General Advertiser* (29 June 1875): 4. See also 'The Deceptions of Spiritualism', *Western Australian Times* (2 April 1875): 5.
54 'A Spiritualistic Exposure *(from the Philadelphia Express, December 17)*', *Sydney Morning Herald* (19 March 1875): 3.
55 'The Balance of Pain and Other Poems by Australie', Rev. of *The Balance of Pain and Other Poems*, *Sydney Morning Herald*, 23 July 1877, 5. Trove, National Library Australia. Accessed 18 April 2011.
56 'The Balance of Pain and Other Poems by Australie', Rev. of *The Balance of Pain and Other Poems*, by Emily Manning, *Town and Country Journal* (4 August 1877): 184.
57 Ibid.
58 Ruskin, 'Of Kings Treasuries', 14.
59 Emily Manning, Letter. 'Boycotting Women', *Sydney Morning Herald* (19 August 1889): 9.
60 Willburn, 'Victorian Women Theologians of the Mystical Fringe', 188–207 (189).
61 This poem is discussed by Andrea Ebel Brozya in *Labour Love and Prayer: Female Piety in Ulster Religious Literature 1850–1914* (1999). The poem was included in a number of nineteenth-century colonial Australian and international periodical publications.
62 The *Town and Country Journal* was a publication to which Eliza Hamilton Dunlop, Emily Manning and Louisa Lawson all contributed.
63 'The Rights of Women', *Australian Town and Country Journal* (8 March 1873): 308.
64 'Women's Rights', *Australian Town and Country Journal* (6 December 1890): 34.
65 Dallas Liddle, *The Dynamics of Genre* (London: University of Virginia Press, 2009), 7.
66 Willburn, 'Victorian Women Theologians of the Mystical Fringe', 191.

Chapter 5 Louisa Lawson: Fin de Siècle Transnational Feminist Poetics and the *Dawn*: 1880–1910

1 Beth Palmer, *Women's Authorship and Editorship in Victorian Culture: Sensational Strategies* (Oxford: Oxford University Press, 2011), 3.
2 Heather Radi, 'Lawson, Louisa (1848–1920)', in *Australian Dictionary of Biography*, vol. 10, ed. Douglas Pike (Melbourne: Melbourne University Press, 1986), n.p.

3   Isobel Armstrong, *Victorian Poetry: Poetry, Poetics and Politics* (London: Routledge, 1993), 346.
4   Louisa Lawson, 'The Home Libraries', *The Dawn* (1 December 1891): 26.
5   Kenneth M. Price and Susan Belasco Smith, eds, 'Introduction: Periodical Literature in Social and Historical Context', in *Periodical Literature in Nineteenth-Century America* (Charlottesville: University Press of Virginia, 1995), 3–16 (3).
6   Walt Whitman, *Walt Whitman's Leaves of Grass*, ed. David S. Reynolds, 150th Anniversary ed. (Oxford: Oxford University Press, 2005), iv.
7   Louisa Lawson, 'To a Bird', *Louisa Lawson Collected Poems with Selected Critical Commentaries*, ed. Leonie Rutherford and Megan Roughley (Armidale: University of New England, 1996), 50. Subsequent references are to this edition and appear in parentheses in the text. Note: Lawson published two different poems with the title 'To a Bird' in the *Dawn*. This refers to the first of these, published in the *Dawn* (15 May 1888): 6. The second poem with this title was published in the *Dawn* (1 February 1892): 22.
8   Christina Rossetti, *Goblin Market, The Princes Progress and Other Poems* (London: Macmillan, 1879), 179.
9   Christina Rossetti, 'Song', *The Dawn* (1 October 1894): 20.
10 Charles Follen Adams's 'Der Oak und der Vine' and Ella Wheeler Wilcox's 'I Bide my time' appeared in *The Dawn* (2 September 1889): 15; Edith M. Thomas's 'Christmas Voices' and Sarah Chauncy Woolsey's 'New Every Morning' (under the pseudonym Susan Coolidge) appeared in *The Dawn* (5 December 1889): 14; Ellen Palmer Allerton's 'Beautiful Things', *The Dawn* (5 March 1890): 17; Julia C. R. Dorr's 'Outgrown' and Wilcox's 'At Set of Sun', *The Dawn* (2 July 1894): 20; Ethel Lynn Beers's 'Old Fashioned Flowers' appears alongside Henry Lawson's 'The Mountain Splitter', *The Dawn* (1 May 1894): 20. Kate Tannatt Woods's 'Dan's Wife' appears in *The Dawn* (6 January 1890): 21.
11 Paula Bennett, *Poets in the Public Sphere: The Emancipatory Project of American Women's Poetry* (Princeton: Princeton University Press, 2003), 207.
12 Tatiana Kontu, *Spiritualism and Women's Writing: From the Fin de Siècle to the Neo-Victorian* (Hampshire: Palgrave Macmillan, 2009), 188.
13 Susan Conley, 'Irony and Liminal Fantasy in the Death Lyrics', 263.
14 Susan Magarey, *Passions of the First Wave Feminists* (Sydney: University of New South Wales Press, 2001), 67.
15 Ibid., 44.
16 Conley, 'Irony and Liminal Fantasy in the Death Lyrics', 265.
17 Ellen Carol DuBois, *Woman Suffrage and Women's Rights* (New York: New York University Press, 1998), 149.
18 Liz Conor, *Skin Deep: Settler Impressions of Aboriginal Women* (Crawley: University of Western Australia Press, 2016), 3.
19 Thomas Nast, 'Get Thee Behind Me Mrs Satan', *Harper's Weekly* 16.790 (17 February 1872): 140.
20 Audrey Oldfield, 'Louisa Lawson and Votes for Women', in *Louisa Lawson Collected Poems with Selected Critical Commentaries*, ed. Leonie Rutherford and Megan Roughley (Armidale: University of New England, 1996), 261–66 (262).
21 Nancy F. Cott, 'Passionlessness: An Interpretation of Victorian Sexual Ideology 1790–1850', *Signs* 4.2 (1978): 219–36.
22 Kate Tannatt Woods, 'Dan's Wife', *The Dawn* (6 January 1890): 21. Subsequent references are to this publication and appear in parentheses in the text.

23 Rodger Streitmatter, *Voices of Revolution: The Dissident Press in America* (New York: Columbia University Press, 2001), 61.
24 Louisa Lawson, 'The Divorce Extension Bill: Or, the Drunkard's Wife', *The Dawn* (5 March 1890): 7.
25 Judith Smart, 'Modernity and Mother-Heartedness: Spirituality and Religious Meaning in Australian Women's Suffrage and Citizenship Movements', in *Women's Suffrage in the British Empire: Citizenship, Nation, and Race*, ed. Ian Christopher Fletcher, Laura E. Nym Mayhall and Philippa Levine (London: Routledge, 2000), 51–67 (53).
26 Magarey, *Passions of the First Wave Feminists*, 7–8.
27 Belinda Wheeler, ed., 'Chronology', in *A Companion to Australian Aboriginal Literature* (New York: Camden House, 2013), xvii.
28 Linda L. Clark, *Women and Achievement in Nineteenth-Century Europe* (Cambridge: Cambridge University Press, 2008), 36.
29 Joan Perkin, *Women and Marriage in Nineteenth-Century England* (London: Routledge, 1985) (Taylor and Francis e-library 2003), 23–24.
30 Brian Matthews, *Louisa* (Ringwood: Penguin, 1987), 152–58.
31 Harriet Kramer Linkin, 'Romanticism and Mary Tighe's "Psyche": Peering at the Hem of Her Blue Stockings', *Studies in Romanticism* 35.1 (1996): 55–72 (56).
32 Mark P. O. Morford and Robert J. Lenardon, *Classical Mythology*, 7th edn (New York: Oxford University Press, 2003), 193.
33 Lady Mary Wroth, 'Late in the Forest I Did Cupid See', *Kissing the Rod: An Anthology of Seventeenth-Century Women's Verse*, ed. Germaine Greer, Susan Hastings, Jeslyn Medoff and Melinda Sansone (New York: The Noonday Press, 1989), 67.
34 Florence Boos, 'Not so Lowly Bards: Working Class Women Poets and Middle Class Expectations', *Key Words: A Journal of Cultural Materialism* 8 (2010): 21–37 (21).
35 Sandra M. Gilbert and Susan Gubar, *The Madwoman in the Attic: The Woman Writer and the Nineteenth-Century Literary Imagination* (New Haven: Yale University Press, 1979), 616.
36 Ibid., 615.
37 Jennifer DeVere Brody, *Impossible Purities: Blackness, Femininity, and Victorian Culture* (Durham: Duke University Press, 1998), 66.
38 Ibid., 69.
39 Bennett, *Poets in the Public Sphere*, 160.
40 Rossetti, *Goblin Market, the Princes Progress and Other Poems*, 15.
41 Robert Dixon, *The Course of Empire* (Melbourne: Oxford University Press, 1986), 2–4.
42 Letters of Mary Gilmore 23. Qtd in Michael Ackland, *That Shining Band: A Study of Australian Colonial Verse Tradition* (St Lucia: University of Queensland Press, 1994), 211.
43 Ackland, *That Shining Band*, 211.
44 Claire Raymond, *The Posthumous Voice in Women's Writing from Mary Shelley to Sylvia Plath* (Burlington: Ashgate, 2006), 169.
45 Sam George, *Botany, Sexuality and Women's Writing 1760–1830* (New York: Manchester University Press, 2007), 6.
46 Debra N. Mancoff, *Flora Symbolica: Flowers in Pre-Raphaelite Art* (New York: Prestel, 2003), 32.
47 Ibid., 36.
48 Toru Dutt, *Ancient Ballads and Legends of Hindustan* (London: Kegan Paul, Trench, 1885), 136.
49 K. T. Sunitha, 'Toru Dutt as a Postcolonial Feminist Poet', in *Indian English Literature*, vol. 7, ed. Basavaraj Naikar (New Delhi: Atlantic, 2007), 5.

50 Dutt, *Ancient Ballads and Legends of Hindustan*, 136.
51 Amelia Bloomer qtd. in Kathleen L. Endres and Therese L. Lueck, eds, *Women's Periodicals in the United States: Social and Political Issues* (Westport, CT: Greenwood Press, 1996), 175.
52 Julie Melnyk, 'Hemans's Later Poetry: Religion and the Vatic Poet', in *Felicia Hemans: Reimagining Poetry in the Nineteenth Century*, ed. Nanora Sweet and Julie Melnyk (New York: Palgrave, 2001), 74–94 (79).
53 Leonie Rutherford, 'Louisa Lawson's Poetry: A Case Study in Revision and Textual Practice', in *Louisa Lawson: Collected Poems with Selected Critical Commentaries*, ed. Leonie Rutherford and Megan Roughley with Nigel Spence (Armidale: University of New England, 1996), 229–44 (231).
54 Louisa Lawson, 'Original Lines (by Dora Falconer)', *The Dawn* (1 August 1902): 18.
55 Ibid.
56 Ella Wheeler Wilcox, *Poems of Passion* (Chicago: Belford Clark, 1890), 3.
57 Ella Wheeler Wilcox, 'I Bide My Time', *The Dawn* (2 September 1889): 15; and Ella Wheeler Wilcox, 'At Set of Sun', *The Dawn* (2 July 1894): 20.
58 Ella Wheeler Wilcox, 'The Rising of Labour', *The Worker* (19 March 1904): 3.
59 Ella Wheeler Wilcox, 'Who Is a Socialist', *The Worker* (9 August 1906): 4.
60 Wilcox, *Poems of Passion*, 63.
61 Raymond, *The Posthumous Voice in Women's Writing from Mary Shelley to Sylvia Plath*, 169.
62 Conley, 'Irony and Liminal Fantasy in the Death Lyrics', 266.
63 Catherine Bernard, 'Dickens and Victorian Dream Theory', in *Victorian Science and Victorian Values: Literary Perspectives*, ed. James G. Paradis and Thomas Postlewait (New Brunswick, NJ: Rutgers University Press, 1985), 197–216 (197).
64 Washington Irving, 'Don Juan: A Spectral Research', *Knickerbocker or New York Monthly Magazine* 17 (1841): 247–53 (250).
65 Ibid., 249.
66 'The Love of a Sister', *The Dawn* (1 July 1904): 7–8 (7).
67 Louisa Lawson, 'To a Libertine', *The Dawn* (1 June 1903): 16.
68 Jill Roe, *Beyond Belief: Theosophy in Australia 1879–1939* (Kensington: New South Wales University Press, 1986), 37.
69 Matthews, *Louisa*, 21.
70 Roe, *Beyond Belief: Theosophy in Australia 1879–1939*, 82.
71 Perkin, *Women and Marriage in Nineteenth-Century England*, 219.
72 Ibid.
73 Ann Vickery, 'A "Lonely Crossing": Approaching Nineteenth-Century Australian Women's Poetry', *Victorian Poetry* 40.1 (2002): 33–54 (36).
74 Louisa Lawson, 'About Ourselves', *The Dawn* (15 May 1888): 1.
75 See, for example, Alfred Tennyson, 'Tears', in *Moreton Bay Courier* (17 June 1848): 4; and 'New Books', *Sydney Morning Herald* (23 June 1848): 1, in which Tennyson's *The Princess* is advertised.
76 Howard W. Fulweiler, *'Here a Captive Heart Busted': Studies in the Sentimental Journey of Modern Literature* (New York: Fordham University Press, 1993), 45.
77 Leslie F. Goldstein, 'Early Feminist Themes in French Utopian Socialism: The St.-Simonians and Fourier', *Journal of the History of Ideas* 43.1 (1982): 91–108 (94–95).
78 Vickery, 'A "Lonely Crossing"', 49.

79 Andrew Leng, 'Millais's *Mariana*: Literary Painting, the Pre-Raphaelite Gothic and the Iconography of the Marian Artist', *Journal of Pre-Raphaelite Studies* 1 (1988): 63–74 (64).
80 Claire Goldberg Moses, *French Feminism in the Nineteenth Century* (Albany: State University of New York Press, 1984), 149.
81 Eliza Cook, 'The Heart That's True', *The Argus* (17 November 1851): 4.
82 Arlene Kisner, *Woodhull & Claflin's Weekly: The Lives and Writings of Notorious Victoria Woodhull and Her Sister Tennessee Claflin* (Washington: Time Change Press, 1972), 27.
83 Julie Ellison, 'Cato's Tears', in *Cato's Tears and the Making of Anglo-American Emotion* (Chicago: University of Chicago Press, 1999), 48–73 (67).
84 Lillian Nayder, *The Other Dickens: A Life of Catherine Hogarth* (New York: Cornell University Press, 2011), 315.
85 Palmer, *Women's Authorship and Editorship in Victorian Culture*, 5.
86 Willah Weddon, 'Michigan Woman's Press Association, 1890–193(8)', in *Women's Press Organizations 1881–1999*, ed. Elizabeth V. Burt (Westport, CT: Greenwood Press, 2000), 114–21 (116).
87 Marion Marzolf, 'Detroit Women Writers 1900 – Present', in *Women's Press Organizations 1881–1999*, ed. Elizabeth V. Burt (Westport, CT: Greenwood Press, 2000), 59–66 (60).
88 Pauline Simonsen, 'Elizabeth Barrett Browning's Redundant Women', *Victorian Poetry* 35.4 (1997): 509–32 (509).
89 Ibid., 509.
90 Juliette Peers, 'Pre-Raphaelitism in Colonial Australia', in *Worldwide Pre-Raphaelitism*, ed. Thomas J. Tobin (New York: State University of New York Press, 2005), 215–33 (215–16).
91 Ibid., 216.
92 Ibid.
93 Susan Sheridan, *Along the Faultlines: Sex, Race and Nation in Australian Women's Writing* (New South Wales: Allen and Unwin, 1995), 31.
94 Talia Schaffer, *The Forgotten Female Aesthetes: Literary Culture in Late Victorian England* (Virginia: University Press of Virginia, 2000), 4–5.
95 Ibid., 4.
96 'Notes and Comments', *The Dawn* (1 May 1889): 8.
97 'Books – new and old by "Elaine"', *The Dawn* (1 December 1899): 28.
98 'Notes and Comments', *The Dawn* (1 May 1889): 8.
99 '"Novel" Nursery Rhyme', *The Dawn* (1 November 1890): 20.
100 Ibid.
101 Palmer, *Women's Authorship and Editorship in Victorian Culture*, 174.
102 Ibid., 161–62.
103 'Answers to Correspondents', *The Dawn* (28 February 1905): 28.
104 Ibid.
105 Judith Johnston and Monica Anderson, *Australia Imagined: Views from the British Periodical Press 1800–1900* (Crawley: University of Western Australia Press, 2005), 157.
106 Mary Arseneau, 'Introduction', in *The Culture of Christina Rossetti: Female Poetics and Victorian Contexts*, ed. Mary Arseneau, Antony H. Harrison and Lorraine Janzen Kooistra (Athens: Ohio University Press, 1999), xiii.
107 Delores Rosenblum, *Christina Rossetti: The Poetry of Endurance* (Carbondale: Southern Illinois University Press, 1986), 17.
108 Boos, 'Not So Lowly Bards', 21–37 (34).

Conclusion: Beyond the *Dawn*

1 Aileen Moreton-Robinson, *Talkin' Up to the White Woman* (Queensland: University of Queensland Press, 2000), 34.
2 Isobel Armstrong, *Victorian Poetry: Poetry, Poetics and Politics* (London: Routledge, 1993), 332.
3 Anne K. Mellor, *Romanticism and Gender* (London: Routledge, 1993), 212.
4 Anne Janowitz, *Lyric and Labour in the Romantic Tradition* (Cambridge: Cambridge University Press, 1998), 1.

BIBLIOGRAPHY

Ackland, Michael. *That Shining Band: A Study of Australian Colonial Verse Tradition*. St Lucia: University of Queensland Press, 1994.
Adams, Charles Follen. 'Der Oak und der Vine'. *The Dawn*, 2 September 1889: 15.
Allerton, Ellen Palmer. 'Beautiful Things'. *The Dawn*, 5 March 1890: 17.
'America: The Katie King Fraud and the Deceptions of Spiritualism (New York Times)'. *Portland Guardian and Normanby General Advertiser*, 29 June 1875: 4.
'Answers to Correspondents'. *The Dawn*, 28 February 1905: 28.
Armstrong, Isobel. *Victorian Poetry: Poetry, Poetics and Politics*. London: Routledge, 1993.
Armstrong, Isobel, Joseph Bristow and Cath Sharrock. *Nineteenth Century Women Poets: An Oxford Anthology*. New York: Clarendon Press, 1996.
Arseneau, Mary. 'Introduction'. In *The Culture of Christina Rossetti: Female Poetics and Victorian Contexts*, edited by Mary Arseneau, Antony H. Harrison and Lorraine Janzen Kooistra, xiii–xxii. Athens: Ohio University Press, 1999.
'Attempts to Sing in a Strange Land'. Rev. of. *Lyra Australis or Attempts to Sing in a Strange Land*, by Caroline Leakey. *Dublin University Magazine* 43, 1854: 741–43.
Auerbach, Nina. *Woman and the Demon: The Life of a Victorian Myth*. Cambridge: Harvard University Press, 1982.
Auerbach, Nina, and U. C. Knoepflmacher, eds. *Forbidden Journeys: Fairy Tales and Fantasies by Victorian Women Writers*. Chicago: University of Chicago Press, 1992.
Bailey, Mary. 'Ariphron's Hymn to Health: By Mrs. Wm Bailey, Over-Hall, Essex'. *Blackwood's Edinburgh Magazine*, 4, September 1833: 424.
———. 'The Death of Pompey'. *Colonial Times*, 19 September 1848: 4.
———. 'The Exile's Wife to Her Husband'. *Hobarton Guardian, or, True Friend of Tasmania*, 3 July 1847: 4.
———. 'Imprisonment for Debt'. *Colonial Times*, 29 August 1848: 4.
———. Letter. 'Contamination! And Pollution! Or England and Tasmania Compared'. *Colonial Times*, 7 May 1847: 4.
———. Letter. 'The Greek Anthology'. *Blackwood's Edinburgh Magazine*, IV, September 1833: 423–4.
———. Letter. 'Keep Down the Poets'. *Colonial Times*, 2 March 1847: 4.
———. 'Odes of Anacreon: Translated from the Original Greek. Ode 1'. *Colonial Times*, 8 May 1849: 4.
———. *Palmyra*, 2nd edn. London: C. G. and F. Rivington, 1833.
———. 'Private Tuition for Young Ladies'. *The Courier*, 18 April 1846: 1.
———. 'A Voice from Ass-Mania or Neddy's Bray'. *Guardian, or True Friend of Tasmania*, 10 July 1847: 4.
———. 'Woman's Love'. *Colonial Times*, 21 August 1846: 3.

'The Balance of Pain and Other Poems, by Australie'. Rev. of *The Balance of Pain and Other Poems*, by Emily Manning. *Illustrated Sydney News*, 18 August 1877: 18. Trove, National Library of Australia. Accessed 18 April 2011.

'The Balance of Pain and Other Poems by Australie'. Rev. of *The Balance of Pain and Other Poems*, by Emily Manning. *Sydney Morning Herald*, 23 July 1877: 5. Trove, National Library of Australia. Accessed 18 April 2011.

'The Balance of Pain and Other Poems by Australie'. Rev. of *The Balance of Pain and Other Poems*, by Emily Manning. *Town and Country Journal*, 4 August 1877: 184. Trove, National Library of Australia. Accessed 18 April 2011.

Barbauld, Anna Laetitia. 'Epistle to William Wilberforce Esq. on the Rejection of the Bill for Abolishing the Slave Trade, 1791'. In *Nineteenth Century Women Poets: An Oxford Anthology*, edited by Isobel Armstrong, Joseph Bristow and Cath Sharrock, 2–4. New York: Clarendon Press, 1996.

Basham, Diana. *The Trial of Woman: Feminism and the Occult Sciences in Victorian Literature and Society*. New York: New York University Press, 1992.

Beers, Ethel Lynn. 'Old Fashioned Flowers'. *The Dawn*, 1 May 1894: 20.

Behrendt, Stephen C. *British Women Poets and the Romantic Writing Community*. Baltimore: Johns Hopkins University Press, 2009.

———. 'Foreword'. In *Romantic Periodicals and Print Culture*, edited by Kim Wheatley, vii–ix. London: Frank Cass, 2003.

———. 'The Gap That Is Not a Gap: British Poetry by Women 1802–1812'. In *Romanticism and Women Poets: Opening the Doors of Reception*, edited by Harriet Kramer Linkin and Stephen C. Behrendt, 25–45. Kentucky: University Press of Kentucky, 1999.

Bennett, Bridget. 'Crossing Over: The Spiritualist Atlantic'. In *Transatlantic Spiritualism and Nineteenth-Century American Literature*, 27–53. Gordonsville: Palgrave Macmillan, 2007.

Bennett, Paula. *Poets in the Public Sphere: The Emancipatory Project of American Women's Poetry*. Princeton, NJ: Princeton University Press, 2003.

Bernard, Catherine. 'Dickens and Victorian Dream Theory'. In *Victorian Science and Victorian Values: Literary Perspectives*, edited by James G. Paradis and Thomas Postlewait, 197–216. New Brunswick, NJ: Rutgers University Press, 1985.

Birkett, Mary. *A Poem on the African Slave Trade: Addressed to Her Own Sex. Part 1*. Dublin: J. Jones, 1792, Brycchan Carey e-text. http://www.brycchancarey.com/slavery/mbc1.htm.

Blain, Virginia, Patricia Clements and Isobel Grundy, eds, *The Feminist Companion to Literature in English: Women Writers from the Middle Ages to the Present*. London: B.T. Batsford, 1990.

Bode, Katherine and Carol Hetherington, eds, '*To Be Continued …*'. *The Australian Newspaper Fiction Database*, http://cdhrdatasys.anu.edu.au/tobecontinued/. Accessed 9 July 2020.

Bonyhady, Tim, and Greg Lehman, 'Exile – Wybalenna'. In *The National Picture: The Art of Tasmania's Black War*, edited by Tim Bonyhady and Greg Lehman, 214–15. Canberra: National Gallery of Australia, 2018.

'Books – New and Old by "Elaine"'. *The Dawn*, 1 December 1899: 28.

Boos, Florence. 'Class and Victorian Poetics'. *Literature Compass* 115, no. 2 (2005): 1–20.

———. 'Not so Lowly Bards: Working Class Women Poets and Middle Class Expectations'. *Key words: A Journal of Cultural Materialism* 8 (2010): 21–37.

Boyce, James. *Van Diemen's Land*. Melbourne: Black, 2008.

Breckenridge, Carol A., Homi K. Bhaba, Sheldon Pollock, and Dipesh Chakrabarty, eds. 'Cosmopolitanisms'. In *Cosmopolitanism*, 1–15. London: Duke University Press, 2002.

Breen, Shayne. 'Extermination, Extinction, Genocide: British Colonialism and Tasmanian Aborigines'. In *Forgotten Genocides: Oblivion, Denial and Memory*, edited by René Lemarchand, 71–90. Philadelphia: University of Pennsylvania Press, 2011.
Brody, Jennifer DeVere. *Impossible Purities: Blackness, Femininity, and Victorian Culture*. Durham: Duke University Press, 1998.
Brontë, Charlotte. 'Part II: Marian v. Zenobia'. In *The Juvenilia of Jane Austen and Charlotte Brontë*, edited by Francis Beer, 195–225. London: Penguin, 1986.
Brown, Susan. 'The Victorian Poetess'. In *The Cambridge Companion to Victorian Poetry*, edited by Joseph Bristow, 180–202. Cambridge: Cambridge University Press, 2000.
Brown, Susan, Patricia Clements and Isobel Grundy, eds. **CAROLINE LEAKEY** entry: Writing screen within *Orlando: Women's Writing in the British Isles from the Beginnings to the Present*. Cambridge: Cambridge University Press, 2006. http://orlando.cambridge.org.ezproxy-m.deakin.edu.au/.
Brozya, Andrea Ebel. *Labour Love and Prayer: Female Piety in Ulster Religious Literature 1850–1914*. Montreal: McGill-Queens University Press, 1999.
Buckley, Ken, and Ted Wheelwright. *No Paradise for Workers: Capitalism and the Common People in Australia 1788–1914*. Melbourne: Oxford University Press, [1988] 1992.
Butterrs, Philip, and Elizabeth Webby, eds. 'Introduction'. In *The Penguin Book of Australian Ballads*, xvii–xxvi. Ringwood: Penguin, 1993.
Byrnes, J. V. 'Howe, George (1769–1821)'. In *Australian Dictionary of Biography*, vol. 1, 557–59. Melbourne: Melbourne University Press, 1966.
'A Catholic, But Not Bigotted'. Letter. 'M.B., Rev. Mr. Gell, and the New College'. *Colonial Times*, 27 October 1846: 4.
'C.D.' Letter. 'To the Editor of the Colonial Times and Tasmanian'. *Colonial Times*, 5 March 1847: 3.
Clark, Linda L. *Women and Achievement in Nineteenth-Century Europe*. Cambridge: Cambridge University Press, 2008.
Clarke, Patricia. *Pen Portraits: Women Writers and Journalists in Nineteenth Century Australia*. Sydney: Allen and Unwin, 1988.
Coleman, Deirdre. *Maiden Voyages and Infant Colonies: Two Women's Travel Narratives of the 1790s*. London: Leicester University Press, 1999.
'The Colonial Times'. Advertisement. *Colonial Times*, 9 February 1847: 2.
Comet, Noah. 'Letitia Landon and Romantic Hellenism'. *Wordsworth Circle* 37, no. 2 (2006): 76–80.
Conley, Susan. 'Irony and Liminal Fantasy in the Death Lyrics'. In *The Culture of Christina Rossetti: Female Poetics and Victorian Contexts*, edited by Mary Arseneau, Antony H. Harrison, and Lorraine Janzen Kooistra, 260–84 (263). Athens: Ohio University Press, 1999.
Connolly, Claire. 'Irish Romanticism, 1800–1830'. In *Cambridge History of Irish Literature*, vol. 1, edited by Margaret Kelleher and Philip O'Leary, 407–8. Cambridge: Cambridge University Press, 2006.
Conor, Liz. *Skin Deep: Settler Impressions of Aboriginal Women*. Crawley: University of Western Australia Press, 2016.
Cook, Eliza. 'The Heart That's True'. *The Argus*, 17 November 1851: 4.
Cooke, Stuart. 'Tracing a Trajectory from Songpoetry to Contemporary Aboriginal Poetry'. In *A Companion to Australian Aboriginal Literature*, edited by Belinda Wheeler, 89–106. New York: Camden House, 2013.
'Cosmopolite'. Letter 'M.B. and Sacred Poetry'. *Colonial Times*, 1 January 1847: 4.

Cott, Nancy F. 'Passionlessness: An Interpretation of Victorian Sexual Ideology 1790–1850'. *Signs* 4, no. 2 (1978): 219–36.

Craciun, Adriana. 'Mary Robinson, the *Monthly Magazine*, and the Free Press'. In *Romantic Periodicals and Print Culture*, edited by Kim Wheatley, 19–40. London: Frank Cass, 2003.

Dalziell, Tanya. *Settler Romances and the Australian Girl*. Fremantle: University of Western Australia Press, 2004.

Damrosch, David. *What Is World Literature?* Princeton: Princeton University Press, 2003.

David, Deirdre. *Intellectual Women and Victorian Patriarchy*. New York: Cornell University Press, 1987.

Davis, Angela Y. *Are Prisons Obsolete?* New York: Seven Stories Press, 2003.

Davis, Richard. 'Exile'. In *The Companion to Tasmanian History*, edited by Alison Alexander, 432–43. Hobart: University of Tasmania, 2005.

Davis, Richard, and Stephan Petrow, eds. *Varieties of Vice-Regal Life (Van Diemen's Land Section) By Sir William and Lady Denison*. Hobart: Tasmanian Historical Research Association, 2004.

Daw, E. D. 'William Bailey and the Free Church of England in New South Wales'. *Journal of the Royal Australian Historical Society* 58, no. 4 (1972): 247–67.

'The Deceptions of Spiritualism'. *Western Australian Times*, 2 April 1875: 5.

De Salis, Margaret. *Two Early Colonials*. Sydney: Author, 1967.

Dixon, Robert. *The Course of Empire*. Melbourne: Oxford University Press, 1986.

———. 'Hostilities between the *Month* and the *Empire*, 1857–8'. *Southerly* 39, no. 4 (1979): 394–416.

Dorr, Julia C. R. 'Outgrown'. *The Dawn*, 2 July 1894: 20.

DuBois, Ellen Carol. *Woman Suffrage and Women's Rights*. New York: New York University Press, 1998.

Dunlop, Eliza Hamilton. 'The Aboriginal Mother'. *The Australian*, 13 December 1838: 4.

———. 'The Irish Mother'. *The Australian*, 30 November 1838: 4.

———. Letter. 'The Aboriginal Mother'. *The Sydney Herald*, 29 November 1841: 2.

———. Letter, 'The Star of the South'. *The Sydney Morning Herald*, 30 August 1842: 3.

———. 'Morning on Rostrevor Mountains'. *Dublin Penny Journal* 4 (1835): 42.

———. 'Morning on Rostrevor Mountains'. *The Atlas*, 25 April 1845: 257.

———. 'Songs of an Exile (No.2)'. *The Australian*, 22 November 1838: 3.

———. 'To the Memory of E.B. Kennedy'. *Maitland Mercury and Hunter River General Advertiser*, 8 August 1849: 4.

———. *The Vase, Comprising Songs for Music and Poems*. N.d. MS. Mitchell Library, Sydney NSW.

Dutt, Toru. *Ancient Ballads and Legends of Hindustan*. London: Kegan Paul, Trench, 1885.

Easley, Alexis. *First-Person Anonymous: Women Writers and Victorian Print Media 1830–1870*. Burlington: Ashgate, 2004.

Eberle, Roxanne. '"Tales of Truth?": Amelia Opie's Antislavery Poetics'. In *Romanticism and Women Poets: Opening the Doors of Reception*, edited by Harriet Kramer Linkin and Stephen C. Behrendt, 71–98. Kentucky: University Press of Kentucky, 1999.

Eliot, George. 'Agatha'. *The Atlantic Monthly* 24 (1869): 199–207.

Ellison, Julie. 'Cato's Tears'. In *Cato's Tears and the Making of Anglo-American Emotion*, 48–73. Chicago: University of Chicago Press, 1999.

Endres Kathleen L., and Therese L. Lueck, eds. *Women's Periodicals in the United States: Social and Political Issues*. West Port, CT: Greenwood Press, 1996.

Esterhammer, Angela. 'The Spectacle of the Romantic Improviser: Corilla, *Corinne*, and British Women Poets of the 1820s'. In *Romanticism and Improvisation, 1750–1850*, 78–103. Cambridge: Cambridge University Press, 2008.
Feldman, Paula R., and Daniel Robinson, eds. *A Century of Sonnets: The Romantic-Era Revival*. Oxford: Oxford University Press, 1999.
Ferguson, Margaret, Mary Jo Salter and Jon Stallworthy. *The Norton Anthology of Poetry*, 4th edn. New York: W.W. Norton, 1996.
Fiorenza, Elizabeth Schüssler. *Congress of Wo/men: Religion, Gender, and Kyriarchal Power*. Cambridge: Feminist Studies in Religion Books, 2016.
Fiske, Shanyn. *Heretical Hellenism: Women Writers, Ancient Greece and the Victorian Popular Imagination*. Athens: Ohio University Press, 2008.
Flinn, E. 'Macdougall, John Campbell (1805–1848)'. *Australian Dictionary of Biography*, vol. 2, edited by Douglas Pike. Melbourne: Melbourne University Press, 1967, n.p., *Australian Dictionary of Biography*, National Centre of Biography, Australian National University. Accessed 16 May 2012.
Fraisse, Geneviève. *Reason's Muse: Sexual Difference and the Birth of Democracy*, trans. Jane Marie Todd. Chicago: University of Chicago Press, 1994.
Fulford, Tim. 'Cobbett, Coleridge, and the Queen Caroline Affair'. *Studies in Romanticism* 37, no. 4 (1998): 523–43.
———. 'The Mission to Civilize and the Colonial Romance'. In *Romantic Indians: Native Americans, British Literature and Transatlantic Culture 1756–1830*, 194–210. New York: Oxford University Press, 2006.
Fulford, Tim, and Peter J. Kitson. 'Romanticism and Colonialism: Texts, Contexts, Issues'. In *Romanticism and Colonialism: Writing and Empire, 1780–1830*, edited by Tim Fulford and Peter J. Kitson, 1–12. New York: Cambridge University Press, 1998.
Fulweiler, Howard W. *'Here a Captive Heart Busted': Studies in the Sentimental Journey of Modern Literature*. New York: Fordham University Press, 1993.
Garrison, William Lloyd. 'The Negro Mother's Appeal, by Anon.'. *The Abolitionist* 1, no. 1 (1833): 160.
Gelder, Ken, and Rachel Weaver. *The Colonial Journals: And the Emergence of Australian Literary Culture*. Crawley: UWA, 2014.
George Gordon, Lord Byron, *Lord Byron: The Complete Poetical Works*, vol. 2, edited by Jerome J. McGann. Oxford: Oxford University Press, 1980.
George, Sam. *Botany, Sexuality and Women's Writing 1760–1830*. New York: Manchester University Press, 2007.
Gilbert, Sandra M., and Susan Gubar. *The Madwoman in the Attic: The Woman Writer and the Nineteenth-Century Literary Imagination*. New Haven: Yale University Press, 1979.
Gilroy, Amanda. 'Women Poets 1780–1830'. In *Romantic Writings*, edited by Stephen Bygrave, 183–204. London: Routledge, 1996.
Goldstein, Leslie F. 'Early Feminist Themes in French Utopian Socialism: The St.-Simonians and Fourier'. *Journal of the History of Ideas* 43, no. 1 (1982): 91–108.
Griswold, Rufus Wilmot, *The Poets and Poetry of England, in the Nineteenth Century*, Philadelphia: Carey and Hart, 1846.
Gunson, Neil. 'Dunlop, Eliza Hamilton (1796–1880)'. In *Australian Dictionary of Biography*, vol. 1, edited by Douglas Pike, 337–38. Melbourne: Melbourne University Press, 1966.
Halloran, Henry. 'The Late Mr Kennedy'. *Sydney Morning Herald*, 31 July 1849: 2.
Harpur, Charles. 'An Aboriginal Mother's Lament'. In *The Bushrangers: A Play in Five Acts and Other Poems*, 113–14. Sydney: W. R. Piddington, 1853.

Heiss, Anita and Peter Minter, eds. 'Aboriginal Literature'. In *Macquarie Pen Anthology of Aboriginal Literature*, 1–9. Crows Nest: Allen and Unwin, 2008.

Hemans, Felicia. *The Poetical Works of Mrs. Felicia Hemans: Complete in one Volume*. Philadelphia: Thomas T. Ash, 1836.

———. *The Works of Mrs. Hemans, With a Memoir of Her Life*, vol. 3. Edinburgh: William Blackwood and Sons and Thomas Cadell, 1839.

Hoberman, Ruth. 'Women in the British Museum Reading Room during the Late Nineteenth and Early Twentieth Centuries: From Quasi – to Counterpublic'. *Feminist Studies* 28, no. 3 (2002): 489–511.

Holloway, Julian. 'Enchanted Spaces: The Séance, Affect and Geographies of Religion'. *Annals of the Association of American Geographers* 96, no. 1 (2006): 182–87.

Howatson, M. C., ed. 'Zenobia'. In *The Oxford Companion to Classical Literature*. Oxford University Press. *Oxford Reference Online*. Accessed 19 March 2012. Deakin University Library.

Ingham, Patricia. *The Language of Gender and Class: Transformation in the Victorian Novel*. London: Routledge, 1996.

'Insolvency Court – Wednesday'. *Hobart Town Daily Mercury*, 11 March 1858: 2.

Irving, Washington. 'Don Juan: A Spectral Research'. *The Knickerbocker or New York Monthly Magazine* 17 (1841): 247–53.

'I Stood among the Glittering Throng'. In *The Irish Melodist: A Collection of the Newest and Most Admired Songs*, 141–42. Dublin: Printed for the Booksellers, 1843.

Janowitz, Anne. *Lyric and Labour in the Romantic Tradition*. Cambridge: Cambridge University Press, 1998.

Jarratt, Susan. C. 'Sappho's Memory'. *Rhetoric Society Quarterly* 32, no. 1 (2002): 11–43.

Jauss, Hans Robert. *Toward an Aesthetic of Reception*, trans. Timothy Bahti. Sussex: Harvester Press, 1982.

Johnston, Anna. 'Mrs Milson's Wordlist: Eliza Hamilton Dunlop and the Intimacy of Linguistic Work'. In *Intimacies of Violence in the Settler Colony*, edited by Penelope Edmonds and Amanda Nettelbeck, 225–47. Cham: Palgrave Macmillan, 2018.

Johnston, Judith, and Monica Anderson. *Australia Imagined: Views from the British Periodical Press 1800–1900*. Crawley: University of Western Australia Press, 2005.

Judson, Emily Chubbuck. 'Lucy Dutton'. In *Alderbrook: A Collection of Fanny Forester's Village Sketches, Poems etc.*, 121–27. Boston: William D Ticknor, 1847. *Google Books*.

Kane, Paul. *Australian Poetry: Romanticism and Negativity*. Melbourne: Cambridge University Press, 1996.

Kemp, Edward. *A Voice From Tasmania*. Hobart: John Moore, 1846.

Kisner, Arlene. *Woodhull & Claflin's Weekly: The Lives and Writings of Notorious Victoria Woodhull and her Sister Tennessee Claflin*. Washington: Time Change Press, 1972.

Kontu, Tatiana. *Spiritualism and Women's Writing: From the Fin de Siècle to the Neo-Victorian*. Hampshire: Palgrave Macmillan, 2009.

Kucich, John J. *Ghostly Communion; Cross-Cultural Spiritualism in Nineteenth Century American Literature*. Hanover: University Press of New England, 2004.

Landon, Letitia. 'To the Author of the Sorrows of Rosalie'. In *The Lyre Fugitive Poetry of the Nineteenth-Century*, 73–76. London: Tilt and Bogue, 1840.

———. *The Improvisatrice and Other Poems*. Boston: Munroe and Francis, 1825.

Lawson, Henry. 'The Mountain Splitter'. *The Dawn*, 1 May 1894: 20.

Lawson, Louisa. 'About Ourselves'. *The Dawn*, 15 May 1888: 1.

———. 'To a Bird'. In *Louisa Lawson Collected Poems with Selected Critical Commentaries*, edited by Leonie Rutherford and Megan Roughley, 50. Armidale: University of New England, 1996.
———. 'To a Bird'. *The Dawn*, 15 May 1888: 6. *Trove, National Library of Australia*. Accessed 9 August 2012.
———. 'The Divorce Extension Bill: Or, the Drunkard's Wife'. *The Dawn*, 5 March 1890: 7.
———. 'A Grave'. *The Dawn*, 1 March 1904: 16.
———. 'The home libraries'. *The Dawn*, 1 December 1891: 26.
———. 'Original Lines (by Dora Falconer)'. *The Dawn*, 1 August 1902: 18.
———. 'Two Dreams – Twenty years Apart'. *The Dawn*, 1 May 1904: 16.
———. 'To a Libertine'. *The Dawn*, 1 June 1903: 16.
Lazarus, Emma. 'The New Colossus'. In *The Norton Anthology of Poetry*, 4th edn, edited by Margaret Ferguson, Mary Jo Salter and Jon Stallworthy, 1068. New York: W. W. Norton, 1996.
Leakey, Caroline. *The Broad Arrow, Being Passages from the Life of Maida Gwynnham, a Lifer.* London: Richard Bentley, 1859.
———. 'God's Tenth'. *Sunday School World* 39, no. 12 (1899): 459.
———. Letters to Octavian Blewitt. 24 February 1871. MS. (MSS/loan/96 RLF/1844/6) Archives of the Royal Literary Fund. British Lib., London.
———. *Lyra Australis or Attempts to Sing in a Strange Land*. London: Bickers and Bush, 1854.
———. 'The Muezzin's Cry'. *Anglo-American Magazine* 6 (1855): 219.
———. 'The Rock of Martin Vaz'. *Sunday Magazine* (1882): 160.
———. 'Sentiment from the Shambles'. *Once a Week* 1 (1859): 505–9.
Leakey, Emily. *Clear Shining Light; a Memoir of C.W. Leakey*. London: John F. Shaw, 1882.
Leask, Nigel. 'Shelley's "Magnetic Ladies": Romantic Mesmerism and the Politics of the Body'. In *Beyond Romanticism: New Approaches to Texts and Contexts, 1780–1832*, edited by Stephen Copley and John Whale, 53–78. London: Routledge, 1992.
Leng, Andrew. 'Millais's *Mariana*: Literary Painting, The Pre-Raphaelite Gothic and the Iconography of the Marian Artist'. *Journal of Pre-Raphaelite Studies* 1 (1988): 63–74.
'The Letters of Mrs Elizabeth Montagu. Part the Second, Published by Matthew Montagu Esq. Volumes III and IV'. Rev. of *The letters of Mrs Elizabeth Montagu*, by Elizabeth Montagu. *Quarterly Review* 10.19 (1814): 32. Accessed 21 August 2012. *Google Books*.
Lever, Susan. 'The Social Tradition in Australian Women's Poetry'. *Women's Writing* 5, no. 2 (1998): 229–39.
Lewis, Sarah. *Woman's Mission*, 2nd edn. New York: Wiley and Putnam, 1840.
Liddle, Dallas. *The Dynamics of Genre*. London: University of Virginia Press, 2009.
Linkin, Harriet Kramer. 'Romanticism and Mary Tighe's "Psyche": Peering at the Hem of Her Blue Stockings'. *Studies in Romanticism* 35.1 (1996): 55–72.
'Literary Women'. *Sydney Gazette*, 9 April 1827, 4.
Loeffelholz, Mary. 'Poetry, Slavery, Personification: Maria Lowell's "Africa"'. *Studies in Romanticism* 38, no. 2 (1999): 171–202.
'The Love of a Sister'. *The Dawn*, 1 July 1904: 7–8.
'Lyra Australis: Or, Attempts to Sing in a Strange Land, by Caroline W Leakey'. Rev. of *Lyra Australis or Attempts to Sing in a Strange Land*, by Caroline Leakey. *Gentlemen's Magazine* 196 (1854): 399.
'Lyra Australis: Or Attempts to Sing in a Strange Land'. Rev. of *Lyra Australis or Attempts to Sing in a Strange Land*, by Caroline Leakey. *The Courier*, 8 September 1854: 2–3.
Macpherson, Geraldine. *Memoirs of the Life of Anna Jameson*. Boston: Roberts Brothers, 1878.

Magarey, Susan. *Passions of the First Wave Feminists*. Sydney: University of New South Wales Press, 2001.
Mancoff, Debra N. *Flora Symbolica: Flowers in Pre-Raphaelite Art*. New York: Prestel, 2003.
Mani, Lata. *Contentious Traditions: The Debate of Sati in Colonial India*. Berkeley: University of California Press, 1998.
Manning, Emily. *The Balance of Pain and Other Poems*. London: George Bell, 1877.
———. 'Harriet Martineau'. *Sydney Morning Herald*, 16 February 1878: 3.
———. Letter. 'Boycotting Women'. *Sydney Morning Herald*, 19 August 1889: 9.
———. 'A Plea for the Ragged Schools'. *Sydney Morning Herald*, 11 August 1873: 2.
———. 'Review. Souvenirs of Madame Vigée Le Brun'. Rev. of *Souvenirs of Madame Vigée Le Brun*, by Louise Elisabeth Vigée Le Brun. *Sydney Morning Herald*, 17 July 1879: 15.
———. 'Unorthodox London'. Rev. of *Unorthodox London*, by Maurice Davies. *Sydney Morning Herald*, 30 April 1874: 6.
Marshall, Gail. 'Women Re-Read Shakespeare Country'. In *Literary Tourism and Nineteenth-Century Culture*, edited by Nicola J. Watson, 95–105. New York: Palgrave Macmillan, 2009.
Martin, A. W. 'Parkes, Sir Henry (1815–1896)'. In *Australian Dictionary of Biography*, vol. 5, edited by Douglas Pike. Melbourne: Melbourne University Press, 1974. *Australian Dictionary of Biography*, National Centre of Biography, Australian National University. http://adb.anu.edu.au/biography/parkes-sir-henry4366/text7099. Accessed 20 August 2019.
Marzolf, Marion. 'Detroit Women Writers 1900 – Present'. In *Women's Press Organizations 1881–1999*, edited by Elizabeth V. Burt, 59–66. West Port, CT: Greenwood Press, 2000.
Mason, Emma. '"Her Silence Speaks": Keble's Female Heirs'. In *John Keble in Context*, edited by Kirstie Blair, 125–42. London: Anthem Press, 2004.
Matthews, Brian. *Louisa*. Ringwood: Penguin, 1987.
May, Caroline. *The American Female Poets: With Biographical and Critical Notices*. Philadelphia: Lindsay and Blakiston, 1848.
McCall, T. B. 'Bailey, William (1806–1879)'. *Australian Dictionary of Biography*, vol. 1, edited by Douglas Pike. Melbourne: Melbourne University Press, 1966. *Australian Dictionary of Biography*, National Centre of Biography, Australian National University. Accessed 16 May 2012.
McCarthy, William. *Anna Letitia Barbauld: Voice of the Enlightenment*. Baltimore: Johns Hopkins University Press, 2008.
McCrae, Hugh. 'I Blow My Pipes'. In *Poetry in Australia Vol 1: From the Ballads to Brennan*, edited by T. Inglis Moore, 234–35. Sydney: Angus and Robertson, 1964.
Mead, Jenna. 'Caroline Woolmer Leakey (1827–1881)'. In *Dictionary of Literary Biography*, vol. 230, edited by Selina Samuels, 245–53. Detroit: Gale Group, 2001.
Mellor, Anne K. *Romanticism and Gender*. New York: Routledge, 1993.
Melnyk, Julie. 'Hemans's Later Poetry: Religion and the Vatic Poet'. In *Felicia Hemans: Reimagining Poetry in the Nineteenth Century*, edited by Nanora Sweet and Julie Melnyk, 74–94. New York: Palgrave, 2001.
Midgley, Clare. *Feminism and Empire: Women Activists in Imperial Britain, 1790–1865*. Oxon: Routledge, 2007.
———. 'British Women, Women's Rights and Empire 1790–1850'. In *Women's Rights and Human Rights*, edited by Marilyn Lake, Katie Holmes and Patricia Grimshaw, 3–15. New York: Palgrave, 2001.
Miller, Lucasta. *The Brontë Myth*. London: Jonathan Cape, 2001.

Miller, Morris. 'Chapter XV: Notes to Chapter VII (Eardley Wilmot)'. In *Pressmen and Governors: Australian Editors and Writers in Early Tasmania*, 281–86. Sydney: Sydney University Press, 1973.

Miller, Morris, and Frederick McCartney. *Australian Literature a Bibliography to 1938*. Sydney: Angus and Robertson, 1956.

Minter, Peter. 'Settlement Defiled: Ventriloquy, Pollution and Nature in Eliza Hamilton Dunlop's "The Aboriginal Mother". In *Text, Translation, and Transnationalism: World Literature in 21st Century Australia*, edited by Peter Morgan, 137–51. Melbourne: Australian Scholarly, 2017.

Moore, Thomas. *The Poetical Works of Thomas Moore*. Paris: A. and W. Galignoni, 1829.

Moreton-Robinson, Aileen, *Talkin' Up to the White Woman*. Queensland: University of Queensland Press, [2000] 2020.

Morford, Mark P. O., and Robert J. Lenardon. *Classical Mythology*, 7th edn. New York: Oxford University Press, 2003.

More, Hannah (attributed). *The Sorrows of Yamba or the Negro Woman's Lamentation*. London: J. Marshall, 1795. The Electronic Text Centre, edited by David Seaman, 1995. University of Virginia Library, 9 March 2010. http://etext.virginia.edu/toc/modeng/public/AnoSorr.html.

Morris, Edward. *A Dictionary of Austral English*. Cambridge: Cambridge University Press, [1898] 2011.

Moses, Claire Goldberg. *French Feminism in the Nineteenth Century*. Albany: State University of New York Press, 1984. *ACLS Humanities e-book*.

Murphy, Howard R. 'The Ethical Revolt against Christian Orthodoxy in Early Victorian England'. *American Historical Review* 60, no. 4 (1955): 800–17.

Nast, Thomas. 'Get Thee Behind Me Mrs Satan'. *Harper's Weekly*, 16, no. 790 (17 February 1872): 140.

Nayder, Lillian. *The Other Dickens: A Life of Catherine Hogarth*. New York: Cornell University Press, 2011.

'New Books'. *Sydney Morning Herald*, 23 June 1848: 1.

Ng, Lynda. 'Inheriting the World: German exiles, Napoleon's Campaign in Egypt, and Australian Multicultural National Identity'. In *Scenes of Reading: Is Australian Literature a World Literature*, edited by Robert Dixon and Brigid Rooney, 156–67. North Melbourne: Australian Scholarly, 2013.

Norton, Caroline. *The Sorrows of Rosalie: A Tale with Other Poems*. London: John Ebers, 1829.

'Notes and Comments'. *The Dawn*, 1 May 1889: 8.

'"Novel" Nursery Rhyme'. *The Dawn*, 1 November 1890) 20.

O'Leary, John. 'Giving the Indigenous a Voice – Further Thoughts on the Poetry of Eliza Hamilton Dunlop'. *Journal of Australian Studies* 82 (2004): 85–93.

———. '"Unlocking the Fountains of the Heart" – Settler Verse and the Politics of Sympathy'. *Postcolonial Studies* 12, no. 1 (2010): 55–70.

Oldfield, Audrey. 'Louisa Lawson and Votes for Women'. In *Louisa Lawson Collected Poems with Selected Critical Commentaries*, edited by Leonie Rutherford and Megan Roughley, 261–66. Armidale: University of New England, 1996.

O'Neill, Sally. 'Manning, Emily Matilda (1845–1890)'. *Australian Dictionary of Biography*, vol. 5, edited by Douglas Pike. Melbourne: Melbourne University Press, 1974. *Australian Dictionary of Biography*, National Centre of Biography, Australian National University. Accessed 16 May 2012.

Owen, Alex., ed. 'Star Mediumship: Light and Shadows'. In *The Darkened Room: Women, Power, and Spiritualism in Late Victorian England*, 41–74. Chicago: University of Chicago Press, 1989.

Palmer, Beth. *Women's Authorship and Editorship in Victorian Culture: Sensational Strategies*. Oxford: Oxford University Press, 2011.

'Palmyra, by Mrs Bailey'. Rev. of *Palmyra*, by Mary Bailey. *The Gentlemen's Magazine* 156 (1834): 202–4.

Pearce, Sharyn. 'From Bush Battler to City Editor: Louisa Lawson and the *Dawn*'. *Journal of Australian Studies* 21, nos. 54–55 (1997): 12–21.

Peers, Juliette. 'Pre-Raphaelitism in Colonial Australia'. In *Worldwide Pre-Raphaelitism*, edited by Thomas J. Tobin, 215–33. New York: State University of New York Press, 2005.

Perkin, Joan. *Women and Marriage in Nineteenth-Century England*. London: Routledge, 1985. Taylor and Francis e-library 2003. Accessed 29 June 2012.

Pfisterer-Smith, Susan. 'The Louisa Factor: The Historical Treatment of Louisa Lawson'. In *Louisa Lawson: Collected Poems with Selected Critical Commentaries*, edited by Leonie Rutherford and Megan Roughley with Nigel Spence, 275–83. Armidale: University of New England, 1996.

'Philalethes'. Letter. 'M.B. and Colonial Poet-Haters'. *Colonial Times*, 9 March 1847: 3.

Price, Kenneth M., and Susan Belasco Smith, eds. 'Introduction: Periodical Literature in Social and Historical Context'. In *Periodical Literature in Nineteenth-Century America*, 3–16. Charlottesville: University Press of Virginia, 1995.

Radi, Heather. 'Lawson, Louisa (1848–1920)'. In *Australian Dictionary of Biography*, vol. 10, edited by Douglas Pike. Melbourne: Melbourne University Press, 1986. *Australian Dictionary of Biography*, National Centre of Biography, Australian National University. Accessed 16 May 2012.

Raymond, Claire. *The Posthumous Voice in Women's Writing from Mary Shelley to Sylvia Plath*. Burlington: Ashgate, 2006.

Rendall, Jane. 'Bluestockings and Reviewers: Gender, Power, and Culture in Britain, c 1800–1830'. *Nineteenth-Century Contexts* 26, no. 4 (2004): 355–74.

———. *The Origins of Modern Feminism: Women in Britain, France and the United States 1780–1860*. Hampshire: Macmillan, 1985.

Reynolds, Henry. *Fate of a Free People*. Victoria: Penguin, [1995] 2004.

Richardson, Alan. '"The Sorrows of Yamba" by Eaglesfield Smith and Hannah More: Authorship, Ideology and the Fractures of Antislavery Discourse'. *Romanticism on the Net* 28 (2002). 'The Rights of Women'. *Australian Town and Country Journal*, 8 March 1873: 308.

Rodgers, Nini. *Ireland, Slavery and Anti-Slavery: 1612–1865*. New York: Palgrave Macmillan, 2009.

Roe, Jill. *Beyond Belief: Theosophy in Australia 1879–1939*. Kensington: New South Wales University Press, 1986.

———. 'Cambridge, Ada (1844–1926)'. Australian Dictionary of Biography, National Centre of Biography, Australian National University. http://adb.anu.edu.au/biography/cambridge-ada-3145/text4691, published first in hardcopy 1969. Accessed 30 August 2019.

Roe, Michael. 'Eardley Wilmot, Sir John Eardley (1783–1847)'. *Australian Dictionary of Biography*, vol. 1, edited by Douglas Pike, n.p. Melbourne: Melbourne University Press, 1966. *Australian Dictionary of Biography*, National Centre of Biography, Australian National University. Web, 16 May 2012.

Rosenblum, Delores. *Christina Rossetti: The Poetry of Endurance*. Carbondale: Southern Illinois University Press, 1986.
Rossetti, Christina. *Goblin Market, The Princes Progress and Other Poems*. London: Macmillan, 1879.
———. 'Song'. *The Dawn*, 1 October 1894: 20.
Roughley, Megan. 'Introduction'. In *Louisa Lawson: Collected Poems with Selected Critical Commentaries*, edited by Leonie Rutherford and Megan Roughley with Nigel Spence, v–xi. Armidale: University of New England, 1996.
Rukavina, Alison. *The Development of the International Book Trade 1870–1895: Tangled Networks*. New York: Palgrave Macmillan, 2010.
Ruskin, John. *Sesame and Lilies: Two Lectures*. New York: John Wiley, 1865.
Rutherford, Leonie. 'Louisa Lawson's Poetry: A Case Study in Revision and Textual Practice'. In *Louisa Lawson: Collected Poems with Selected Critical Commentaries*, edited by Leonie Rutherford and Megan Roughley with Nigel Spence, 229–44. Armidale: University of New England, 1996.
Ryan, Brandy. '"Echo and Reply": The Elegies of Felicia Hemans, Letitia Landon and Elizabeth Barrett'. *Victorian Poetry* 46, no. 3 (2008): 249–77.
Ryan, Lyndall. *Tasmanian Aborigines: A History since 1803*. Sydney: Allen and Unwin, 2012.
Schaffer, Talia. *The Forgotten Female Aesthetes: Literary Culture in Late Victorian England*. Virginia: University Press of Virginia, 2000.
Servant or Slave. Documentary film. Director: Steven McGregor. Producers: Hetti Perkins and Mitchell Stanley, No Coincidence Media Pty. Ltd., 2015.
Setzer, Sharon M., ed. *A Letter to the Women of England and the Natural Daughter, by Mary Robinson*. Ontario: Broadview Press, 2003.
Shakespeare, William. *The Dramatic Works of William Shakespeare: With the Corrections and Illustrations of Dr. Johnson, G. Steevens and Others*, edited by Isaac Reed. New York: H. Durell, 1817.
Shelley, Percy Bysshe. 'A Defence of Poetry'. In *A Defence of Poetry and Other Essays by Percy Bysshe Shelley*, 29–48. Project Gutenberg. Accessed 15 April 2012.
———. *The Poetical Works of Percy Bysshe Shelley*, edited by Mrs Shelley. London: Edward Moxon, 1839.
Sheridan, Susan. *Along the Faultlines: Sex, Race and Nation in Australian Women's Writing*. New South Wales: Allen and Unwin, 1995.
Simonsen, Pauline. 'Elizabeth Barrett Browning's Redundant Women'. *Victorian Poetry* 35, no. 4 (1997): 509–32.
Sladen, Douglas B. W., ed. *Australian Poets 1788–1888*. London: Griffith, Farran, Okeden and Welsh, 1888.
Smart, Judith. 'Modernity and Mother-Heartedness: Spirituality and Religious Meaning in Australian Women's Suffrage and Citizenship Movements'. In *Women's Suffrage in the British Empire: Citizenship, Nation, and Race*, edited by Ian Christopher Fletcher, Laura E. Nym Mayhall and Philippa Levine, 51–67. London: Routledge, 2000.
Smith, Charlotte. *Emmeline the Orphan of the Castle*. London: Oxford University Press, 1971.
Smith, Rosalind. 'Australie (Emily Manning)'. In *Australian Dictionary of Biography: Australian Literature 1788–1914*, edited by Selina Samuels, 20–26. Detroit: Gale Group, 2001.
Smith, Henry Stooks. *The Register of Contested Parliamentary Elections*, 2nd edn. London: Marshal, 1842.
Sparling, H. Halliday. *A Facsimile Reproduction of Irish Minstrelsy Being a Selection of Irish Songs, Lyrics and Ballads*. London: Walter Scott, 1887.

Spender, Dale. 'A Difference of View'. In *Writing a New World: Two Centuries of Australian Women Writers*, 60–65. London: Pandora Press, 1988.
'A Spiritualistic Exposure *(from the Philadelphia Express, December 17)*'. *Sydney Morning Herald*, 19 March 1875: 3.
Staël, Germaine de. *Corinne, or Italy*, trans. and ed. Sylvia Raphael. Oxford: Oxford University Press, 1998.
Stauffer, Andrew. *Anger, Revolution, and Romanticism*. Cambridge: Cambridge University Press, 2005.
Stephenson, Glennis. 'Letitia Landon and the Victorian Improvisatrice: The Construction of L.E.L.'. *Victorian Poetry* 30, no. 1 (1992): 1–17.
Streitmatter, Rodger. *Voices of Revolution: The Dissident Press in America*. New York: Columbia University Press, 2001.
Summers, Anne. *Damned Whores and God's Police: The Colonization of Women in Australia*. Ringwood, Victoria: Penguin, 1975.
Sunitha, K. T. 'Toru Dutt as a Postcolonial Feminist Poet'. In *Indian English Literature*, vol. 7, ed. Basavaraj Naikar, 1–7. New Delhi: Atlantic, 2007.
Tennyson, Alfred. 'Tears'. *Moreton Bay Courier*, 17 June 1848: 4.
Thomas, Edith M. 'Christmas Voices'. *The Dawn*, 5 December 1889: 14.
van Toorn, Penny. *Writing Never Arrives Naked: Early Aboriginal Cultures of Writing in Australia*. Canberra: Aboriginal Studies Press, 2006.
Vickery, Ann. 'Feminine Transports and Transformations: Textual Performances of Women Convicts and Emigrants to Australia from 1788–1850'. *JASAL* 7, no. 3 (2007): 71–83.
———. 'A "Lonely Crossing": Approaching Nineteenth-Century Australian Women's Poetry'. *Victorian Poetry* 40, no. 1 (2002): 33–54.
———. *Stressing the Modern*. Cambridge: Salt, 2007.
Vincent, Patrick. 'First Last Songs: The Public Voice of Sentiment'. In *The Romantic Poetess: European Culture, Politics and Gender 1820–1840*, 52–71. Durham: University of New Hampshire Press, 2004.
Voltaire. *A Philosophical Dictionary from the French of M De Voltaire*. 2nd vol. London: W Dugdale, 1843.
Walker, Shirley. '"Wild and Wilful" Women: Caroline Leakey and The Broad Arrow'. In *A Bright and Fiery Troop: Australian Women Writers of the Nineteenth Century*, edited by Debra Adelaide, 85–99. Victoria: Penguin, 1988.
Webb, Timothy. 'Romantic Hellenism'. In *The Cambridge Companion to British Romanticism*, edited by Stuart Curran, 148–77. Cambridge: Cambridge University Press, 1993.
Webby, Elizabeth. 'Australian Literature and the Nation'. Rev. of *The Oxford Literary History of Australia*, by Bruce Bennett, Jennifer Strauss and Chris Wallace-Crabbe. *Southerly* 59, no. 1 (1999): 167.
———. 'Born to Blush Unseen: Some Nineteenth Century Women Poets'. In *A Bright and Fiery Troop: Australian Women Writers of the Nineteenth Century*, edited by Debra Adelaide, 41–52. Victoria: Penguin, 1988.
———. *Early Australian Poetry: An Annotated Bibliography*. Sydney: Hale and Iremonger, 1982.
———. 'Writers, Printers, Readers: The Production of Australian Literature before 1855'. *Australian Literary Studies* 13, no. 4 (1988): 113–25.
Weddon, Willah. 'Michigan Woman's Press Association, 1890–193(8)'. In *Women's Press Organizations 1881–1999*, edited by Elizabeth V. Burt, 114–21. West Port, CT: Greenwood Press, 2000.
Welter, Barbara. 'The Cult of True Womanhood'. *American Quarterly* 18, no. 1 (1966): 151–74.

———. 'The Feminization of American Religion 1800–1860'. In *Clio's Consciousness Raised*, edited by Mary S. Hartman and Lois W. Banner, 137–57. New York: Octagon Books, 1974.
Wheatley, Kim, ed. *Romantic Periodicals and Print Culture*. London: Frank Cass, 2003.
Wheeler, Belinda, ed. *A Companion to Australian Aboriginal Literature*. New York: Camden House, 2013.
White, Richard. *Inventing Australia: Images and Identity 1688–1980*. Sydney: George Allen and Unwin, 1981.
Whitman, Walt. *Walt Whitman's Leaves of Grass*, edited by David S. Reynolds. 150th Anniversary edn. Oxford: Oxford University Press, 2005.
Wilcox, Ella Wheeler. 'I Bide My Time'. *The Dawn*, 2 September 1889: 15.
———. 'At Set of Sun'. *The Dawn*, 2 July 1894: 20.
———. *Poems of Passion*. Chicago: Belford Clark, 1890.
———. 'The Rising of Labour'. *The Worker*, 19 March 1904: 3.
———. 'Who Is a Socialist', *The Worker*, 9 August 1906: 4.
Willburn, Sarah. 'Victorian Women Theologians of the Mystical Fringe: Translation and Domesticity'. In *Women's Theology in Nineteenth Century Britain: Transfiguring the Faith of their Fathers*, edited by Julie Melnyk, 188–207. New York: Garland, 1998.
Wilson, John. 'An Hour's Tete-a-Tete with the Public'. *Blackwood's Edinburgh Magazine* 8 (1820): 78–105.
'Women's Rights'. *Australian Town and Country Journal*, 6 December 1890: 34.
Woods, Kate Tannatt. 'Dan's Wife'. *The Dawn*, 6 January 1890: 21.
Woolsey, Sarah Chauncy (under the pseudonym Susan Coolidge). 'New Every Morning'. *The Dawn*, 5 December 1889: 14.
Wroth, Lady Mary. 'Late in the Forest I Did Cupid See'. In *Kissing The Rod: An Anthology of Seventeenth-Century Women's Verse*, edited by Germaine Greer, Susan Hastings, Jeslyn Medoff and Melinda Sansone, 67. New York: Noonday Press, 1989.

Visual Works Cited

Bailey, Mary. *View from Sandy Bay* c.1850. Watercolour. National Library of Australia, Canberra.
Bruce, Charles. *Miss Debney's Establishment For Young Ladies*. 1831. Engraving printed in black ink. National Gallery of Australia, Canberra.
De Morgan, Evelyn. *Love the Misleader*. 1889. Oil on canvas. Private collection.
Hosmer, Harriet. *Zenobia in Chains*. c.1859. Marble. Saint Louis Art Museum, Missouri.
Millais, John Everett. *The Somnambulist*. 1871. Oil on Canvas. Private Collection.
———. *A Huguenot on St. Bartholomew's Day Refusing to Shield Himself from Danger by Wearing a Roman Catholic Badge*. 1852. Oil on Canvas. Private Collection.
Nast, Thomas, 'Get Thee Behind Me (Mrs.) Satan!' Cartoon. *Harper's Weekly*, 17 February 1872.
Strutt, William. *The Burial of Burke*. 1911. Oil on canvas. State Library of Victoria, Melbourne.
Vigée-Le Brun, Elisabeth. *Portrait of Madame de Staël as Corinne*. 1809. Oil on Canvas. Musée d'Art et d'Histoire, Geneva.

INDEX

Note: Page numbers in *italics* denote figures.

abolitionism 18–19, 23, 24, 27–28, 29, 32, 42, 49, 54, 55, 66, 180
The Abolitionist 27
Aboriginal authorship 2
Ackland, Michael 4, 5, 120, 156, 157
   That Shining Band: A Study of Colonial Verse Tradition 5
Act of Union 38, 42
Adams, Charles Follen 142
Addison, Joseph, *Cato* 170
Adelaide, Debra 4
   A Bright and Fiery Troop: Australian Women Writers of the Nineteenth Century 5
aesthetics 1, 20–21, 71, 141, 142–43, 158, 168, 169, 173–74, 177
Aikin, Lucy 71
Alcaeus 65
Allerton, Ellen Palmer 142
Altick, Richard D., *The English Common Reader: A Social History of the Mass Reading Public, 1800–1900*, 17
Analectic Magazine 74
Ancient Ballads and Legends of Hindustan 159
ancient Greece 19, 51, 67, 156
Anderson, Hans Christian, *The Little Mermaid* 99
Anthony, Susan B. 149
antiquity, Greco-Roman 19, 53, 55–56, 58, 62, 64–66, 76, 80, 109, 154, 156
anti-slavery discourses 8, 14–15, 19, 23, 27–33, 34–35, 38, 42, 48, 54–57, 114
archival research 11–12
Argus 17, 173

Armstrong, Isobel 7, 13, 37, 41, 85–86, 89, 94, 96, 115, 127, 140, 180
   Nineteenth Century Women Poets 13
   Victorian Poetry: Poetry, Poetics and Politics 7
Arseneau, Mary, *The Culture of Christina Rossetti* 177
Atlantic 141
Atlantic Monthly 9
Atlas 23, 43
Auerbach, Nina 97, 98, 99
Aurora Leigh 89
Austen, Jane 45
AustLit 11, 12
Australasian 9
The Australian 23, 26, 30, 38, 39
Australian colonial literature 4–11
Australian Dictionary of Biography 5, 16–17
Australian Ladies Annual 9
Australian Literature 105
Australian national identity 3, 5, 81
Australian Town and Country Journal 136

Bailey, Mary 1, 2, 7, 8, 9, 10–11, 12, 14, 17, 18, 19, 51, 110, 135, 156, 183
   concern with convict transportation 54
   'Contamination! And Pollution! Or, England and Tasmania compared' 52–53
   on conviction status of her husband 55, 58
   on convict rights and women's rights 54
   dark humour of 64–65
   'The Death of Pompey' 64–65, 66, 67, 70

INDEX

Bailey, Mary (*cont.*)
  and Eardley-Wilmot 60–61
  on education and gender 77
  'The Exile's Wife to her Husband' 61
  feminist transnationalism and cosmopolitanism, approach to 66
  gender, approaches to 53
  'Hymn to Health', translation 70
  imprisonment, approaches to 53
  'Keep Down the Poets' 72
  linking women and intellect through Romantic Hellenism 68
  'Monody on Sir John Eardley-Wilmot' 60–61, 72–73
  The Months, Palmyra 51
  natural environment, approaches to 53
  'Odes of Anacreon', translations of 51, 62, 66
  opposition to slavery and transportation 54–55
  Palmyra 62, 68–70
  and periodicals 72–76
  poetic practice 56
  problematization of wealth and appearance 77
  references to de Staël 58
  Reflections Upon the Litany of the Church of England 51
  and Romantic Hellenism 51–54, 57–67
  translations by 51, 57, 62–63, 70
  translations of the 'Odes of Anacreon' 62–63
  use of classical models of women's intellect 70
  View from Sandy Bay 53, 53
  'A Voice, from Ass-Mania!! Or Neddy's Bray' 58, 60, 80
  'Woman's Love' 61
Bailey, Reverend William 51
Bailey, William 55
Barak, William 118
Barbauld, Anna Laetitia 29
  'Epistle to William Wilberforce, Esq. on the Rejection of the Bill for Abolishing the Slave Trade' 31–32
Barrett, Elizabeth 47
Basham, Diana 120, 122
Beers, Ethel Lynn 142

Behrendt, Stephen 4, 13, 16, 32, 41, 42, 56, 74
  British Women Poets and the Romantic Writing Community 13
Belfast Magazine 23
Bengal Hurkaru 24
Bennett, Bridget 131–32
Bennett, Paula 142, 155
  Poets in the Public Sphere: The Emancipatory Project of American Women's Poetry, 1800–1900, 7
Bentley, Richard 104–5
Bernard, Catherine 166
Birkett, Mary 29, 33
  A Poem on the African Slave Trade Addressed to Her Own Sex 33
Black War 54, 91
Blackwood's Magazine 18, 24, 51, 57, 70, 71, 76
Blake, William 13
Blewitt, Octavian 98
Bloomer, Amelia 144
  The Lily 160
Bode, Katherine 11, 12
Bonyhady, Tim 91
Boos, Florence 40, 154, 175, 178
Bowles, Caroline (later Southey) 81, 85, 86, 87, 89, 178
  Ellen Fitzarthur 81, 86, 87, 99
Boyce, James 54, 91
Brady, Andrea 142
Breen, Shayne 54
Brennan, Christopher 122
Brereton, John Le Gay 122
Bristow, Joseph, *Nineteenth Century Women Poets* 13
British Museum Reading Rooms 76, 78
British Romanticism 12, 13, 16, 19, 20, 47, 56–57, 79, 81, 94, 133, 180, 181, 183
British Romantic Women's Poetry Project 12
Brody, Jennifer DeVere 9, 23, 92, 131, 155
  Impossible Purities: Blackness, Femininity and Victorian Culture 9
Brontë, Charlotte 68, 78, 106
  'Marian v. Zenobia' 68
the Brontës 113
Brown, Susan 58

Browne, Felicia Dorothea. *See* Hemans, Felicia
Browning, Elizabeth Barrett 4, 81, 88, 89, 113, 126, 142
  'My Heart and I' 172
Bruce, Charles, *Miss Debney's Establishment for Young Ladies 101*
Brun, Elisabeth Vigée-Le 113
Buckley, Ken 89–90
Bull, John 73
Bulletin 8, 18, 139
Burke, Robert O'Hara 46
bush nationalism 5, 182
Butterss, Philip, *The Penguin Book of Australian Ballads* 4
Byron, Lord 13, 17, 33, 57, 58, 66–67, 95, 113, 167
  Don Juan 57, 167, 180
  The Giaour 180
  Hebrew Melodies 33

Cambridge, Ada 6, 9
  Hymns on the Holy Communion 9
  Hymns on the Litany 9
  The Manor House and Other Poems 9
  Unspoken Thoughts 9
Cameron, Bessie 118
Carter, Elizabeth 57
Cassalligi, Carmen, *Romanticism: A Literary and Cultural History* 13
Castle, Terry 143
Christianity 30, 48, 68, 82, 116, 121, 136
Christianization 91
The Chronicles of Wolfert's Roost 167
civilizing role, of women 7, 49, 92, 182
Clark, Linda L. 150
Clarke, Marcus 82, 105
  His Natural Life 82
Clarke, Patricia 4, 111, 126
class-conscious approach 20, 95, 115, 141, 178
classical culture 67, 156
classical scholarship 75
Coleman, Deirdre 55
Coleridge, Samuel Taylor 13, 17, 98, 128
colonial newspaper poetry 72–76
Colonial Times 16, 17, 19, 51, 52, 54, 55, 56, 57, 58, 61, 72, 73, 74, 77

Comet, Noah 71
Conley, Susan 144, 157, 165
Connolly, Claire 38
Conor, Liz 146
Constance School 7
Cook, Eliza 4, 15, 17, 133, 170
Cook, Florence 133
Cooper-Oakley, Isabel 168
Copeland, W. T. 34
Corelli, Marie 175
Cott, Nancy F. 108–9, 148
Courier 51, 104, xxxiv
Cousins, Sara 146
Craciun, Adriana 77, 78
Cupid 152, 153, 156
Curran, Stuart 4, 13, 57, 75

Dalziell, Tanya 29
Damrosch, David 3
David, Deirdre 126
Davies, Andrew Jackson 168
Davies, Rev. Maurice, *Unorthodox London* 113
Davis, Angela 12, 55
Davis, Richard 85
Daw, E. D. 61
Dawn 6, 16, 17, 134, 139, 141, 144, 145, 146, 149, 150, 156, 160, 161, 163, 164, 167, 168, 169–78
Deamer, Dulcie 6
De Morgan, Evelyn, *Love the Misleader* 156, *157*
Denison, William 91–92
De Salis, Margaret 23, 33, 34, 38, 41
de Staël, Germaine 57
  Corinne, or, Italy 58, 129–30
Devotion is a strong theme in Bailey's poetry 61–62
Dickinson, Emily 155, 166
Dictionnaire Philosophique 64
digital resources 11–12
divorce 9, 14, 16, 113, 122, 141, 145, 148–61, 171, 177
Dixon, Robert 18, 44–45, 156
domestic ideal 1, 9, 33, 43, 48, 50, 52, 67, 79, 80, 82, 89–90, 103–4, 109, 110, 111, 112–13, 119, 120, 121, 122–28, 130, 131, 135, 136, 160, 180

Dorr, Julia C. R. 142
dreams, and spiritualism 161–66
Driscoll, Cornelius 72
Dublin Penny Journal 23, 24, 41
The Dublin University Magazine 104
DuBois, Ellen Carol 145
Duffy, Sir Charles Gavan, *The Ballad Poetry of Ireland* 39
Dunlop, Eliza Hamilton 1, 2, 6, 7, 9, 10, 13, 14, 16, 17, 18–19, 23, 27, 49, 54, 57, 73, 109, 110, 183
   'The Aboriginal Father' 34
   'The Aboriginal Mother' 6, 16, 18, 23, 24–26, 27–29, 32, 36–37, 46, 48–49
   The Aboriginal Mother and Other Poems 10
   anti-slavery and Romanticism 27–29
   'Carlingford Bay' 18
   and Copeland 34–35
   criticism 27, 32
   'The Emigrant Mother' 39
   Hermans' influence 31
   'Hints from Horace' 180
   ideological representations of nature 36–37
   on Indian culture 42–43
   Irish identity and nationalism 38–44
   'The Irish Mother' 23, 38, 39
   Maitland Mercury and Hunter River General Advertiser 23, 46
   'Morning on Rostrevor Mountains' 23, 41–42, 43–44, 180
   nationalist poem 44–50
   'Native Poetry' 45
   'Pialla Wollombi' 34
   as reflection of Romantic women poets 29–33
   response to criticism 32–33
   'Songs of an Exile' 30, 38, 39–41, 49
   'Star of the South' 44
   'To the Memory of E.B. Kennedy' 46, 47–48
   The Vase, Comprising Songs for Music and Poems 10, 24, 33, 47
   'The Virginia Voyager to his Mistress' 34
   women's Romantic tradition and colonial context 33–38
Dutt, Toru, 'The Lotus' 159

Eardley-Wilmot, John 58–59, 58–61
Easley, Alexis 2
Eberle, Roxanne 29–30
Edinburgh Review 18, 70
Eggert, Paul 11, 12
elegy 34, 39, 44, 46–48, 47, 63, 64, 67
Eliot, George 20, 114, 116, 126
   Agatha 116
Eliza Cook's Journal 170
emotional pain 31, 102, 103, 110, 150, 153
empathy 48
Empire 17, 18, 23, 44, 50
The Englishwoman's Review of Social and Industrial Questions 177
Erinna 99
Erle, Marian 89
Esterhammer, Angela 130
exilic theme 15, 20, 30, 38–40, 49, 61, 80, 83, 89–90, 98, 109

Falconer, A. S. *See* Lawson
Falconer, Dora. *See* Lawson
fallen woman 14, 19–20, 81–84, 85–88, 89–100, 102, 105–10, 140, 143, 145, 152–53, 158, 161, 168, 171, 180
Feldman, Paula R., *British Women Poets of the Romantic Era* 13
feminist discourse 68–71
feminized religiosity 112–22, 131
Fermanis, Porscha, *Romanticism: A Literary and Cultural History* 13
Fiorenza, Elizabeth Schüssler 8, 53
Fiske, Shanyn 52, 78
Flinn, E. 56
floral symbolism 4, 81, 82, 84–85, 141, 143, 152, 154–56, 158, 159–60, 161, 166, 177, 179
Foott, Mary Hannay, *Where the Pelican Builds* 11
Forester, Fanny (Emily Chubbuck), 'Lucy Dutton' 108
Forsyth, W. 101
Fourier, Charles 168, 169
Fraisse, Geneviève 68
French Revolution 52, 113
French utopian socialist feminists 66
Friedman, Susan Stanford 3
Fulford, Tim 31, 35, 98

INDEX

Fullerton, Mary 6
Fulweiler, Howard W. 169
Furphy, Joseph, *Such Is Life* 173

Gaskell, Elizabeth, *Life of Charlotte Brontë* 106
Geelong Advertiser and Squatters' Advocate 51
Gelder, Ken, *Colonial Journals and the Emergence of Australian Literary Culture* 11
gender 44, 52, 77, 78, 112, 158
 and culture 67
 and libertine 143–48
gender roles 7, 111, 112, 114, 117, 128, 135, 175, 179
Gentleman's Magazine 68, 92
George, Sam 84, 158
Gilbert, Sandra 155
Gilfillan, George 79
Gilmartin, Kevin, *Print Politics: The Press and Radical Opposition in Early Nineteenth-Century England* 17
Gilmore, Mary 6, 156
Gilroy, Amanda 78–79
Gipps, Lady Helena 34
Globe 24
Godwin, William 76
Goldstein, Leslie F. 169
Greece 19, 51, 52, 57, 67, 71, 78, 156
Grimstone, Mary Leman 17
Gubar, Susan 155
Gunson, Neil 38

Hades 165
Halloran, Henry 44, 46, 48
 'The Late Mr Kennedy' 46, 48
 'Rosette' 46
Hamilton, Solomon 41
Hamilton's Gazeteer 3
Hampton, Susan, *The Penguin Book of Australian Women Poets* 6
Harold, Childe, *Pilgrimage* 57, 58, 66
Harper's Magazine 17
Harper's Monthly 141
Harper's Weekly 146
Harpur, Charles 18, 34, 35–36, 44, 45, 46, 58

'An Aboriginal Mother's Lament' 35–36, 46
The Bushrangers: A Play in Five Acts and Other Poems 35
'A Wail from the Bush' 35
Head, Guy, *Zenobia, Queen of Palmyra in chains* 68
Heiss, Anita, *Macquarie Pen Anthology of Aboriginal Literature* 2
Hemans, Felicia 4, 13, 17, 20, 30–31, 46, 47, 48, 58, 67, 71, 73, 75, 78, 81, 85, 95, 96, 98, 100–101, 103, 127, 133, 136, 145
'The American Forest Girl' 31
'Arabella Stuart' 95, 96
'The Bride of the Greek Isle' 30
'Flowers and Music in a Room of Sickness' 160
'The Image in Lava' 67
'Indian Woman's Death Song' 30, 31
Records of Woman 30, 96
'The Siege of Valencia' 46, 48
'A Tale of the Fourteenth Century' 98
Heney, Helen 43
Hill, Fidelia, *Poems and Recollections of the Past* 9, 17, 79
Hobarton Guardian 17, 51, 80
Hobart Town Courier and Van Diemen's Land Gazette 51, 100
Hoberman, Ruth 76
Holloway, Julian 122, 131
Hosmer, Harriet, *Zenobia in Chains* 68, *69*, 70
Howatson, M. C., *The Oxford Companion to Classical Literature* 68
Howe, George 16
Hunt, William Holman, *Light of the World* 173

Illustrated Sydney News 112
imperial feminism 1, 3, 9, 13, 18, 21, 26, 29, 37–38, 42, 46, 48, 54, 62, 82, 100, 111, 112–13, 114, 121, 137, 178, 179, 181–82, 183
imprisonment 50, 53, 55, 56, 79, 80, 81, 86–88, 94–96, 105, 109
Indian culture 3, 30, 31, 42, 158–59
Ingelow, Jean 142

Ingham, Patricia 90, 126
Ingram, Patricia, *The Language of Gender and Class: Transformation in the Victorian Novel* 9
international feminist trends 134
Irving, Washington, 'Don Juan: A Spectral Research' 167

Jackson, J. R. de J., *Romantic Poetry by Women: A Bibliography 1770–1835* 12, 51
Jameson, Anna 70, 88
   Memoirs of Celebrated Female Sovereigns 70
Janowitz, Anne, *Lyric and Labour in the Romantic Tradition* 14
Janowitz, Anne 14, 40, 180
Jarratt, Susan C. 65
Jauss, Hans Robert 7, 8
Jewsbury, Maria Jane, 'Song of the Hindoo Women, While Accompanying a Widow to the Funeral Pile of Her Husband' 42
Jones, Reverend William 51
Judson, Emily Chubbuck 81
   'Lucy Dutton' 81, 108

Kane, Paul 35, 36, 37, 75
'Katie King' 132–33
Keats, John 13, 24
   Ode on a Grecian Urn 24
   'Ode to Psyche' 152
Keble, John 102
Kemp, Edward 58–59, 80
   'A Voice from Tasmania' 58, 59–60, 80
Kennedy, E. B. 44, 48
Kindersley, Caroline 88
Kitson, John 35
Knoepflmacher, U. C. 99
Knowles, Claire, *Sensibility and Female Poetic Tradition* 13
Kontou, Tatiana 143
Kucich, John 117–18
Kyriarchy 8, 53

Lake, Marilyn 145
Landon
   'The Female Convict' 96
   The Lyre; Fugitive Poetry 88

'Sappho's Song' 63
Landon, Letitia, 'To the Author of the Sorrows of Rosalie' 87–88
Landon, Letitia Elizabeth 3, 4, 13, 17, 30, 42, 47, 48, 58, 63, 71, 73, 75, 81, 85, 87–88, 96, 99, 127
   'The Fairy of the Fountains' 98
   'Hurdwar, a place of Hindoo Pilgrimage' 3, 42
   The Improvisatrice 58, 96
Law, James 38
Law, Mary Georgina 38–39
Lawson, Henry 6–7
Lawson, Louisa 1, 4, 6, 9, 11, 14, 16, 17, 18, 20–21, 61, 122, 134, 139, 140, 158, 161, 164, 171, 179, 180, 183
   activism around legislature and laws 150–51
   aesthetes and 'New Woman' writers 173–78
   'After Many Days' 161
   'All's Well' 172
   approaches as a poet 177–78
   'Buried Love' 164, 165–66
   'The Common Lot' 152
   'Consider the Lilies of the Field' 156
   cynicism towards love 142–43
   and *Dawn* 169–72
   'The Dead Baby' 174
   Dert and Do 175
   'The Digger's Daughter' 159
   and divorce 148–61
   'Dolley Dear' series 175–76
   'A Dream' 161–64, 165, 166
   dreams and spiritualism 161–66
   faith, approach to 160
   female sexuality 145
   feminist approach 147–48
   feminist discourse around masculinity, and colonial racism 145
   floral symbolism 141, 143, 152, 154–56, 158, 159–60, 161, 166, 177
   'The Flower and the Book' 152, 154, 155, 166
   on gender inequality 158
   gender roles 175–76
   'A Grave' 158
   home life 167–68

influence of Tennyson on 168–69
'In Memoriam' 154, 165
'A Libertine' 159, 167
liberty concept of 170–71
'A Life's Dream' 161, 165
'Lines Written during a Night in a Bush Inn' 169
'The Lonely Crossing' 165
The Lonely Crossing and Other Poems 11, 139, 141, 142, 145, 149, 155–56, 164, 165, 170
'A Mother's Answer' 160–61
'My Nettie' 172
'The Petunia' 160, 161
political approaches to sexuality 141
Pre-Raphaelite aesthetics 142–43
and print culture 169–72
'Renunciation' 142–43, 148, 164
representations of masculinity 146
The Revolution 149
romantic love, approach to 153, 156–57, 165
'Song of Bacchus' 144, 166
'The Squatter's Wife' 16, 145–52, 164
'To a bird' 141
'To a Libertine' 165, 166–67, 177
'To My Sister' 165
transnationalism 171–72
use of Psyche and Cupid 152, 153
Worker 139, 164
Lazarus, Emma, 'The New Colossus' 15
Leakey, Caroline 1, 4, 5, 6, 7, 9, 11, 14, 17, 19–20, 33, 52, 80, 81, 83, 94–95, 109, 113, 145, 158, 180, 183
and Agnew (Leakey's doctor) 100
'Blanche and Other Tales' 82
The Broad Arrow, Being Passages from the Life of Maida Gwynnham, a Lifer 5, 81, 82, 86, 95, 96, 101, 104, 107, 109
on convictism in Tasmania 95–96
dedication to Lady Denison 100
on Denison 91–92
'Dora' 82, 86–88, 95, 108–9
'English Wild Flowers' 84
exilic theme of 89–90
'The Fallen Jasmine Blossom' 82–83, 85
fallen woman theme 89–100
flowers imagery 84–85

framing of penal system and transportation 103–4
'God's Tenth' 100
'In the Morning' 103
Lyra Australis, or Attempts to Sing in a Strange Land 5–6, 11, 33, 81, 84, 86, 88, 89, 92, 100, 102, 104, 105, 108, 109, 168
'The Muezzin's Cry' 100
'Not here. Far away' 97
Oliné Keese (pseudonym) 98
'On Tasmania's Receiving the Writ of Freedom' 93
'The Prisoner's Hospital, Van Diemen's Land' 93–94
'Queen Ina' 96, 97–98, 99–100, 105
reference of Shakespeare 97
and religion 100–10
resistance to gender and class-based oppression through sexuality 92–93
'The Rock of Martin Vaz' 100, 105–6
'Romantic' 102
'Sentiment from the Shambles' 107–8
'Shadows of Death' 95
Tasmanian Aboriginal people acknowledgement 90
'Tasmania's Writ of Freedom' 94
use of mermaid 97–99
use of symbolism 82
and white women's civilizing role 92
'Who Sweetest Sing their Songs of Home?' 95
on woman suffering through a period of illness 88–89
Leakey, Emily 83, 88, 94, 106, 107
Clear Shining Light: A Memoir of C.W. Leakey 83, 88, 106
Leask, Nigel 128
legal double standards 150–51
Leggett, Lucy 140, 171, 172
reference to Browning's poem 172
'Tired' 172
Lehman, Greg 91
Leighton, Angela 165
Leng, Andrew 169
Lever, Susan 6, 7
The Oxford Book of Australian Women's Verse 6
'The Social Tradition in Australian Women's Poetry' 7

Lewis, Sarah 66, 119
  Woman's Mission 125, 135
Liddle, Dallas 137
Linkin, Harriet Kramer 152
literary movements 20, 89
Llewellyn, Kate, *The Penguin Book of Australian Women Poets* 6
Loeffelholz, Mary 27
Long, Major, *Narrative of an Expedition to the Source of St. Peter's River* 31
Lyall, Edna 175
Lytton, Bulwer 34, 142

Macdougall, John Campbell 56
Magarey, Susan 150
Mancoff, Debra N. 158
Mani, Lata 42
Manning, Emily 1, 5, 6, 7, 9, 11, 14, 15, 17, 20, 52, 109, 110, 111, 142, 164, 183
  'The Angel's Call' 121
  'The Balance of Pain' 111, 112–13, 114–15, 121, 122, 123, 125, 127–28, 129
  The Balance of Pain and Other Poems 11, 20, 111, 112, 114, 116, 118, 126, 127, 130, 133, 136
  'Blind Little Joe: The Unconscious Missionary' 130
  'Books Worth Reading' 113
  'Cupid on a Swiss Tour' 113
  depiction of Sydney 118–19
  on gender roles 114–15, 135
  on material injustice in relation to ideas of maternal suffering 124–25
  and occultism 122–28, 128–31
  and periodical culture and spiritualism 131–37
  'A Plea for the Ragged Schools' 118–19, 130–31
  plurality of religious varieties 113–14
  review of Harriet Martineau's Autobiography 114
  review of Rev. Maurice Davies' Unorthodox London 113–14
  review of Elisabeth Vigée-Le Brun 113
  on social inequality, gender inequality and marriage 112

  'The Story of a Royal Pendulum' 113
  use of mesmerism 126–28, 129
  use of theatrical dialogue 117
  view of religion and appeal to maternal sympathy 119
  on women's inequality 123–24
Manning, Sir William Montagu 112
marriage 112, 153, 156–57
  egalitarian marriage 113
  middle-class domestic marriage 182
Marshall, Gail 87
Martin, Aimé, *Woman's Mission* 66, 119, 126
Martin, A. W. 34
Martineau, Harriet 20, 113, 114, 126, 137, 164
Marx, Karl 169
'Mary Mary Quite Contrary' 175
Marzolf, Marion 172
masculine nationalism 1, 3, 14, 15, 18, 21, 44–50, 85, 94, 105, 109, 182–83
Mason, Emma 102–3
maternal and religious themes 29
Matthews, Brian 150, 167–68
Maxwell, William Hamilton, *The Dark Lady of Doona* 34
May, Caroline, *The American Female Poets* 75–76
McCarthy, William 32
McCartney, Frederick 105
McGann, Jerome 13
Mead, Jenna 6, 82, 85, 86, 93, 94, 101, 107
Mellor, Anne 4, 13–14, 37, 180
Melnyk, Julie 102, 103, 160
middle-class women 2, 90, 109, 126, 180, 181
Midgley, Clare 10, 23, 29, 37–38, 42
  Feminism and Empire 3
Millais, John Everett 150, 152, 161
  A Huguenot on St. Bartholomew's Day 150, 151, 169
  'Mariana' 106, 169
  The Somnambulist 161, *162*
Miller, Lucasta 74, 105, 106
Miller, Morris 11, 60, 72
Minter, Peter 10, 29
  Macquarie Pen Anthology of Aboriginal Literature 2

'Mistress Ward' 175
Montagu, Elizabeth 75
Month 18, 44
The Monthly Magazine 78
Moore, George 174
Moore, John 58
Moore, Thomas 63–64, 70
morality 66, 90, 94, 114, 143, 146, 153, 161, 169, 181
More, Hannah 28, 29, 73
Moreton-Robinson, Aileen 179
Morgan, Peter, *Text, Translation, and Transnationalism: World Literature in 21st Century Australia* 10
Morris, Edward E., *A Dictionary of Austral English* 89
Moses, Claire Goldberg 65–66, 77, 170
motherhood 26–31, 37–41, 48–49, 94, 116, 117, 119, 144, 181
Murphy, Howard 114, 116, 117, 119
Myall Creek Massacre 14, 16, 18, 26, 31, 35, 37, 39, 44, 46, 49

Nairn, Carolina 178
Nast, Thomas, *Get Thee Behind Me (Mrs.) Satan!* 146–48, *147*
Nathan, Isaac 33–34
Nathan, Rosetta 34
Nayder, Lillian 126–27
  The Other Dickens: A Life of Catherine Hogarth 171
'The Negro Mother's Appeal' 27–28
'New Woman' writers 21, 136, 140, 173–78
New York Times 133
Ng, Lynda 3
Niboyet, Eugenie 170
NINES (Networked Infrastructure for Nineteenth Century Electronic Scholarship) 12
Nixon, Francis 91, 100
Norton, Caroline 81, 85, 86, 87–88, 89, 106, 110
  English Laws for Women in the Nineteenth Century 87
  'The Name' 87
  The Sorrows of Rosalie 81, 86, 87, 88, 109
  The Undying One 110
'"Novel" Nursery Rhyme' 174

occultism 20, 111–12, 120, 122–28, 128–31, 132, 134, 136–37, 161
O'Connell, Daniel 38
Oldfield, Audrey 148
O'Leary, John 10, 26, 31, 33–34, 37, 46, 49
  'Giving the Indigenous a voice: Further thoughts on the poetry of Eliza Hamilton Dunlop' 10
Once a Week 107
O'Neill, Sally 112
Opie, Amelia 29
Other 36
Ouida (pseudonym of Marie Louise de la Ramée) 173, 174, 175
Owen, Alex 120, 133

pacifism 8, 19, 51, 65–66, 67
Palmer, Beth 171, 176
  Women's Authorship and Editorship in Victorian Culture: Sensational Strategies 176
Parkes, Henry 17, 18, 34
Pascoe, Judith 13
passionlessness 148, 155
Peacock, Thomas Love, *Palmyra and Other Poems* 68
Pearce, Sharyn 6–7
Peers, Juliette 173
The Penguin Anthology of Australian Poetry 10
periodical culture, and spiritualism 131–37
periodical journalism 2
periodical publishing 18, 40, 55, 134
periodicals 10, 72–76
Perkin, Joan 150, 168
Pfisterer-Smith, Susan 5
Philautia 143
Poetess Archive 12
political voice 1, 3, 7, 9, 17–18, 34, 48, 50, 70, 79–80, 111, 128–31, 136, 137, 145, 179, 180, 181
Portland Guardian and Norman by General Advertiser 133
posthumous voice 123, 142, 159, 165–66, 178
Pre-Raphaelitism 141, 158–59, 168, 173
Price, Kenneth M., *Periodical Literature in Nineteenth-Century America* 140

print culture 2, 3, 14, 15–21, 23, 77, 112, 118, 120, 131, 134–35, 136, 139, 140, 154, 160, 169–72, 176, 177, 182
Probationism 58
Psyche 152–54
purity 9, 21, 62, 90, 91, 92, 97, 109, 125, 126, 131, 145, 146, 150, 154–56, 155, 158, 159, 160–61, 166, 181, 182

racism 9, 21, 29, 43, 117, 135, 145–46, 155, 178, 181
Radi, Heather 139
rationalism 114–15, 123, 136
Raymond, Claire 157, 165
  The Posthumous Voice in Women's Writing from Mary Shelley to Sylvia Plath 157
Rayne, Martha 172
religion/religiosity 48, 82, 87, 100–10, 115
Rendall, Jane 29, 70, 71, 113
Reynolds, Henry 91
Richards, Thomas 56
Richardson, Alan 28
Robinson, Mary 4, 29, 63, 71, 76, 77, 78
  Sappho and Phaon 63
Rodgers, Nini 38
Roe, Jill 9, 61, 122, 167, 168
  Beyond Belief: Theosophy in Australia 1879–1939 167
Roe, Michael 58
Romantic Hellenism 19, 51–52, 56, 57–67, 80
Romanticism 13–15, 55–56, 180
Romantic Sociability: Social Networks and Literary Culture in Britain 13
Rosenblum, Dolores 178
Rossetti, Christina 4, 21, 103, 140, 142, 144, 155–56, 157, 165, 166
  'After Death' 157, 166
  'Song' 141–42
Rossetti, Dante Gabriel, 'The Blessed Damozel' 158
Rossetti Archive 12
Roughley, Megan, *Louisa Lawson: Collected Poems with Selected Critical Commentaries* 5, 11
Rukavina, Alison 104–5

Ruskin, John 20, 126, 134
  'Of Queens' Gardens' 126
  Sesame and Lilies 125
Rutherford, Leonie 5, 11, 161
  Louisa Lawson: Collected Poems with Selected Critical Commentaries 5, 11
Ryan, Brandy 47
Ryan, Lyndall 26, 54, 91, 92

Sacrae, Musae 51
Saint Simonians 8, 65, 77
sati 42, 48
Schaffer, Talia 173–74
Schoenfield, Mark, *British Periodicals and Romantic Identity: 'The Literary Lower Empire'* 16
Scott, Rose 168
Scott, Walter 45
seduction 89, 97, 98, 107, 108–9
sentimental poetry 30, 31, 33, 96, 102, 107–8, 121, 142, 143, 155, 175, 178
separate spheres 76–80, 111, 125–26, 134, 136–37, 182
Setzer, Sharon M. 76
sexual double standard 76, 81, 85, 91, 98, 108, 140, 143, 145, 146, 156, 158, 167, 168, 177
sexual purity 62, 154, 158, 166
Shakespeare, William 87, 97
  The Dramatic Works of William Shakespeare: With the Corrections and Illustrations of Dr. Johnson, G. Steevens and Others 97
  Hamlet 87
  A Midsummer Night's Dream 97
Shelley, Percy Bysshe 13, 17, 68, 106, 128
  'Defence of Poetry' 129
  'The Magnetic Lady to her Patient' 128
  Queen Mab 68
  'To the Moon' 106
Sheridan, Susan 45, 173
  Along the Faultlines 173
Simonsen, Pauline 172
Sladen, Douglas B., *Australian Poets 1788–1888* 105
Smart, Judith 149–50
Smith, Charlotte 78, 81, 100, 106
Smith, Eaglesfield, 'The Sorrows of Yamba' 28–30

Smith, James 173
Smith, Rosalind 5
Smith, Susan Belasco, *Periodical Literature in Nineteenth-Century America* 140
socialist politics 168, 169–72
Sparling, H. Halliday, *A Facsimile Reproduction of Irish Minstrelsy Being a Selection of Irish Songs, Lyrics and Ballads* 39
spectral symbolism 143
Spence, Nigel 5
  Louisa Lawson: Collected Poems with Selected Critical Commentaries 5, 11
Spender, Dale 42–43, 82
spiritualism 20, 111–12, 117–18, 122, 141
  and dreams 161–66
  and erotic poetic discourse 166–69
  and periodical culture 131–37
spiritual love 143
Stanton, Elizabeth Cady 144, 149
Stauffer, Andrew 67
Stephenson, Glennis 99
Streitmatter, Rodger, *Voices of Revolution: The Dissident Press in America* 149
Strutt, William 46
  The Burial of Burke 46, *47*
Summers, Anne 117, 126
The Sunday-School World 100
Sunitha, K. T. 159
Sydney Electronic Text and Image Service (SETIS) project 11, 12
Sydney Freeman's Journal 51, 70
Sydney Gazette and New South Wales Advertiser 16, 17, 30, 34, 74, 75
Sydney Herald 27, 32, 33
Sydney Mail 17, 111
Sydney Morning Herald 17, 23, 44, 46, 49, 73, 113, 114, 118, 132, 133, 134
symbolism 43, 47, 71, 82, 90, 91, 94–95, 96–97, 102, 103–4, 105, 111, 125, 140, 141–43, 147, 152, 154–56, 158–60, 173, 177, 179
sympathy 31, 37, 84, 85–86, 181–82

Tait's Edinburgh Magazine 79
Tasmania
  and the fallen woman 89–100
  genocide in 19, 52, 54, 91

Tasmanian Romanticism 20, 56, 78
Tennyson, Alfred 106, 113, 169
  influence on Lawson 169
  'Love and Death' 168
  'Mariana in the South' 163
  The Princess 152, 169
theology 20, 111, 112, 117, 125, 126, 130, 133, 134, 136, 166, 178, 179
theosophical movement 168
Thomas, Annie, *Only Herself* 171
Thomas, Edith M. 142
Tighe, Mary 47
  'Psyche' 152
Times 16
Tobin, Thomas J., *Worldwide Pre-Raphaelitism* 173
Town and Country Journal 17, 111, 133, 135, 139
transnational circulation 3
The Turning Wave: Poems and Songs of Irish Australia 10

upper-class women 40, 180
utopia 8, 19, 66, 169, 170

Van Diemen's Land 10, 14, 51, 53, 61, 91, 93
van Toorn, Penny, *Writing Never Arrives Naked: Early Aboriginal Cultures of Writing in Australia* 2
Vickery, Ann 4, 5, 6, 8, 96, 168, 169
  'A "Lonely Crossing": Approaching Nineteenth-Century Australian Women's Poetry' 6
  Stressing the Modern 6
Victorian Poetry 6
Vigée-Le Brun, Elisabeth, *Portrait of Madame de Staël as Corinne* 59
Vincent, Patrick 13, 130
  The Romantic Poetess: European Culture, Politics and Gender 1820–1840 13
La Voix des Femmes 170
Voltaire 64

Walch, J. 105
Walker, G. W. 100
Walker, Shirley 5–6, 82, 83, 107
Waterhouse, John William 152

Weaver, Rachel, *Colonial Journals and the Emergence of Australian Literary Culture* 11
Webb, Timothy 57, 63, 77
Webby, Elizabeth 4, 5, 6, 10, 17–18, 31, 44, 49, 73
  'Born to Blush Unseen: Some Nineteenth Century Women Poets' 5
  Early Australian Poetry: An Annotated Bibliography 2, 10, 55
  The Penguin Book of Australian Ballads 4
  'Writers Printers Readers: The Production of Australian Literature before 1855' 17–18
Weddon, Willah 172
Weekly Register 35
Welter, Barbara 109, 120, 121, 135
  'The Cult of True Womanhood' 20, 120, 131, 134–35
Western Australian Times 133
Wheatley, Kim 16, 56–57
  Romantic Periodicals and Print Culture 16
Wheelwright, Ted 89–90
White, Richard, *Inventing Australia* 5
whiteness 21, 92, 146, 154, 158
Whitman, Walt 141
Wilcox, Ella Wheeler 4, 15, 140, 142, 164, 178
  'Communism' 164
  'From the Grave' 165
  Poems of Passion 164
  'The Rising of Labour' 164
Wilde, Oscar 174
Willburn, Sarah 125, 134
Wilson, John 70, 71
Windeyer, Lady Mary 168
Windeyer, Sir William 168
Wirrayaraay people, massacre of. *See* Myall Creek Massacre
Wollstonecraft, Mary 76, 158, 179–80
  A Vindication of the Rights of Woman 158

Wolstenholme, Maybanke 144
Woman's Journal 177
Woman's Voice 144
Woman's World 174
women
  aesthetes and 'New Woman' writers 173–78
  purity of 9, 62, 90, 91, 126, 145, 146, 150, 154–55, 160, 182
  rights activism 29, 110
  rights of 67
  Romantic tradition and colonial context 33–38
  sexuality of 20, 21, 80, 81, 84, 85, 88, 89, 90, 92, 94, 96, 100, 104, 109, 110, 143, 145, 152, 158, 159
  suffrage movement 21
  virtue of 67, 144–45
'Women's Rights' 135
Woodhull, Victoria 146, 164, 170
Woodhull & Claflin's Weekly 170
Woods, Kate Tannatt 140, 142, 178
  'Dan's Wife' 148–49
Woolley, Charlotte 168
Woolley, Margaret 122
Woolsey, Sarah Chauncy (Susan Coolidge) 140, 142
Wordsworth, William 13, 16, 17
  'Somnambulist' 16
working-class women 9, 90, 126, 180
Wroth, Lady Mary, 'Late in the Forest I did Cupid see' 153
Wu, Duncan, *Romantic Women Poets: An Anthology* 13

Yearsley, Ann 29
Yellow Book 174
Yonge, Charlotte
  Golden Hours 111
  Monthly Packet of Evening Readings 111, 112

www.ingramcontent.com/pod-product-compliance
Lightning Source LLC
Chambersburg PA
CBHW021824300426
44114CB00009BA/306